100 BOOKS

that changed the world

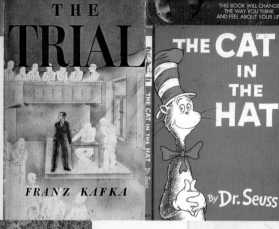
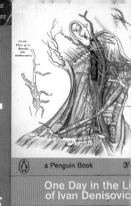

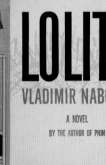
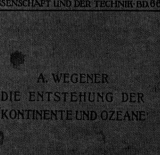

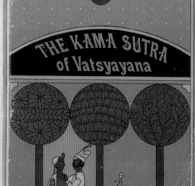

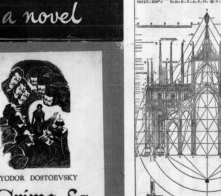

First published in the United Kingdom in 2018 by Batsford,
an imprint of Pavilion Books Group Limited,
43 Great Ormond Street
London, WC1N 3HZ

Produced by Salamander Books, an imprint of Pavilion Books Group Limited.

ISBN: 9781849944519

A CIP catalogue record for this book is available from the British Library.

10 9 8 7 6 5 4 3 2 1

Reproduction by Rival Colour Ltd, UK
Printed by 1010 Printing International Ltd, China

This book can be ordered direct from the publisher at the website:
www.pavilionbooks.com or try your local bookshop.

100 BOOKS

that changed the world

Scott Christianson and Colin Salter

BATSFORD

This book is dedicated to
Scott Christianson (1947–2017)

Contents

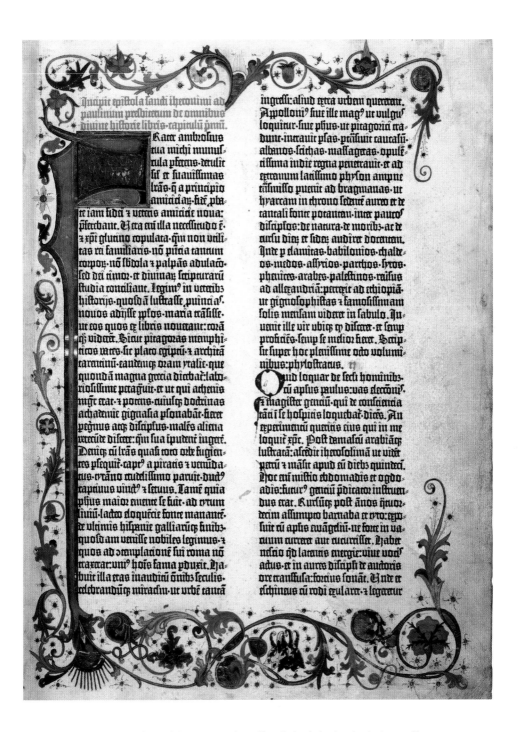

ABOVE: An original copy of the 1450s Gutenberg Bible – the first book to be printed using movable type.
Colourful hand-painted decorations have been added to this opening page. (See page 48.)

ABOVE: *A nineteenth-century woodblock print by Utagawa Kunisada showing a scene from what is often hailed as the world's first novel,* The Tale of Genji *(c. 1021) by Murasaki Shikibu.* *(See page 42.)*

Introduction

What's your favourite book? Why did it inspire you? Did it make you laugh? Or cry? Or gasp with wonder? Did it change your world? Now imagine trying to choose a hundred, not just from your own shelves, not just from your local library, but from the entire history of the written word.

So how do you choose? Where do you start? This book starts at the very beginning with a 4,800-year-old text, the divinatory *I Ching*, which predicts the future based on the toss of six coins. We end ninety-nine books later in the twenty-first century with another prediction, Naomi Klein's *This Changes Everything*, which forecasts the end of the planet if we don't act collectively to mend our ways. On the pages in between, our list is drawn from every age, in every style and on every subject. All of them have changed their readers' worlds, and ours.

The oldest printed texts were stamped into clay while it was still wet, then baked into permanence. As handwriting developed, it became easier to copy texts out onto sheets of papyrus, vellum, or paper. But it would still take a team of monks several years to produce a single beautifully illustrated manuscript copy of the Bible. The world was truly changed with the invention of printing. The Bible was the first book to be printed with movable type, in the 1450s. Although it took Gutenberg three years to print roughly 180 copies of it, it was significantly faster than a team of monks.

SCIENCE AND MAGIC

Mass production of books not only lowered the cost but enabled the faster spread of knowledge and the exchange of ideas. In the wake of Gutenberg's invention, the first scientific volumes start to appear on our list of world-changing books. Copernicus leads the way in the modern era with *On the Revolutions of the Heavenly Spheres* (1543). We've included Robert Hooke's microscopic images (*Micrographia*, 1665), Isaac Newton's mathematics (*Philosophiae Naturalis Principia Mathematica*, 1687) and Carl Linnaeus's classification of species (*Species Plantarum*, 1753). Each of them benefited from the exchange of ideas in books, combined with the insights of their own particular genius. Each in turn was read by others; Henry Gray's *Anatomy, Descriptive and Surgical* (1858), Charles Darwin's *On the Origin of Species* (1859) and Albert Einstein's *Relativity* (1917) were all, as Newton put it, 'standing on the shoulders of giants' who had gone before them. Books carry new knowledge forward into the future.

Printing had the same world-shrinking impact as the development of the Internet five hundred years later. Nowadays, you can share information or ask questions with friends and colleagues on the other side of the

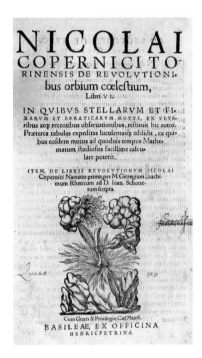

ABOVE: The publication of Copernicus's On the Revolutions of the Heavenly Spheres *in 1543 contradicted fourteen centuries of belief by stating that the Sun, not the Earth, was at the centre of the universe. (See page 52.)*

ABOVE: A plate from William Henry Fox Talbot's The Pencil of Nature *(1844–46), the first commercially published book illustrated with photographs. (See page 98.)*

globe almost instantly. Or you can send emojis: not all text messages change the world, after all.

Nor do all books. But the oldest-known work of literature, *The Epic of Gilgamesh* (c. 2100 BC) is here. It's a Sumerian tale of gods and men that today might be described as magic realism. Joining it are more recent combinations of magic and reality, including *The Arabian Nights* from the ninth century and Gabriel García Márquez's 1967 novel *One Hundred Years of Solitude.* Literature makes magic across the millennia.

INNER AND OUTER WORLDS
Storytelling makes up a large part of our list. Looking back, we admire the fiction of earlier centuries for what it reveals about the times in which it was written. Geoffrey Chaucer's *The Canterbury Tales* (1390s), for example, or Jane Austen's *Pride and Prejudice* (1813), are snapshots of time and place. But for their first readers, as well as their modern ones, those ancient works of literature captured something more: the human condition. The best literature shows us the best and worst of ourselves. We are all flawed, and it is easier to see the flaws in others than in ourselves, especially if, as in Jonathan Swift's *Gulliver's Travels* (1726), they are transferred to completely imaginary worlds. But we all have goodness, too, embodied in fiction's heroes. Don Quixote shows us a remarkable nobility of spirit, no matter how misguided. Harry Potter, another character on a quest, is a model for the moral strength we all wish we had.

Good literature changes our inner world by helping us to understand human behaviour. Sometimes it goes further and changes the world around us. Charles Dickens's observations of Victorian poverty were instrumental in improving the conditions of the working class. Alexsander Solzhenitsyn's *One Day in the Life of Ivan Denisovitch* (1962) was the first chink of light to be shed on the secretive cruelty of Stalin's gulags, a revelation that contributed eventually to the breakup of the Soviet Union.

Books can be exquisitely beautiful objects, but what concerns us here is their inner beauty, the power of their words, their capacity to startle us into new ways of thinking with just a few well-chosen letters. Words can be powerful in many ways: evocative, emotive, persuasive, prescriptive, informative, misleading, lyrical, musical, incomprehensible, revealing. Words can do whatever a good author wants them to do for his or her readers.

Religious writing is perhaps the most powerful of all and therefore the most dangerous, as well as the most inspiring. The Torah, the Quran and the Bible all make it onto our list; but so too do books that show the ugliness of excessive religious zeal. Anne Frank's *Diary of a Young Girl* (1947) and Art Spiegelman's *Maus* (1991) are very different but equally compelling records of the Nazi persecution of the Jews. Salman Rushdie lives under constant threat of assassination because his 1988 novel, *The Satanic Verses*, offended devout Muslims.

BIG IDEAS AND HELPING HANDS

Books of both fiction and fact can change the world. Somewhere between them, it could be argued, lies philosophy, another way of trying to explain the human condition. Each age seems to throw up its own way of interpreting how we behave, or ought to behave. Times change, and we change with them, with the help of books. Sun Tzu's *The Art of War* (c. 512 BC) gives way to Machiavelli's *The Prince* (1532); Adam Smith's *The Wealth of Nations* (1776) is challenged by John Maynard Keynes's *The General Theory of Employment, Interest and Money* (1936); Karl Marx's *Das Kapital* (1867) is revisited in Thomas Piketty's *Capital in the Twenty-First Century* (2013).

Books have been particularly instrumental in changing the attitude of men toward women, and of women towards themselves. Thomas Paine's 1791 political thesis *The Rights of Man* was followed a year later by Mary Wollstonecraft's *A Vindication of the Rights of Woman*, an early feminist milestone. Our selection also includes Simone de Beauvoir's *The Second Sex* (1949) and Betty Friedan's *The Feminine Mystique* (1963).

Books don't have to contain big ideas to change their worlds. Some books just want to help you with everyday life at work and at home. So we've included the domestic bible *Mrs. Beeton's Book of Household Management* (1861), which transformed the lives of middle-class women in the nineteenth century, as Elizabeth David's *A Book of Mediterranean Food* (1950) did in the twentieth. Dale Carnegie's business advice from 1936 still teaches us *How to Win Friends and Influence People* more than eighty years after its publication. The *Kama Sutra* (400 BC–AD 200) and the *Kinsey Reports* (1948 and 1953) on sexual behaviour are two very different approaches to the same subject, two thousand years apart.

CHANGING YOUR WORLD

Of our one hundred books, there are fifty that everyone would agree should be included. About the other fifty, almost everyone will disagree. Should Jung be in and Freud out? Should it be *David Copperfield* or *Great Expectations*? Robert M. Pirsig's *Zen and the Art of Motorcycle Maintenance* or Mark Zimmerman's *Essential Guide to Motorcycle Maintenance*? Why *The Cat in the Hat* over *Green Eggs and Ham*? Why Mao and not Lenin?

There are a lot of books out there. In the United States, every year roughly one book is published for every thousand people in the population. That's more than 300,000 new books every year. In the United Kingdom it's even more: one book for every 350 people. And in China the figure falls even further, to just over 300 people per book – that's 440,000 new books or new editions every year, in China alone. The global total is about 2.25 million new publications. Every year. We hope that *100 Books that Changed the World* is a modest but worthy addition to the world's library. If it makes you question your own choices or ours, or introduces you to a book that eventually changes your world, then our work is done.

ABOVE: The publication of D.H. Lawrence's unexpurgated Lady Chatterley's Lover *in 1960 marked a crucial step towards the freedom of the written word and helped usher in the sexual revolution of the 1960s. (See page 152.)*

I Ching

(c. 2800 BC)

No other book in history has so much embodied the culture that produced it and influenced that culture for so long as China's ancient divination text, the *I Ching*.

The creation of the *I Ching*, or *Book of Changes*, is thought to lie as far back as 2800 BC, making it the oldest text still in continuous use. Its origins remain shrouded in legend, but it is generally agreed that the diagrams date to around 2800 BC, the text to 1000 BC, and the philosophical commentaries on it to 500 BC. The diagrams are credited to Emperor Fu Hsi, who was inspired by the markings on a tortoise to create the hexagrams that formed the basis of the *I Ching*.

For centuries it was known as the *Zhou Yi*, until in 136 BC, Emperor Wu of the Han dynasty named it the first among the classics, pronouncing it the *Classic of Changes*, or *I Ching*. The *I Ching* is a book of divination, or geomancy, where objects – originally yarrow stalks – are cast on the ground and the patterns they form are interpreted through the use of hexagrams, which are given meaning and significance by reference to the book.

Although there is no verified author, the text of the *I Ching* is thought to have originated in the Western Zhou period (1046–771 BC). What started out as a method of predicting the future, of interpreting good and bad omens, was given deeper meaning by the addition of philosophical commentaries known as the 'Ten Wings'.

The most important element of the Ten Wings is the Great Commentary. This elevated the spiritual significance of the *I Ching*, describing it as 'a microcosm of the universe and a symbolic description of the processes of change.' An individual who takes part in the spiritual experience of the *I Ching*, it maintained, could understand the deeper patterns of the universe.

The Ten Wings were traditionally attributed to Confucius, giving

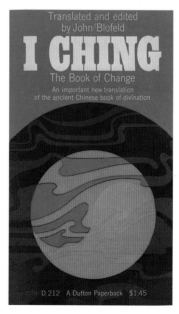

gravitas to the text and helping to maintain its importance throughout the Han and Tang dynasties.

The *I Ching* offers a unified understanding of China's two main contending spiritual traditions – Confucianism and Taoism – both of which are rooted in it. It considers the dynamic of two opposite principles: one negative, dark and feminine (yin); one positive, bright and masculine (yang), whose interaction influences the destinies of creatures and whose harmony gives birth to other creations. The text examines the infinite range of dynamic reactions set up by the interplay of yin and yang, within the sixty-four possible six-line statements that make up the *I Ching*.

Its philosophy is said to include three basic concepts: change, ideas and judgements, which indicate whether a given action will bring good fortune or misfortune, remorse or humiliation. The *I Ching* stresses the importance of caution, humility and patience in one's daily living. It reminds the reader that great success is often followed by difficulty, and great hardship is often necessary for subsequent achievement.

After the Xinhai Revolution deposed the last emperor in 1911 and China became a republic, the *I Ching* was no longer considered part of mainstream Chinese political philosophy. However, psychologist Carl Jung was fascinated by it and introduced an influential 1923 German translation by Richard Wilhelm. The book was taken up by the counterculture of the 1960s and has continued to influence writers through the twentieth century, including Philip K. Dick and Herman Hesse.

ABOVE: *This annotated copy of the* I Ching *dates from the twelfth century AD, when it was being redefined as a work of divination rather than philosophy.*

OPPOSITE: *John Blofield's 1965 translation coincided with the emerging countercultural movement that was looking to the East for spiritual meaning and direction.*

The Epic of Gilgamesh

(c. 2100 BC)

This four-thousand-year-old tale of gods and men was rediscovered by archaeologists in the Middle East during the nineteenth century. It is the oldest work of literature ever recorded and contains universal characters and themes that would not be out of place in any modern cinematic epic.

Gilgamesh was a real person, a Sumerian king of the city-state of Uruk around 2700 BC. The earliest examples of writing, from 3300 BC, have been found in Uruk, the ruins of which lie in modern-day Iraq. In the centuries following Gilgamesh's death he achieved a mythical, godlike status in popular memory.

The earliest known stories about him, stamped by unknown authors onto clay tablets, date from around 2100 BC. Over time these stories and others were combined to form *The Epic of Gilgamesh* that we know today. Fragments of this combined history have been found dating from 2000 BC. Modern translations are based largely on an almost-complete version of the epic written down on twelve tablets in about 1200 BC – some 1,500 years after Gilgamesh's death – which was discovered in 1853 by archaeologists.

The Epic of Gilgamesh is a tale of two halves. The first is a sort of buddy movie. The gods, alarmed at wicked King Gilgamesh's despotic behaviour, create an opposite to rein him in, a morally upright man called Enkidu. After fighting, the two become firm friends. In the course of their subsequent adventures they offend the gods, who decide to punish Enkidu with death.

Gilgamesh is grief-stricken and contemplates his own mortality. Part two is a classic road movie in which he sets off to find the secret of eternal life from Utnapishtim, the only survivor of a great flood. After many encounters and dangers along the way, Gilgamesh is forced to accept that death is built into every man's life, but that humanity, and human achievement, will endure. He returns to Uruk a changed man and becomes the mature, wise ruler whom his people (and we) will remember long after his passing.

The themes of *The Epic of Gilgamesh* – friendship, mortality, a voyage of self-discovery – are eternal and can be traced in the literature of every age from then until now. The story of Gilgamesh had a direct influence on two other ancient texts: the Bible and the works of Homer. Homer's *Iliad* and *Odyssey* are both tales of epic journeys with lessons learned on the way. The Old Testament of the Bible contains several episodes that almost copy passages from *The Epic of Gilgamesh*, notably descriptions of the Garden of Eden and the Great Flood in which Utnapishtim becomes Noah.

The Epic of Gilgamesh is the oldest written story so far discovered, and its value is enhanced by the existence of so many versions written over a period of 900 years. The use in its text of often-repeated phrases suggest that it comes from an even older oral tradition of storytelling dating back to the time of Gilgamesh himself. And if nineteenth-century archaeologists could find this epic, who knows what others remain to be discovered?

LEFT: Known as Tablet V, this 2000–1500 BC fragment from The Epic of Gilgamesh *was discovered in 2015 by the Sulaymaniyah Museum in Iraq.*

Torah

(c. 1280 BC)

The guide to Jewish daily life for more than three thousand years, the Torah provides the basis for Jewish law and practice. Jewish scholars have summed up its overall teaching in a single sentence: 'Love thy neighbour as thyself.'

The Torah consists of five books – Bereshit, Shemot, Vayikra, Bamidbar and Devarim – which correspond to the first five books of the Christian Bible: Genesis, Exodus, Leviticus, Numbers and Deuteronomy. The books describe the origin of mankind in the Garden of Eden and the early leaders of the tribe of Israel, including Abraham, Isaac and Jacob. It describes the escape from Egypt to Mount Sinai; the delivery of the Torah, including the Ten Commandments and other instructions; and the punishment for not obeying them. The Torah concludes with the death of Moses and the entry of the Israelites into Canaan, the land promised to them by God.

Although often translated from the Hebrew as 'law', the word 'Torah' more accurately means 'instruction' or teaching. Specifically, the Torah consulted by Jews is the Torah of God or the Torah of Moses. By tradition this Torah existed before the world was created. God offered it to all the peoples of Earth, but only Israel accepted. Moses, leader of the Israelites, received it from heaven in 1312 BC and wrote it down over the next thirty to forty years.

Modern scholars believe more prosaically that the five books were written by several different authors over many centuries before coalescing as the Torah around 700 BC. While orthodox Jews hold it to be the strict law of God, more liberal Jews see it as a set of guidelines rather than rules, in the same way that some Christians no longer accept the literal truth of the Bible. Islam also accepts the historic existence of the Torah. There are several references to it in the Quran, although Muslims hold it to have been corrupted by human error – the careless transcription of it by scribes over the ages.

The Torah is still transcribed by hand onto scrolls. Tradition demands strict accuracy of the 304,805 Hebrew characters that make it up. It is a painstaking process, a work of profound faith and calligraphic art, executed according to precise rules of style and lettering, which can take eighteen months to complete.

It is a requirement of Judaism that every Jew own such a copy of the Torah. For at least two thousand years Jews have heard or spoken the same prescribed passage of the Torah on the same day in a year-long cycle of readings. The Torah not only embodies the tenets of the Jewish religion but emphasizes its ancient tradition. It is, with Hinduism and Zoroastrianism, one of the oldest systems of belief in the world, and the Torah is its book.

RIGHT: Like all scrolls of the Torah, this nineteenth-century North African copy is handwritten in ink on parchment. If an error is introduced in transcription, it renders the text invalid.

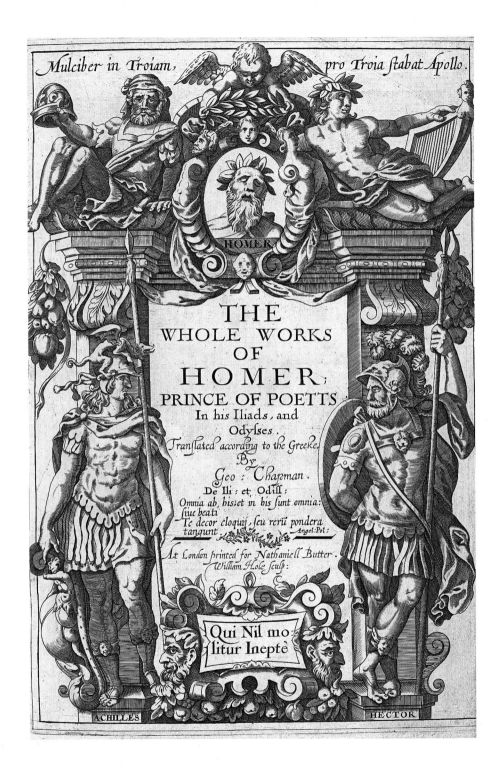

Mulciber in Troiam, pro Troia stabat Apollo.

HOMER

THE
WHOLE WORKS
OF
HOMER;
PRINCE OF POETTS
In his Iliads, and
Odysses.
Translated according to the Greeke,
By
Geo: Chapman.
De Ili: et Odiss:
Omnia ab, his,et in his sunt omnia:
siue beati
Te decor eloquij, seu rerŭ pondera
tangunt. *Angel:Pol:*

At London printed for Nathaniell Butter.
William Hole sculp:

Qui Nil mo
litur Ineptê

ACHILLES   HECTOR

*ABOVE: The title page of the first English-language edition of Homer's works, published in
London in 1616, with translations by the English dramatist and poet George Chapman.*

The Iliad and The Odyssey
Homer

(c. 750 BC)

Two of the greatest epic poems were composed three thousand years ago by a mysterious blind man in ancient Greece. These seminal works of Western literature tell the heroic stories of characters caught up in a city's brutal siege and a warrior's long and perilous journey home.

Precious little is known about Homer, including whether he even existed or if he was a composite character. Some accounts say he was born around the eighth to ninth century BC on the island of Chios in the Aegean Sea and probably lived in Ionia, an ancient region of what is now Turkey. In a field rich in academic speculation, some believe he was a court singer and storyteller who became blind.

Homer is credited with having composed the two great epic narrative poems, *The Iliad* and its sequel *The Odyssey*, around 750 BC. The date has been arrived at from statistical modelling of the evolution of language, although some historians believe it to be older. What is almost certain is that both works arose from the oral tradition and were intended to be performed, not written down.

The Iliad, sometimes known as *The Song of Ilion*, depicts a few weeks in the final year of the ten-year siege of the city of Troy. Organised into twenty-four books, it tells the story of the great warrior Achilles and his heroic battle against Hector of Troy and his quarrel with King Agamemnon.

The Odyssey tells the story of the Trojan War hero Odysseus (known as Ulysses in Roman translations) as he makes a perilous ten-year journey home to Ithaca, a small island off the west coast of Greece, once the siege is ended. After his long absence, it has been assumed that Odysseus is dead, and his wife, Penelope, and son, Telemachus, must contend with a group of ardent suitors who compete for Penelope's hand in marriage.

'Tell me, muse, of the man of many resources who wandered far and wide after he sacked the holy citadel of Troy, and he saw the cities and learned the thoughts of many men, and on the sea he suffered in his heart many woes.'

Odysseus, like Achilles before him in *The Iliad*, is offered a choice: he may either live in comfort and be immortal like the gods, or he may return to his wife and his country and be mortal like the rest of us. After choosing the latter, he struggles to complete his journey and is constantly confronted with questions about human mortality and the meaning of life.

Both books were composed in Homeric Greek – an amalgam of Ionic Greek and other ancient Greek dialects. The oldest known fragments of *The Iliad*, written on papyri and discovered rolled up in the sarcophagi of mummified Greek Egyptians, date to 285–250 BC and are displayed at the Metropolitan Museum of Art in New York.

The Iliad and *The Odyssey* are the two oldest extant works of Western literature. They represent the earliest recorded form of storytelling and have inspired writers from every generation, from Euripides and Plato, to James Joyce with *Ulysses* (1922) and Margaret Atwood with *Penelopiad* (2005), a retelling of the *Odyssey* from Penelope's perspective.

LEFT: Venetus A is the oldest complete manuscript of The Iliad. *Dating to AD 900, it is preserved at the Biblioteca Nazionale Marciana in Venice.*

Aesop's Fables

(620–560 BC)

One of the earliest and greatest collections of fables was written in prose in ancient Greek and traditionally ascribed to a deformed slave named Aesop, who gained great fame for his storytelling ability. The distinctive tales were originally performed for adults but later became standard bedtime fare for young children.

A fable is a short, simple tale that features animals or inanimate objects as characters to impart a truth and teach a moral lesson about the human condition. Isaac Bashevis Singer, the great modern Jewish fabulist, called the fable maybe 'the first fictional form' and noted that ancient man believed myths and fables were true but not necessarily factually accurate, just as a child can grasp that such a lesson might contain a deep truth beneath an obvious falsehood. Fables are also pessimistic in their point of view.

As Aesop tells it, in 'The Wolf and the Lion': 'A Wolf, having stolen a Lamb from a fold, was carrying him off to his lair, when he was stopped by a Lion, who seized the Lamb from him. The Wolf protested, saying, "You have unrighteously taken that which was mine!" To which the Lion jeeringly replied, "It was righteously yours, eh? The gift of a friend?"'

The Greek historian Herodotus (c. 484–c. 425 BC) mentioned 'Aesop the fable writer', whom he described as a slave from Phrygia (now Turkey) who had won his freedom by telling fables and enjoyed the company of the beautiful courtesan Rhodopis. Aesop's fame was so great that his name was also cited by Socrates, Aristotle, Aristophanes, Plato, Pliny and a host of other ancient writers.

Many historians believe that Aesop's fables had been passed on by oral tradition dating back in some instances much further than the sixth century BC; a few have been traced back on papyri 800 to 1,000 years earlier. The ones he told apparently were not collected and written down until three centuries after his death. Throughout later periods, including the Middle Ages and the Renaissance, additional fables were added to the list ascribed to Aesop, although they had actually come from other times and cultures that had no relation to the former slave. Over time they had been refined and adapted, while retaining their original simplicity and cogent message.

Ancient Greek and Latin manuscripts repeated Aesop's fables, and versions of the tales were among some of the earliest subjects translated and printed across Europe, further enhancing his reputation as a fabulist. To be accepted into the genre, subsequent additions had to meet a number of criteria: They had to be plain and unadorned, brief and true to nature in their depiction of animals and plants. Their context and concluding moral were also crucial. And they had to impart timeless, universal truths.

Versions have been published in countless forms and languages. Aesop's fables have been dramatised on the stage and in movies, set to verse and music, adapted in cartoons, and performed in dance.

For centuries the fables were primarily aimed at adults, but in 1693 the English philosopher John Locke advocated tailoring them to 'delight and entertain a child', along with illustrations that would appeal to young people. Since then Aesop's fables have been a staple of children's literature, and the names of the stories ('The Wolf in Sheep's Clothing', 'The Goose that Laid the Golden Egg', 'The Boy Who Cried Wolf') have become a part of common vernacular.

LEFT: In 'The Raven and the Fox', the vain bird is smooth-talked into dropping its morsel of cheese. This woodcut illustration is from William Caxton's printing of 1484.

ABOVE: *A woodcut portrait of Aesop from the first English edition of the fables, printed in 1484 by William Caxton.*

法 兵 子 孫

SUN TZŬ

ON THE

ART OF WAR

THE OLDEST MILITARY TREATISE IN THE WORLD

TRANSLATED FROM THE CHINESE WITH INTRODUCTION
AND CRITICAL NOTES

BY

LIONEL GILES, M. A.
Assistant in the Department of Oriental Printed Books & MSS.
in the British Museum.

LONDON
LUZAC & Cº.
1910

*ABOVE: The first English edition to gain recognition was
Lionel Giles's 1910 translation. It is still in print today.*

The Art of War
Sun Tzu

(c. 512 BC)

Although it was written two and a half millennia ago, an ancient Chinese treatise that is packed with wise advice about warfare strategy and tactics has remained a must-read by generations of military commanders, business leaders and competitors of all sorts. Its tenets are credited with many victories, large and small.

Sun Tzu, or Sunzi, is reputed to have lived during the Spring and Autumn period of Chinese history that ran from about 722 to 470 BC, at the height of ancient China's golden age. Little is known about him or the sources of his expertise, other than that he was a military general and philosopher who is credited as the primary author of *The Art of War*.

In his day, as dozens of small feudal principalities developed their own competing ideas and philosophies, they increasingly battled one another for supremacy, and warfare assumed a more central role. After Sun Tzu's death, one of his descendants, Sun Ping of Chi, repopularised the wise philosopher's treatise in about 350 BC. It's said that *The Art of War* played a large role in reshaping and unifying ancient China, which became history's most stable and peaceful empire.

As one of China's Seven Military Classics, Sun Tzu's work achieved such fame in Asia that even illiterate peasants knew it by name, and generations of combatants memorised much of its contents. Over time the book has remained one of the definitive classics on waging war.

The author considered war as a necessary evil that must be avoided whenever possible. He also offered sage advice about how to win a war and what not to do when contending with one's enemies. 'The art of war is of vital importance to the State,' he wrote. 'It is a matter of life and death, a road either to safety or to ruin. Hence it is a subject of inquiry which can on no account be neglected.' In his view, 'The supreme art of war is to subdue the enemy without fighting.'

The text is composed of thirteen chapters, each of which is devoted to instructing commanders on a specific key aspect of warfare. Sun Tzu presents five constant or fundamental factors to be taken into account in warfare deliberations: the way (moral law), heaven (seasons), earth (terrain), leadership (the commander), and management (method and discipline), as well as seven elements that determine the outcomes of military engagements.

Although Sun Tzu is generally agreed to be the primary author, many historians argue that the treatise may have been modified over time as new developments occurred in warfare, such as the introduction of cavalry. The earliest known bamboo copy of the work, known as the Yinqueshan Han Slips and unearthed in Shandong in 1972, has been dated to the Western Han dynasty of 206 BC to AD 220, and it is nearly identical to modern editions of *The Art of War*. The first European edition occurred in France in 1772, and the most famous English version, by Lionel Giles, first appeared in 1910.

Many of the book's precepts hold true for activities besides warfare. 'If you know the enemy and know yourself, you need not fear the result of a hundred battles. If you know yourself but not the enemy, for every victory gained you will also suffer a defeat. If you know neither the enemy nor yourself, you will succumb in every battle.'

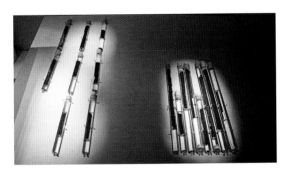

LEFT: These inscribed bamboo strips are the oldest known copy of The Art of War. *Known as the Yinqueshan Han Slips, they date from 206 BC to AD 220.*

The Analects of Confucius

(475–221 BC)

An ancient Chinese philosopher compiled a collection of wise sayings that offered ethical principles to regulate the five relationships of life – the relationships of prince and subject, parent and child, brother and brother, husband and wife, and friend and friend – and his guidance has been followed for thousands of years.

Confucius (c. 551–479 BC) was a philosopher and politician who had grown up in the *shi* (gentry) class and spent many years compiling wise sayings to guide individuals in their daily lives, according to ethical principles.

'Analect' means a fragment or extract of literature, or a collection of teachings. In the case of Confucius it also refers to a discussion or verbal exchange of moral and ethical principles. *The Analects of Confucius* took the form of Confucian teachings and thoughts, along with fragments of dialogues between the philosopher and his disciples.

Compiled and written by Confucius's followers during the Warring States period (c. 475–221 BC), *The Analects* are considered among the most representative works of Confucian thought, and they still exert great influence on Chinese culture and East Asia. Many scholars believe that the analects were later refined into their final form during the mid-Han dynasty (206 BC–220 AD) to become a central text of Chinese culture. Regarded as a foundational work in Chinese education for nearly two thousand years, the *Analects* continued to be officially used in civil service examinations until the early twentieth century. Although they were frowned upon under the Cultural Revolution of the 1960s, they continue to shape the morality and thoughts of millions of Chinese, upholding the central virtues of decorum, justice, fairness and filial piety.

One of the key concepts of

Confucianism is *ren*, which stands for a comprehensive set of ethical values that include kindness, benevolence, humaneness, altruism and goodness. *The Analects* teach how to cultivate and practise *ren* in speech, action and thought. Modesty, self-deprecation, humility, and self-discipline are prized as essential virtues, which flow from the Chinese equivalent of the Bible's Golden Rule: 'Do not do to others what you would not like done to yourself.'

The Analects use the term 'junzi' for an ideally ethical and capable person, while 'dao' is a teaching, skill, or art that is a key to some arena of action. 'Zhong' denotes loyalty; 'xin' stands for trustworthiness; 'jing' for respectfulness and attentiveness; 'xiao' means obedience to one's elders; 'yong' is courage or valour.

The Analects provided guidance in dealing with others in every aspect of an individual's life, including self-awareness: 'Have no friends not equal to yourself.'

The hallmark of Confucian teaching was its emphasis on education, study and knowledge. 'When you know a thing, to hold that you know it; and when you do not know a thing, to allow that you do not know it – this is knowledge.'

The Analects is one of the four great Confucian texts known as the Four Books, and it has been one of the most widely studied works in China for the past two millennia. Its combination of wisdom, philosophy and social morality continue to influence Chinese culture and values today.

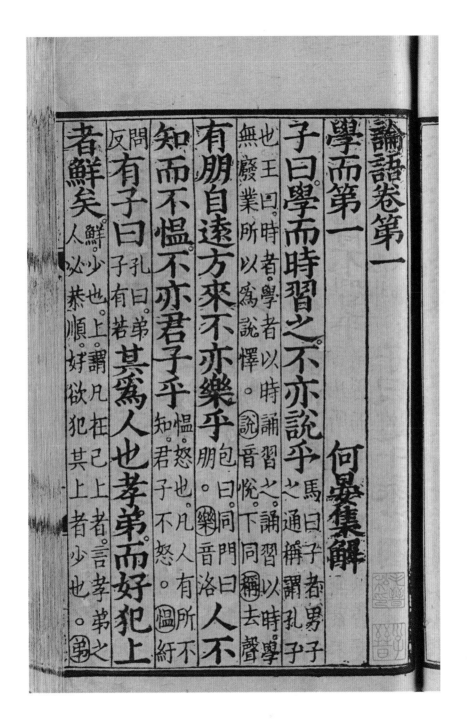

ABOVE: A late seventeenth-century illustration of the Kama Sutra *attributed to the Rajput school of painting.*

OPPOSITE: A 1964 edition of Sir Richard Burton's famous translation of the

Kama Sutra, *which was first published privately in 1883.*

Kama Sutra
Vatsyayana
(400 BC–AD 200)

Written in ancient Sanskrit two thousand years ago and stashed in a cave in northern India, this explicit and highly literary sex manual was first published in 1883 but wasn't issued in the United States until 1962. Although it's long been tagged as a showcase of exotic coital positions, today's readers are discovering that its contents and style make for a remarkably modern guide to the art of living.

Everyone who hasn't read the *Kama Sutra* knows it as an illustrated Indian tutorial of exotic sexual intercourse techniques. Yet the original manuscript didn't include any drawings, and its text actually offered a great deal more than expert advice about coital relations.

Found in a cave in northern India in the nineteenth century, the work was translated from an archaic form of ancient Sanskrit by an English orientalist and linguist, Sir Richard Burton, and privately published in 1883. The title combines desire or pleasure (*kama*) and a thread that holds things together (*sutra*). In some Eastern religions such as Buddhism and Hinduism, sutras also signify an aphorism or a compendium of aphorisms.

Little is known about the *Kama Sutra*'s author, Vatsyayana, who claimed to be a celibate monk who had compiled all of the accumulated sexual knowledge from several previous authors as a form of his own meditation and contemplation of the deity. Most scholars place the work's origin between 400 BC and AD 200, which makes it the oldest surviving text from that period of ancient Indian history.

The *Kama Sutra* consists of thirty-six chapters organised into seven parts containing 1,250 verses. It examines four *purusharthas* (basic ends of worldly human action) – *dharma* (virtue and righteousness), *artha* (wealth and power), *kama* (pleasure) and *moksha* (liberation) – and offers comprehensive advice for a good and pleasurable life.

Although the guidance is offered

from the vantage point of a worldly but virtuous male, it also pertains to women, with tips that cover virtually every aspect of living, from youth through courtship, romance, sex and marriage. It tells males and females what to wear, what to eat, with whom to socialise, and how to act in order to achieve the power that will attract others. Members of both genders are counselled to become well-versed in the arts of pleasure in all of its forms.

As after-dinner warm-up entertainments, he particularly recommends a list of 'well-known games peculiar to different regions, like plucking the mango, eating roasted grain, nibbling lotus stems, collecting new leaves, squirting water, pantomimes, the silk-cotton tree game, and mock-fights with wild jasmine flowers.'

When it comes to sexual intercourse, he devotes extensive attention to different techniques of embracing, kissing, scratching, biting, hitting and moaning, oral sex and coital positions. Four of the 'embraces at the time of actual sexual union', for example, include the 'twining creeper', the 'climbing a tree', the 'sesame seeds and rice grains', and the 'milk and water'. Another involves using the thighs 'like a pair of tongs'.

It endorses sexual relations on grounds of pleasure, not just procreation, and allows that females can also achieve orgasm. Given that it was written so long ago, in a culture with deeply misogynist traditions, the *Kama Sutra*'s philosophy of gender relations seems remarkably progressive.

The Republic
Plato

(c. 380 BC)

A masterpiece of philosophy and political thought, which asks questions about society that are still debated today. Plato's imagined conversation about the nature of justice in a city republic was inspired by his own traumatic experience of state injustice.

Plato (c. 428–348 BC) was born in Athens, where he became a student of Socrates, one of the founding fathers of Western philosophy. When Socrates criticized the Athenian government he was tried on trumped-up charges in a kangaroo court and sentenced to death. Plato witnessed the final days of his mentor and was so disgusted with the injustice meted out by the state that he left Athens in search of fairer societies. He wrote *The Republic* after his return.

Plato's writing generally takes the form of a Socratic dialogue – that is, an imaginary conversation as Socrates would have conducted it. Socrates, the central character in *The Republic*, asks a question of his companions and identifies the flaws in their answers. The process is repeated until, it is hoped, a consensus is reached about a flawless truth. In *The Republic*, the question is 'What is justice?'

The Republic includes one of Plato's most enduring allegories – the fire in the cave. Imagine some prisoners who have spent their whole life in a cave, chained so that they face only its back wall. They watch shadows cast on the wall by a campfire and imagine the objects that might have made them. The shadows are the prisoners' only reality.

But suppose one of the prisoners is released from the cave. He can now see the fire and the actual objects, although he cannot at first accept their reality compared to the shadows to which he has been used. Leaving the cave he finds an even more intense reality in the blindingly bright daylight, and finally sees the sun itself, the ultimate symbol of goodness. On returning to the cave he is blinded now by the darkness, but he has literally been enlightened. He is a philosopher now, with a duty to share the light.

Plato makes a distinction between shadows and objects, which echoes the distinction between mere objects or social constructs and the ideal forms or ideas that they attempt to represent. It is the philosopher's task to identify these ideals.

The Socratic discussion flows naturally from justice to the nature of the common good, and to the rights and responsibilities of the state and its citizens. Failing to find a real example of a properly just society, Socrates and his friends set about constructing a hypothetical city-state from scratch. The ideal leader is, they speculate, a philosopher-king.

More important than the conclusion of *The Republic* is the process and the value of discussing ideas. It is historically and philosophically the single most influential work of its kind ever written and still widely read today. Its impact on Western thinking is summed up by twentieth-century philosopher A.N. Whitehead, who wrote: 'The safest general characterisation of the European philosophical tradition is that it consists of a series of footnotes to Plato.'

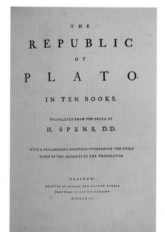

RIGHT: Title page of the oldest complete copy of The Republic. *This ninth-century AD manuscript is held at the Bibliothèque Nationale de France in Paris. There are earlier fragments of* The Republic *written on papyrus that date to the third century AD.*

LEFT: The first English translation, published in Glasgow in 1763.

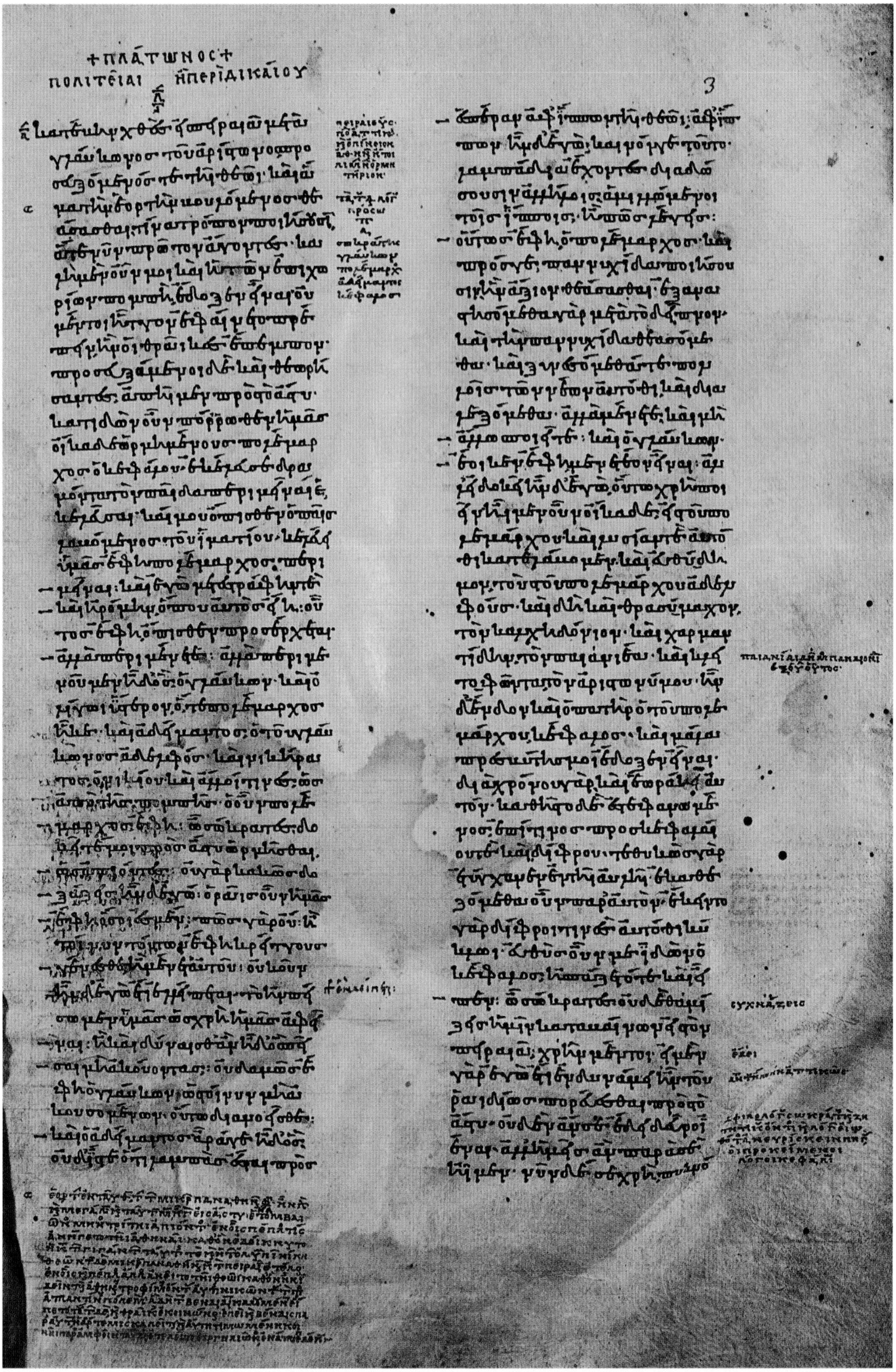
+ΠΛΑΤΩΝΟϹ+

ΠΟΛΙΤΕΙΑΙ ΗΠΕΡΙΔΙΚΑΙΟΥ

3

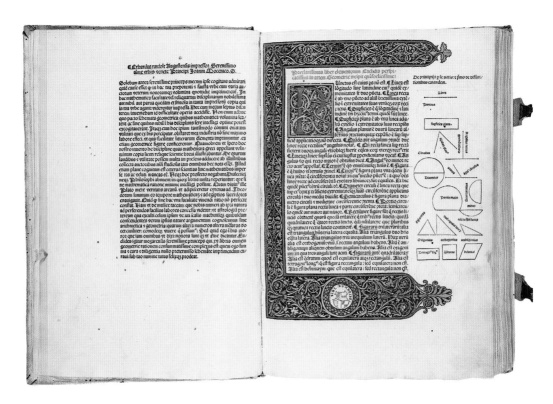

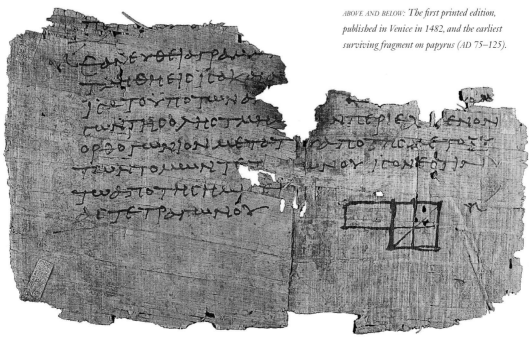

ABOVE AND BELOW: The first printed edition, published in Venice in 1482, and the earliest surviving fragment on papyrus (AD 75–125).

Elements of Geometry
Euclid
(c. 300 BC)

The facts about Euclid's life are unclear, yet he compiled the great treatise that for two thousand years has been the most successful textbook in history and the foundational work in mathematics and logic – with fans who have run the gamut from Abraham Lincoln to Albert Einstein.

Euclid (meaning 'renowned, glorious') was a great ancient Greek mathematician who lived in Alexandria, Egypt, near the mouth of the Nile. He is presumed to have been born around 330 BC in Tyre, and some accounts say that he attended Plato's former school in Athens and was trained by Plato's students. Most historians claim that he worked as a tutor in Alexandria.

Regardless of his physical roots, his masterpiece, *Elements of Geometry*, indicates that he was well versed in the works of other mathematicians, including Thales, Pythagoras, Eudoxus, Hippocrates, Autolycus and Theaetetus. What made his achievement so great was not some new discovery but the fact that it codified existing mathematical knowledge into a single coherent system that became the model for all future deductive, mathematical reasoning. Although the version of his text that is used today was also probably modified by others who followed, Euclid's stature in geometry is unrivalled.

Passed down for centuries as handwritten manuscripts, the first printed edition, based on Campanus of Novara's 1260 Latin translation, appeared in Venice in 1482, shortly after the introduction of the printing press, and it remained second only to the Bible in its number of published editions.

Elements of Geometry consists of thirteen books with 465 propositions dealing with geometry, plane and solid, and number theory, which Euclid had compiled as a concise encyclopaedia of geometry definitions, axioms (or 'common notions'), postulates, and other essential mathematical knowledge, all of which he had confirmed through his own rigorous mathematical proofs.

Books one to six deal with plane (two-dimensional) geometry. The first two set out the basic properties of triangles, parallels, parallelograms, rectangles and squares. Three and four deal with circles. Book five examines proportion and magnitude, and book six looks at applications of the results of book five to plane geometry. Seven to nine cover number theory; ten examines irrational numbers; eleven to thirteen cover solid (three-dimensional) geometry.

While the Egyptians and the Babylonians had used geometry to solve specific problems, Euclid took the study further by stating theories and general rules that could be used to guide the practice of mathematics. His book was remarkable for the clarity with which the theorems are stated and proved.

For centuries the textbook has helped to shape the thinking of students of maths and logic at every level of understanding. Abraham Lincoln wrote about studying his copy under the lamplight, saying: 'You never can make a lawyer if you do not understand what demonstrate means; and I left my situation in Springfield, went home to my father's house, and stayed there till I could give any proposition in the six books of Euclid at sight.'

Albert Einstein recalled that as a boy the two gifts that made the greatest impression on him were a magnetic compass and a copy of Euclid's *Elements*.

LEFT: The first English translation, published in London in 1560.

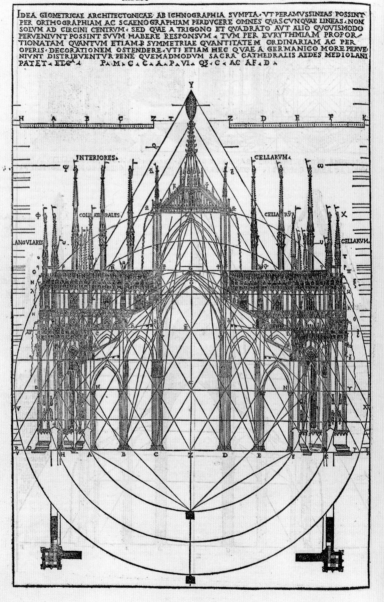

*ABOVE AND OPPOSITE: Pages from the 1521 edition showing Vitruvius's principles
as applied to Milan Cathedral (above), and his workings on the proportions of
the human body (opposite), which were later refined by Leonardo da Vinci.*

34_____100 Books that Changed the World

De Architectura
Vitruvius
(20 BC)

A ten-volume treatise compiled in the first century BC, *De Architectura* presented an illustrious architect's personal account of magnificent construction projects throughout the Roman Empire, along with a detailed manual and history of ancient engineering.

As the only significant work on architecture to survive from antiquity, *De Architectura* is unique. Very little is known about its author, Marcus Vitruvius Pollio (c. 80–15 BC), beyond what is set down in the book he wrote. Trained in architecture at the height of the Roman Empire, he served with the engineering corps in Caesar's army as it besieged its way across Europe around 50 BC. In Roman times the role of an architect stretched across many disciplines and a knowledge of engineering and surveying was paramount when building military camps, bridges, roads and aqueducts. Vitruvius also turned his hand to designing siege weapons such as ballista or catapults for firing metal bolts at the enemy.

Vitruvius is sometimes loosely referred to as the first architect, but he was less of an original thinker and more a recorder, someone who extensively catalogued existing Roman architectural practice. The only great building he worked on was the basilica in Fano, Italy, completed in 19 BC but no longer standing. His most famous credo for the ideal building was *firmitas, utilitas, venustas* (sturdy, useful, beautiful). He detailed Roman architectural practices in ten separate and diverse books that make up *De Architectura*. Apart from writing on materials, location, security, acoustics, water supply and central heating, among many things, there is a touch of politics in there, too. Vitruvius makes a recurring point that the work of some of the most talented are unknown, while lesser talents become famous. This was mostly true of his own magnum opus, which was obscured from history for more than a thousand years. Even so, Frontinus mentions him in his AD 100 book on aqueducts, *De Aquaeductu*, in relation to the standardisation of pipework.

De Architectura stands alone as the most comprehensive account of ancient Greek and Roman architectural principles and building techniques. It was written before the Romans devised cross vaulting, domes, or used concrete, but in all other aspects it is peerless. When it was rediscovered in 1414, it became an inspiration to the leading thinkers and artists of the Renaissance. The text was first published in 1486, followed by an illustrated edition in 1511. Leonardo da Vinci used Vitruvius's definition of human proportions to create his own Vitruvian Man: the human body inscribed in a circle and square. For the great sixteenth-century architect Palladio, Vitruvius was his 'master and guide'.

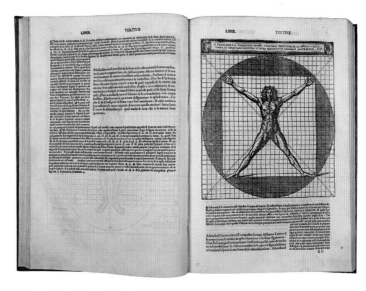

Naturalis Historia
Pliny the Elder
(AD 79)

The world's first scientific encyclopaedia was a remarkable achievement for a man who also held a full-time post as a high-ranking civil servant in the Roman Empire. Pliny's thirty-seven-volume magnum opus contains everything that the Romans knew about the natural world.

Pliny the Elder (c. AD 23–79) is so called to distinguish him from his nephew Pliny the Younger, also a noted author, on whom we rely for many details of his uncle's life. In a letter from the younger Pliny to the Roman historian Tacitus, he wrote, 'Blessed are those who either do what is worth writing of, or write what is worth reading; above measure blessed those on whom both gifts have been conferred. Amongst the latter is my uncle.'

Pliny the Elder led a full life. At twenty-three he began a twelve-year career as a cavalry officer in the Roman army's campaigns in Germany. During his military service he wrote his first book, on the art of throwing a javelin on horseback. On his return to Rome he practised law while writing a biography, several plays, a history of the German campaign in twenty volumes, and a book on the art of public speaking. Coming to the attention of the emperor Vespasian, he was appointed governor of a succession of Roman provinces from Africa to Belgium. Returning to Rome again he was made an admiral of the Roman fleet, completed and expanded another author's history of the city, and began compiling his last work, *Naturalis Historia* (*Natural History*) in AD 77.

Of Pliny's remarkable output, only the thirty-seven books of *Natural History* survive. All the others are lost, and we know of them only because later authors refer to them or quote them in their own writings. Tacitus, for

example, relies heavily on Pliny's German history, and Pliny's nephew mentions several of his uncle's works in his letters. *Natural History* is such a towering achievement that it makes the absence of any other of Pliny's works all the more tragic.

Pliny covered astronomy, geography, zoology, botany, medicine, geology, arts and much more in his survey of the natural world. He did not, it must be said, distinguish between actual facts, mere public opinion, and his own conjecture about some things. But as a comprehensive assembly of what the Roman world believed to be true, it was unrivalled. Two innovative features further distinguish it – an index of its contents and a list of sources. Pliny was rigorous in noting them, and the bibliography of *Natural History* records some four thousand different authors.

All encyclopaedias are modelled on this one. Over the centuries that followed, many of Pliny's original sources were, like his own works, lost or destroyed. Only the *Natural History* survived, to be quoted or plagiarised by future writers who believed it to be the fount of all knowledge. For example, his observations about exotic wild animals form the basis for many medieval bestiaries.

Not until the end of the fifteenth century did some authors begin to question its accuracy. Science may finally have overtaken Pliny in many respects, but his record of the world as his fellow Romans understood it is an invaluable snapshot of another era.

LIBRO PRIMO DELLA NATVRALE HISTORIA DI. C.
PLINIO SECONDO TRADOCTA IN LINGVA FIOREN
TINA PER CHRISTOPHORO LANDINO FIORENTI
NO ALSERENISSIMO FERDINANDO RE DI NAPOLI.
PREFATIONE

ITERMINAI O GIOCONDISSIMO
imperadore con epistola forse di troppa licétia
narrarti elibri della historia naturale: opera no
uella alle muse romane:nata apresso di me nel
lultima genitura. Sia adunq; questa prefatióe
uerissima di te métre che gia inuecchia nel grá
dissimo tuo padre : per che usando el uerso di
Catullo mio compatriota tu soleui pure stima
re qualche chosa le mie ciácie. Tu conosci que
sta castrense & militare parola. Et lui chome tu
sai mutando le prime syllabe si fece alquanto
piu duro che non uolea essere stimato da tuoi
familiari & serui . Per questo adunq; ditermi
nai scriuerti:& áchora per che le nostre chose apparischino & sieno manifeste p questa
mia audacia maxime dolédoti tu che pel passato non lhabbi facto in una altra nostra
procace epistola. Et accio che tutti glhuomini sappino quanto di pari lomperio techo
uiua : Tu elquale hai triomphato & se stato censore & sei uolte cósolo & participe del
la tribunitia potesta:Se stato prefecto del pretorio:ilche hai facto piu nobile che tutti
glaltri magistrati:perche per piacere a tuo padre & allordine equestre lacceptasti : Et
tutte queste cose per rispecto della republica hai facto : Et me chome nel contubernio
castrense tractasti? Et certo niéte ha mutato inte lamplitudine & grandezza della tua
fortuna:se non che tanto piu possi & uogla giouare:quáto quella e maggiore. Adúq;
béche a tutti glaltri huomini sia aperta la uia a impetrare ogni chosa da te uenerádoti:
Niente di meno solo laudacia fa che io piu familiarmente te honori. Questa audacia
adunq; imputerai a te medesimo:& a te medesimo nel nostro fallo perdonerai. Io mi
stropicciai la faccia:& niente di meno nessuno proficto ho facto: perche per unaltra
uia mapparisti grande:& di lontano mi rimuoui con le faccelline del tuo ingegno . Et
certo in nexuno piu sfolgora quella:laquale piu ueramente e decta in te che in altri for
za deloquentia.In te e quella facundia che alla tribunitia potesta si conuiene:Con qta
risonantia tuoni le laude paterne? Có quanta(non sanza amore)dimostri quelle di
tuo fratello?Quanto se excellente & sublime nella poetica faculta ? O gran fecondita
danimo. Certo hai trouato inche modo possi imitare tuo fratello . Ma queste chose
chi potrebbe sanza paura considerare : hauendo a uenire al giudicio dellongegno
tuo : maxime essendo quello dame prouocato? Certamente non sono in simile
conditione quegli che publicano alchuno libro:& quegli che ate glintitolano. Impero
che se io publicassi & non lo intitolassi ate:potrei dire perche leggi tu queste chose o
imperadore:lequali sono scripte albasso uulgo & alla turba de glagricultori & de glar
tefici & a quegli che cósumano elloro otio negli studii?Perche adunq; ti fa tu giudice:
concio sia che quando io scriueuo questa opera:non thaueuo posto nella tauola doue
sono descripti egiudici:Et eri di tanta excellentia : che non stimauo che tu ti degnassi
scendere si basso?Preterea quando bene non fussi in si excelso grado:nientedimeno gli
scriptori comunemente fuggono el giudicio de docti . Questo fa Cicerone:elquale e
di tanta eloquentia:che puo sottomettere longegno al giuocho della fortuna : & quel

ABOVE: *This early printed edition, published in Venice in 1476, was
specially illuminated for banker Filippo Strozzi.*
OPPOSITE: *The first English translation, published in London in 1601.*

100 Books that Changed the World_____37

The Quran

(AD 609-632)

Muslims revere the Quran as the word of Allah and the sacred verses form the centre of their daily religious worship. The rhymed medieval text imparts the religion's basic tenets and provides the strict rules to guide every believer's faith and conduct.

Islamic tradition says that the Prophet Muhammad received his first divine revelation from Allah through Gabriel the archangel in a cave on Mount Hira near Mecca where he had gone by himself to meditate and pray. For the next twenty-three years, until Muhammad's death in AD 632, he received and recited more divine verses and went on to share them with others. Some of his companions also committed the verses to memory, and scribes were later used to put the revelations into writing in Arabic. The verses were eventually published as the Quran, which spread the faith and helped to turn Arabia into a more literate society that rose to become a great power, making Islam a powerful force in that part of the world.

Muslims regard the Quran as the culmination of divine revelations put forth in the Torah and the Bible. Islam teaches that God revealed his will through divine messengers, known as prophets, including Moses, Jesus and Muhammad. However, Islam also instructs that the previous messengers were flawed, whereas the Prophet Muhammad was the only one to accurately convey the complete and unquestionable word of God. Although the work reflected conditions in the early Islamic community of Arabia, its passages were, and still are, considered to be infallible, transcending time and space in the minds of its believers. All Muslims are commanded to submit to the will of Allah as the Prophet Muhammad commands.

The structure of the Quran consists of 114 *surahs* (chapters). Each *surah* has a heading with a title indicating whether its verses were revealed to Muhammad before or after the *hijrah* (his

emigration from Mecca to Medina). The verses provide detailed guidance regarding marriage, divorce, inheritance, funerals and political meetings. Teaching is favoured over narrative. Unlike stories in the Bible, however, the text of the Quran doesn't seem to have any beginning, middle, or end.

After the Prophet Muhammad's death, his followers carried on his mission, and the Islamic faith spread very quickly. But theological conflicts emerged among various factions. Some of the schisms occurred as efforts were made to translate the Quran into dialects and languages other than the original Arabic, and there were many intense disputes among the believers over different shades of meaning. Deep-seated schisms still exist today.

The oldest handwritten fragments of the text, known as the Birmingham Quran, have been radiocarbon-dated to before AD 645. The first Latin translation appeared during the Crusades of the 1100s. The first printed edition occurred between 1537 and 1538 in Venice. By the 1900s, translations had occurred in several major languages besides Arabic, although Muslim scholars classify these foreign translations as 'commentaries or interpretations' to distinguish them from the original text. Today there are large Muslim populations throughout the globe.

Islam instructs its worshippers to conform to certain rules governing their Quranic recitations. The reciter must sit, facing Mecca, and proceed according to an acceptable tempo. Although Islam views men and women as spiritual equals, it presents many different requirements for each gender.

Arabian Nights

(AD 800–900)

The tales of the Arabian Nights – the first-ever collection of bedtime stories – introduced storytelling tricks that authors take for granted today. They have had a greater influence on Western literature than in the Eastern countries, where they were originally written.

The contents of the *Arabian Nights* (originally known as *One Thousand and One Nights*) have evolved over a thousand years. Its earliest stories are from eighth- or ninth-century Persia and India. Genuinely Arabian tales were added in the tenth century, to be joined in the thirteenth century by contributions from Egyptian and Syrian traditions.

One common feature throughout its history has been the use of a literary device found in early Sanskrit writings, the frame story, whereby a character in one story tells a further story. In the *Arabian Nights* a sultan, Shahryar, executes a new wife every night to prevent her from being unfaithful to him. His latest wife Scheherazade hits on the idea of telling him a new story every night, saving the ending for the following evening so that he will not kill her. What follows are the stories that she tells, and after a thousand and one of them Shahryar decides not to kill her.

The *Arabian Nights* asserts the power of storytelling, to release the reader from dull reality, convey moral messages, and above all, entertain. There are examples in the *Arabian Nights* of early crime fiction, farcical comedy, erotic fiction, gothic horror – and some stories are the earliest ever to include ghosts.

Several themes unify the book, despite the diversity of its sources. Many tell of rises from rags to riches and of downfalls because of greed. Many, such as 'Aladdin', are fantastical, or rely on magic. Others, like 'Ali Baba', hinge on the good luck of the central character, but also on his ability to take advantage of that luck.

'Ali Baba' and 'Aladdin', which we think of as typical *Arabian Nights* tales, are actually very late additions to the book. The first European translation of the *Arabian Nights* was published in French in 1704. It was written by Antoine Galland, who followed in the footsteps of many before him in adding a couple of his own stories to the collection. In his case, 'Aladdin' and 'Ali Baba'.

An English translation based on Galland's work appeared in 1706, the first to use the title *Arabian Nights*. But the definitive English version was translated in 1885 by the explorer Sir Richard Burton, who also published the first English edition of the *Kama Sutra*. Burton gleefully restored the erotic elements that Galland and others had omitted on grounds of decency, adding footnotes to explain Eastern sexual practices.

The many editions available today are testament to its enduring appeal, while its ability to shock has not diminished. In 1985, Egypt banned an unexpurgated version of the text on the grounds that it violated pornography laws. But as Salman Rushdie observes: 'Sometimes great, banned works defy the censor's description and impose themselves on the world – *Ulysses, Lolita*, the *Arabian Nights*.'

OPPOSITE: *'The Fisherman and the Genie' from a 1907 edition illustrated by Edmund Dulac.*

BELOW: *An English edition from 1811, based on the first European translation by Antoine Galland, which was published in twelve volumes between 1704 and 1717.*

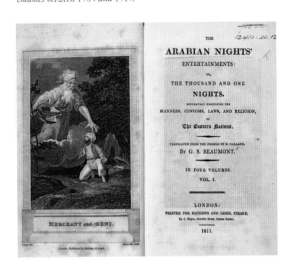

The Tale of Genji
Murasaki Shikibu

(c. 1021)

An early masterpiece of Japanese literature, sometimes hailed as the world's first novel, *The Tale of Genji* is still read by every Japanese schoolchild a thousand years after it was first circulated. Twentieth-century translations revealed its brilliance to a global audience.

Genji, the central character of Murasaki's novel, is a handsome young man, the son of an emperor but who is obliged to live as a commoner. *The Tale of Genji* is a simple narrative of his life, a mixture of political intrigue and romantic adventure. Its overarching theme is 'the sorrow of human existence', a phrase that recurs in the text more than a thousand times. Genji's fortunes at court wax and wane, occupying the first two parts of the story. The third follows the tribulations of his son after his death. The book was originally written in at least fifty-four instalments and completed over a decade.

Like much great literature, *The Tale of Genji* excels not only by its rich poetry and storytelling but because it is a window on the times in which it was written. Murasaki (c. 973–1031) lived during Japan's Heian period, a time of relative stability. She was a member of the powerful Fujiwara clan, which controlled the country. The imperial court, which she joined as a lady-in-waiting, led a life of cultured, hedonistic isolation from the rest of the population.

Women were further isolated by virtue of their sex. They were not permitted to be seen in public; a woman lived with her father even after marriage, visited there occasionally only by her husband. Women were considered intellectually inferior to men and were therefore not taught Chinese, the official language of state and commerce. Instead, they were encouraged to read stories written in *kana*, the earliest form of Japanese script, which first emerged during the Heian period. Romantic tales were admired, and it is probably because of her reputation as an author that she was admitted to court as a companion for the emperor's daughter.

Murasaki began to write for other ladies-in-waiting, cut off as they all were from society and stimulation. Her readers in turn copied out the text and passed it on to their friends. Thus, the tale's fame quickly spread far and wide. Although the original manuscript is lost, some three hundred early copies of it survive, all with fascinating variations in detail. Previously undiscovered copies still turn up from time to time in dusty archives.

The epic tale shows the influence of classic Chinese historical poetry and the prose stories of Murasaki's Japanese contemporaries. Her great innovation was to write about purely earthly subjects, excluding the supernatural and the magical elements of her predecessors' stories. This was a modern world, a world entirely understood by her readers.

The first complete English translation was published in 1933, and on reading it Jorge Luis Borges noted that Murasaki wrote 'with an almost miraculous naturalness, and what interests us is not the exoticism ... but rather the human passions of the novel.' It is rooted in eleventh-century Japan, but its understanding of human psychology make it entirely relevant to the twenty-first century.

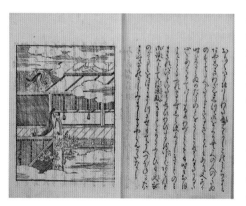

LEFT: Pages from the first printed edition of The Tale of Genji *with woodcuts by Yamamoto Shunshô (1610–82), published in Kyoto in 1654.*

ABOVE: *A woodblock print by the famous Japanese artist Utagawa Kunisada (1823–80) showing a scene from chapter forty-one of* The Tale of Genji, *'Maboroshi' ('The Wizard').*

The Divine Comedy
Dante
(1308-21)

The greatest literary creation of the Middle Ages is a huge allegorical poem that envisions a trip through Hell, Purgatory and Heaven, guided by the Roman poet Virgil. Based on its breathtaking scope, detail and divine inspiration, critics have called it a language equivalent to a Gothic cathedral.

Dante Alighieri (1265–1321) was a poet born in Florence who in 1308 embarked on an epic tale about an imaginative journey through the afterlife, originally entitled *La Commedia* (*The Comedy*). He finished it twelve years later in 1320. The work had a profound effect on Giovanni Boccaccio (1313–75), author of *The Decameron*, who added the word 'Divine' to the title in appreciation for its poetry, making it *La Divina Commedia* (*The Divine Comedy*).

The epic poem followed the medieval world's view of the afterlife as promulgated by the Catholic Church in the fourteenth century. It describes Dante's imaginary travels through Inferno (Hell), Purgatoria (Purgatory) and Paradiso (Heaven), representing the soul's journey from sin to purification.

His vision was drawn from a vast encyclopaedia of knowledge taken from religious literature, history, art and cosmology. Into the three parts he inserted notable figures from mythology, history and philosophy, as well as some of his own friends and enemies.

Dante wrote in the first person, which was unusual in literature at that time, and he gave his account as an explorer might do, starting on the night before Good Friday and ending on the Wednesday after Easter in the spring of 1300, when Dante would have been thirty-five years old and midway through his expected life span.

In the beginning of the poem Dante becomes lost in the woods when he is confronted by three dangerous beasts – a lion, a leopard and a wolf – and becomes unable to find the right path to his salvation.

'All hope abandon, ye who enter here!' says an inscription on the gates of Hell.

> There, sighs and lamentations and loud wailings resounded through the starless air, so that at first it made me weep; strange tongues, horrible language, words of pain, tones of anger, voices loud and hoarse, and with these the sound of hands, made a tumult which is whirling through that air forever dark, as sand eddies in a whirlwind.

The fact that he wrote in a Tuscan dialect, rather than the traditional Latin, further added to its popularity and helped make Tuscan the lingua franca of Italy.

Although *The Divine Comedy* was viewed as a masterpiece in the centuries that followed its publication, by the time of the Enlightenment it had fallen out of critical favour. Artist William Blake helped restore its lustre when he was commissioned to illustrate several passages in 1826, and it was taken up once more by the nineteenth-century romantic writers. Henry Wadsworth Longfellow was the first American translator and fellow poet T.S. Eliot was convinced of the writer's stature among the literary greats. 'Dante and Shakespeare divide the world between them,' he wrote. 'There is no third.'

ABOVE: A circa 1470 illustration of Dante's Inferno, showing Lucifer torturing sinners.
LEFT: Domenico di Michelino's 1456 portrait of Dante, La Commedia Illumina Firenze *(The Comedy Illuminating Florence) is in Florence Cathedral. The fresco is divided, like the poem, into three parts: Inferno, Purgatorio and Paradiso.*

Of dubbyl worstede was hys semy cope
That rounde was as a belle out of presse
Somwhat he lispyde for hys wanwlonesse
To make hys englysshe swete vpon hys tonge
And in hys harpynge whan he hadde y sunge
Hys eyen twynklyde in hys hed a ryght
As don the sterris in the frosty nyght
Thys worthy frere was callyde hukberde

A Marchaunt ther was wyth a forkyde berde
In motley on hygh on hys hors he sat
Vp on his hed a flaundres beuer hat
Hys bootis claspyde feyr and fetuysly
Hys resons he spack ful solempnely
Shewynge alway the encresse of hys wynnynge
He wolde the see were kept for ony thynge
Betwyx Myddelburgh and orewelle
Welle coude he in hys eschaunges selle

*ABOVE: A woodcut image of the Knight from William
Caxton's 1483 edition of* The Canterbury Tales.

46 _____ 100 Books that Changed the World

The Canterbury Tales
Geoffrey Chaucer
(1390s)

Penned at a time of turbulent social change in English history, a royal clerk's path-breaking collection of tales in verse and prose about a motley group of characters on a religious pilgrimage changed the form of English literature and left a vivid portrait of English society in the late fourteenth century.

By 1386, Geoffrey Chaucer (c. 1343–1400) had led an extremely active life and held many different positions and occupations when he was named Controller of Customs, Justice of Peace, a member of Parliament, and, three years later, Clerk of the King's Works. It was in that latter period of his life that he began working on a major collection of related poems, *The Canterbury Tales*, bringing to it great literary powers that were marked by his qualities of keen observation, sharp humour, solid realism, deep psychological insight, excellent technical ability and grace.

One of the work's distinguishing features was that, unlike other works at the time, including his own previous literary attempts, it was crafted in vernacular Middle English, not French or Latin, although he borrowed from French, Italian and ancient traditions. In the process he refined Middle English language.

The Canterbury Tales comprises twenty-four stories amounting to more than 17,000 lines of verse and prose recounting a pilgrimage made by thirty-one travellers, including himself, from the Tabard Inn in Southwark to Saint Thomas à Becket's shrine at Canterbury Cathedral. In the telling Chaucer uses a story-within-a-story literary device. To help pass the time, the host of the inn creates a contest whereby each pilgrim will tell two tales on the way out and two on the way home, and the best storyteller will win a free supper upon their return.

Thus the poems reflect a diversity of voices as well as stories, providing a cross-section of local English society. Some of the notable characters include a cook, a knight, a carpenter, a nun and a friar. The characterisations cover a wide range of personal qualities across the different classes and occupations, mixing humour, vulgarity, piousness, erudition, wit and other traits. Chaucer indicates how the classes and characters interact and how they differ from each other in their manner of speaking. The General Prologue (translated here from Middle to Modern English) explains:

> He who repeats a tale after a man,
> Is bound to say, as nearly as he can,
> Each single word, if he remembers it,
> However rudely spoken or unfit,
> Or else the tale he tells will be untrue,
> The things invented and the phrases new.

The Canterbury Tales offers a full and critical portrait of English society, including commentary about changing views of the Church, which also reflects Chaucer's mastery of a broad range of different literary forms, devices and linguistic styles. His elegant use of Middle English to deliver beautiful poetry elevated the language's standing in literature.

Chaucer died before he was able to complete his original plan of one hundred tales, and although no copy of the tales in Chaucer's hand survive, no fewer than eighty-three known manuscripts of the work from the late medieval to early Renaissance periods have been preserved. The oldest is in the Hengwrt Chaucer manuscript held in the National Library of Wales, which is believed to have been written in 1400, around the time of Chaucer's death. The copy most often used as a base text for editions of *The Canterbury Tales* is the early 1400s Ellesmere manuscript, named for its former owner, the Earl of Ellesmere, which is now in the Huntington Library, San Marino, California.

The first printed version of *The Canterbury Tales* was published in 1478, and ten copies are known to exist.

The Canterbury Tales is undoubtedly one of the most ambitious works of literature, and it continues to be studied and enjoyed for its dazzling range of literary styles that vividly evoke life in medieval England.

Gutenberg Bible

(1450s)

Johann Gutenberg's Bible was the first major book to be printed using movable type. Its publication demonstrated conclusively the advantages of the process, which drove enormous cultural, economic and intellectual changes in the centuries that followed.

It goes without saying that the Bible has been extremely influential, both as a historical record and as a religious handbook. The version printed by Johann Gutenberg (c. 1400–68) ushered in a technical revolution that, it could be argued, had an even greater impact on society.

Before Gutenberg transformed the process, printing was done with painstakingly carved woodblocks, one for each page. This worked well for images but was far too time-consuming for text of any length; one spelling mistake, for example, would mean starting all over again, literally from scratch. Large bodies of text such as the Bible were instead written out by hand on parchment. Each copy took years to produce, and the work was only conducted by a few literate monks in monasteries. Religious orders thus retained great power over the spread of knowledge and literacy.

Gutenberg was born in Mainz, Germany, into a family of skilled metalworkers. He may have begun his experiments with movable type – type in which each letter is a separate, reusable piece cast in metal – as early as the 1430s. After some trial runs with single sheets of text, and then a few small books, Gutenberg felt confident enough to attempt the Bible. It was a huge undertaking. Its 1,286 pages were printed two pages at a time. Each copy of each pair of pages was typeset and pressed by hand, then the type was dismantled and reset for the next two. It is estimated that Gutenberg took three years to print the 180 or so copies of his Bible – the time a monk might take to write out just one.

Gutenberg probably cast each letter in a mould of fine sand, a delicate process still used today for detailed cast-iron work. His font required 270 different characters, including uppercase and lowercase, punctuation, and abbreviations. Gutenberg found that traditional water-based inks would not stick to the metal letters before it was pressed onto the paper, so he devised a new oil-based ink that gave a depth of colour on the page never seen before.

The impact of this new printing, or 'multiplying of books' as it was first known, is impossible to overstate. Books of all kinds could now be reproduced in large

quantities for a fraction of the cost and labour of a single handwritten one. Literacy increased as more people had access to the printed word. The ideas and knowledge within books could be exchanged, discussed and developed faster than ever. The publication of the Gutenberg Bible led directly to the Renaissance and to the birth of modern science. Its enormous effect on society is comparable with the invention of the Internet.

Remarkably, forty-nine copies of Gutenberg's Bible still survive. The last one to come up for auction was sold in 1978 for $2.2 million. In the unlikely event of one becoming available today, it would cost you up to $35 million.

IL PRINCIPE DI NICCOLO MA/
CHIAVELLI AL MAGNIFICO
LORENZO DI PIERO
DE' MEDICI.

LA VITA DI CASTRVCCIO CA/
stracani da Lucca a Zanobi Buondelmonti, & à
Luigi Alamanni, composta per il medesimo.

IL MODO CHE TENNE IL DVCA
Valentino per ammazare Vitellozo, Oliverotto da
Fermo, il. S. Pagolo, & il Duca di Grauina
di scritta per il medesimo.

I RITRATTI DELLE COSE DEL/
la Francia, & della Alamagna per il medesi/
mo, nuouamente aggiunti.

*ABOVE AND RIGHT: The title page of the original Italian edition (above),
published in 1532, and the first English translation (right) from 1640.*

The Prince
Machiavelli
(1532)

Machiavelli's political treatise on the art of getting and keeping power was based on his own observations of the machinations of kings, princes and popes. It caused controversy with its unethical recommendations, but five hundred years later it is still widely read by aspiring politicians.

Italy in the time of Machiavelli (1469–1527) was not the unified country we know today but a diverse collection of kingdoms centred on Naples, Rome, Venice, Milan and Florence. This fragmented political landscape was the target of regular invasions by neighbouring countries. Feuds between the Italian states and even within them were commonplace: for example, Florence, Machiavelli's home, was the setting during his life of a long-running power struggle between the Medici and Borgia families.

On a diplomatic mission to France in 1500, he was impressed by the relative peace and stability of the country, ruled as a single nation by Louis XII. France frequently interfered in Italian affairs, and in a deal with the pope, Louis installed Cesare Borgia as ruler of Romagna, the province neighbouring Florence to the east. Borgia had a reputation for ruthless cruelty and cunning in pursuit of power, qualities that Machiavelli believed would be necessary to achieve his ideal of an Italy as united and stable as France.

He began to develop his ideas on paper, and an early handwritten draft of *Il Principe* (*The Prince*) was in circulation in 1513. Where previous authors argued that high office should be guided by high ethical morality, Machiavelli argued that too moral a sense of purpose could actually hinder a man's ability to seize and exercise power.

Using real examples from Italian history, he made the case for strong, merciless rule in which it was only necessary for a leader to appear morally virtuous to retain the goodwill of the people. In a world of constant war between nations and states, he believed that efficient warfare, combined with tactical diplomacy, was the basis for successful statehood. War, rather than being an evil inevitability, was a necessary tool of government.

In short, the end – power – justified the means. This was political theory rooted in the real world, a practical manual for princes that only in the centuries following its publication has become a philosophy of political theory. When it was finally printed, five years after Machiavelli's death, it was condemned for being immoral and unethical. An English-language edition was not printed until 1640, although several manuscript translations were thought to be in circulation by the end of the sixteenth century. Machiavelli's understanding of human nature won admirers among the leaders of the English Civil War, the American Revolution, and the Chicago and New York mobs: John Gotti described it as the Mafia bible. *The Prince* has had a profound influence on world leaders from Henry VIII to Josef Stalin.

We use the word 'Machiavellian' to mean politically cunning or ruthlessly devious. In fact, his ideas are more complex than that, invoking concepts of civic pride and patriotism, which Machiavelli hoped would guide princes towards a strong and stable united Italy. Italy was finally unified in 1871.

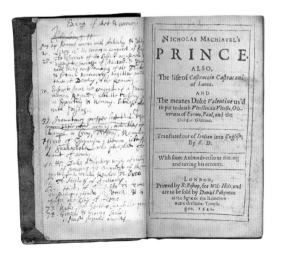

On the Revolutions of the Heavenly Spheres
Copernicus
(1543)

The Renaissance astronomer and mathematician waited until he was safely on his deathbed before publishing his book that would literally change the world's place in the universe. His heliocentric theory was credited with starting the Scientific Revolution in Western culture, its implications convincing modern thinkers, from Marx to Einstein and Freud, that man and his superstitions no longer ruled as supreme lord of the universe.

The Polish-born geometrist Nicolaus Copernicus (1473–1543) secretly worked on his theory of the universe as early as 1514, and had written substantial portions in the 1530s, but he hesitated to publish it, knowing that the Church could bring charges against him. His heliocentric model of the solar system, where the sun, not Earth, is at the center of the universe, would contradict Ptolemy's Earth-centered geocentric model that had held sway for fourteen centuries. As rumours circulated about Copernicus's blasphemous thesis, Martin Luther referred to it in 1539, saying: 'People gave ear to an upstart astrologer who strove to show that the earth revolves, not the heavens or the firmament, the sun and the moon … This fool wishes to reverse the entire science of astronomy; but sacred Scripture tells us that Joshua commanded the sun to stand still, and not the earth.'

One of the few persons who had actually read and understood Copernicus's manuscript was his assistant, Georg Joachim Rheticus. The young mathematician convinced his mentor to deliver it to Copernicus's close friend, Bishop Tiedemann Giese, for him to have it printed in Nuremberg, Germany. The final papers included a dedication and a preface to Pope Paul III, in which Copernicus acknowledged the likely theological rejection of his theory. But he was careful to state that mathematics should be the basis on which his theory was understood and accepted, and the technical nature of his book made understanding difficult for priests who were not highly trained in geometry.

De Revolutionibus Orbium Coelestium (On the Revolutions of the Heavenly Spheres), written in Latin, appeared in 1543, shortly after Copernicus's death. The title page contained this note, which couched the theory's impact in mathematical terms:

> Diligent reader, in this work, which has just been created and published, you have the motions of the fixed stars and planets, as these motions have been reconstituted on the basis of ancient as well as recent observations, and have moreover been embellished by new and marvellous hypotheses. You also have most convenient tables, from which you will be able to compute those motions with the utmost case for any time whatever. Therefore buy, read and enjoy. Let no one untrained in geometry enter here.

The work was organised into six books, following the same format as Ptolemy's *Almagest*, which had ruled Western thought for centuries. The first eleven chapters of Book I presented Copernicus's basic outline of heliocentric theory and explained his cosmology.

The initial response to Copernicus's book was muted. Written in highly technical terms, it was above most readers' heads, and the first print run of 400 copies didn't sell out. In time, however, its controversial conclusions sank in and provoked a torrent of criticism from scientists on doctrinal grounds. While not formally banned, it remained largely suppressed by the Catholic Church until 1758, and Luther also denounced it.

Although the book has long been hailed for starting the Scientific Revolution, some historians of science have recently downgraded Copernicus's achievements in view of the work that already had been done by Arab astronomers from the school in Maragheh.

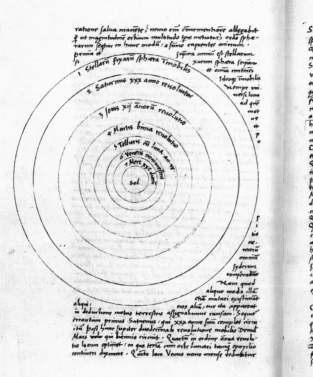

ABOVE AND LEFT: Copernicus's handwritten manuscript (above) and the first printed edition from 1543 (left), showing his controversial heliocentric model of the solar system, where the sun, not the Earth, is at the centre of the universe.

Lives of the Artists
Vasari

(1550)

Lives of the Artists was the first book to examine the history of art. The analysis that Vasari presented is still used today, and his book is an unparalleled source of information about the golden age of Italian art.

Giorgio Vasari (1511–74) was born in the Italian hill town of Arezzo and trained as a painter. At the age of sixteen he migrated to the big city, Florence, where Michelangelo took him under his wing. He established a reputation as an artist, particularly for his patrons, the ruling Medici family. Today, Vasari is better remembered for his architecture. Among his designs were the *uffizi* (offices) for Florence's magistrates, which now house the Uffizi Gallery. Centred on the Medicis' private collection, the Uffizi is one of the finest art galleries in the world. Vasari's courtyard there is a masterpiece of space, focus and perspective.

On trips to Rome and Venice, Vasari saw work by the greatest artists of his age. He became interested in their lives and their influences, collected old drawings and studied ancient Roman art and architecture. Gradually he began to develop ideas about the path from ancient art to modern.

In 1550 he published his book *Lives of the Artists* – in full, *Le Vite de' Più Eccellenti Pittori, Scultori, ed Architettori* (*The Lives of the Most Eminent Painters, Sculptors and Architects*). Biographies of artists had been published in the past; Vasari's great innovation was a series of introductory articles describing the historical trends that his choice of artists illustrated. With the publication of his book, Vasari became the world's first art historian.

He broke his history down into three phases: the classical period of Roman antiquity, a high point; the decline of art thereafter in the Dark Ages; and its rebirth from the fourteenth century onward, thanks to Cimabue and Giotto, culminating in the genius of Leonardo da Vinci and Michelangelo. At the time, his friend and teacher Michelangelo was the only living artist included in the encyclopaedia.

A second, expanded edition appeared in 1568, which included more living artists and even some from Venice. This version, widely translated, remains the template for biographical encyclopedias to this day. The first English translation was a short plagiarised version, published in 1685 and presented as William Aglionby's own work under the title *Painting Illustrated in Three Dialogues*.

Aglionby did, however, add some German and English artists to the contents. Vasari was undeniably biased in favour of Italian art, and in particular Florentine art. In the first edition he did not include a single artist from Venice, Florence's rival city-state. He was the first to use the word 'Renaissance' in a cultural context; and he also coined the term 'Gothic Art' in describing the creative resurgence of northern Europe. The biographies of earlier artists were rather poorly researched and have been much corrected by later art historians.

But Vasari's writing about the artists of the Renaissance is a rich resource, as are his descriptions of the artistic techniques of the day. His analysis of the development of the Renaissance is still the accepted history of the period, even if modern scholars now allow that it happened not just in Vasari's Rome and Florence but throughout Europe.

MICHELAGNOLO BVONARRVOTI   717

Vita di Michelagnolo Buonarruoti Fiorentino Pittore, Scultore, & Architetto.

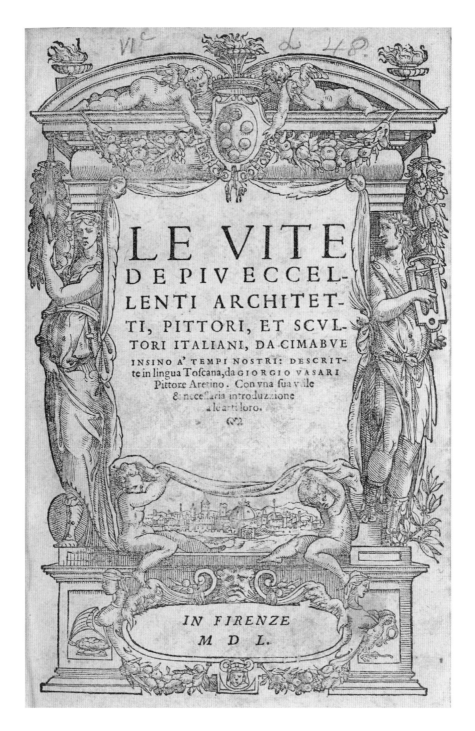

LE VITE

DE PIV ECCEL-
LENTI ARCHITET-
TI, PITTORI, ET SCVL-
TORI ITALIANI, DA CIMABVE

INSINO A' TEMPI NOSTRI: DESCRIT-
te in lingua Toscana, da GIORGIO VASARI
Pittore Aretino. Con vna sua vtile
& necessaria introduzzione
a le arti loro.

IN FIRENZE
M D L.

OPPOSITE AND ABOVE: *A portrait of Michelangelo (opposite), the only living artist included in the book, and the title page (above), both from the first edition. Vasari's book was the first to use the word 'Rinascita' (Renaissance) to describe the rebirth in art and culture that had started in Italy in the fourteenth century.*

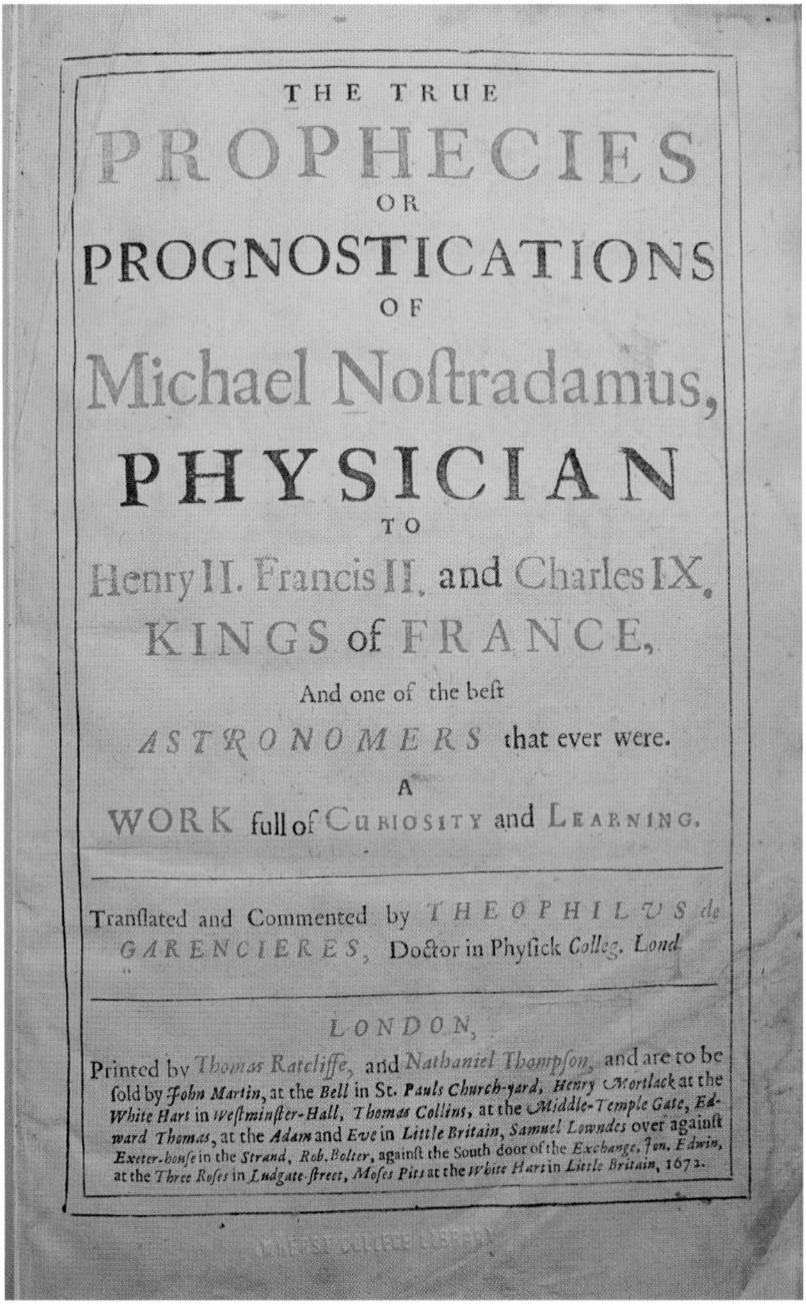

THE TRUE

PROPHECIES

OR

PROGNOSTICATIONS

OF

Michael Noſtradamus,

PHYSICIAN

TO

Henry II. Francis II. and Charles IX.

KINGS of FRANCE,

And one of the beſt

ASTRONOMERS that ever were.

A

WORK full of CURIOSITY and LEARNING.

Tranſlated and Commented by *THEOPHILVS de GARENCIERES*, Doctor in Phyſick *Colleg. Lond*

LONDON,

Printed by *Thomas Ratcliffe*, and *Nathaniel Thompſon*, and are to be sold by *John Martin*, at the Bell in St. *Pauls Church-yard*, *Henry Mortlack* at the *White Hart* in *Weſtminſter-Hall*, *Thomas Collins*, at the *Middle-Temple Gate*, *Edward Thomas*, at the *Adam* and *Eve* in *Little Britain*, *Samuel Lowndes* over againſt *Exeter-houſe* in the *Strand*, *Rob. Bolter*, againſt the South door of the *Exchange*, *Jon. Edwin*, at the *Three Roſes* in *Ludgate-ſtreet*, *Moſes Pits* at the *White Hart* in *Little Britain*, 1672.

AMHERST COLLEGE LIBRARY

ABOVE AND RIGHT: The first English translation (above), published in London in 1672, and the original French edition (right) from 1557.

The Prophecies
Nostradamus

(1557)

A French mystic relied on ideas drawn from several exotic fields in an effort to save people from the plague that was sweeping Europe. Outlawed by the Inquisition for his activities, he went into hiding and began publishing grim prophecies that made him famous as history's greatest seer.

Michel de Nostredame (1503–66), or Nostradamus, was raised in a Jewish household in Avignon, France, though the family practised their religion in secret because King Louis XII had ordered all Jews to become baptised or be expelled, and his father, a prosperous merchant, elected to remain. As a youth Nostradamus studied mathematics, literature, medicine, astrology, alchemy and Kabbalah – an ancient Jewish tradition of mystical interpretation of the Bible that was considered a forbidden art in France.

Using a combination of mystical methods, he dedicated himself to treating victims of the bubonic plague that was sweeping Europe at that time. For a time he appears to have enjoyed some success, until the deaths of his own wife and children injured his medical reputation, and he became targeted by the Inquisition. As a result he had to flee.

While roaming through Europe he began to make prophecies, which he compiled into quatrains (four

lines), the sources for which his biographer, Stéphane Gerson, later attributed to a mix of 'astrology, prophecy, melancholy poetry, magic and history.' His prophecies appear to have been based on biblical stories and other literature he read as he moved from place to place.

In 1550 he changed his name from Nostredame to Nostradamus and published an almanac containing calendars and prophecies, which became so popular he issued them on an annual basis.

Nostradamus also wrote a book of 353 quatrains, which was published in 1557 as *Les Propheties* (*The Prophecies*), in which he foretold natural disasters, wars, conflagrations, plagues and other major problems far into the future. As a means of protecting himself from possible persecution by the Church, he used a mixture of different languages, including Greek, Italian, Latin and Provençal, as well as syntactical tricks and other methods to deliberately create ambiguity.

The book received a mixed reaction when it was published. One critic charged that Nostradamus conspired to 'wrappe hys prophesyes in such darke wryncles of obscuritye that no man could pyke out of them either sence or understandying certayn.' But others accepted his prophesying. Catherine de Médicis, wife of the king of France, was one of his most influential admirers.

Some readers later credited Nostradamus with foretelling the Great Fire of London, the rise of Napoléon and Hitler, and the September 11 attacks on the World Trade Center.

Although there is much skepticism about the accuracy of Nostradamus's predictions, the popularity of his published prophecies has not diminished. The deliberate ambiguity of his pronouncements continues to make them appear relevant to past, present and future world events.

Don Quixote
Cervantes
(1605)

Even those who have never read *Don Quixote* know something of its sympathetic central characters – the thin man on a skinny horse and the fat servant on a tubby donkey, tilting at windmills – but the novel is far more than a series of tragicomic episodes befalling a deluded fool and his companion.

Don Quixote is a novel that grows in wisdom and humanity the further you read. It starts out as a comic attack on the prevailing literature of the day – nostalgic, chivalrous romances about knights in shining armour fighting monsters and saving maidens. Don Quixote, driven mad by reading such stories, believes himself to be such a knight-errant and sets off into the world to right wrongs. His mighty steed is in reality a barnyard nag called Rosinante, his faithful squire a bumbling farm labourer called Sancho Panza, and his noble lady, Dulcinea, merely a farmer's daughter. He attacks windmills believing they are giants, and flocks of sheep that look to him like armies.

But these are not simple stock characters in a farce. Having created them, Cervantes (1547–1615) allows them to grow in emotional intelligence and experience with each life lesson that he puts them through. The reader, and Cervantes, seem to watch this process of maturing unfold, and the result is a rich range of very human players in the drama. Cervantes writes with great economy, not commenting but simply describing events with just enough colour and detail to let the reader's imagination take over. The famous windmill episode, for example, lasts only a few lines, but remains much larger and more vivid in our minds. His characters thus have lives of their own, and it is no wonder that Don Quixote himself has entered our culture and language. To be quixotic is to be an unconventional, or impractical, visionary.

Don Quixote also attacks the divisions of class and the attitudes of the Church; and although the book is in part a parody of those chivalrous tales of old, it is the values of ordinary decency embodied by Don Quixote and Sancho Panza that touch the reader – the very values that inspired the outdated ideals of chivalry.

The first part of the book, published with the promise of a sequel in 1605, was an immediate success. It was translated into English as early as 1612, and in Spain it was so popular that a fake part two was written and published by another author, before Cervantes had finished the real one. When that did finally appear in 1615, only a few months before Cervantes's death, it

introduced characters who knew of Don Quixote because they had read part one and who criticised the false tales of him put about by the fake sequel – a very modern literary device of self-reference.

As a sign of the book's enduring appeal, at least fourteen movie adaptations of it have been released, alongside twelve plays, operas and ballets. In the twenty-first century alone four new English translations of it have already been published. *Don Quixote* lives on.

LEFT: The first English edition, translated by Thomas Shelton, was printed in 1612.

EL INGENIOSO

HIDALGO DON QVI-
xote de la Mancha.

*Compuesto por Miguel de Ceruantes
Saauedra.*

DIRIGIDO AL DVQVE DE
Bejar, Marques de Gibraleon, Conde de Benalcaçar, y
Bañares, Vizconde dela Puebla de Alcozer, Señor
de las villas de Capilla, Curiel,
y Burguillos.

Impreſſo con licencia, en Valencia, en caſa de
Pedro Patricio Mey, 1605.

A coſta de Iuſepe Ferrer mercader de libros,
delante la Diputacion.

*ABOVE: The first edition, printed in Valencia in 1605. Two other editions
came out the same year, printed in Madrid and Lisbon.*

King James Bible

(1611)

Four hundred years after it first went to press, the King James Bible remains the finest expression of Christian faith: a crowning literary achievement for the English language, and one of the most influential books of all time. It also performed useful political functions for the sovereign.

In 1604 the new King of Great Britain, James I (1566–1625), commissioned a large and contentious committee of scholars and clergymen, who met in intensive working sessions, to carry out an extraordinarily complex and sensitive theological task. Their job was to produce an authorised new translation of the holy Bible from the original Greek, Hebrew, Aramaic and Latin, crafted into a meticulously revised and more readable version that would provide a common standard for a diverse spectrum of Protestant denominations and sects.

The sovereign's motives were also political, for he hoped his project would foster greater unity in his kingdom, thereby making it stronger and easier for a secular power to rule.

The complicated process took seven years to complete, but the results were spectacularly successful. No previous work had been so painstakingly edited by a large committee. In 1611, following its approval by English church authorities, the book was first printed by the king's printer, Robert Barker, as 'THE HOLY BIBLE, Containing the Old Testament, and the New: Newly translated out of the Originall Tongues: and with the former Translations diligently compared and revised by his Majesties speciall Commandment.' The ponderous work stood sixteen inches tall and was sold in a loose-leaf version for ten shillings, and the bound copy cost twelve.

The spread of new printing technology led to the book's wide dissemination throughout the realm and beyond, resulting in its appearance in households as

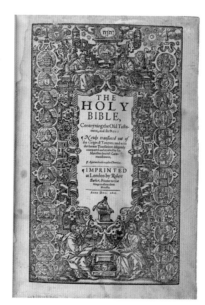

well as churches and fine libraries. The text fuelled the growth of the Protestant faith, not only in Great Britain, but across the globe that was then being colonised. In the process it established a new universal standard for the language of the Bible and English 'religious speech'.

Victor Hugo, the nineteenth-century French novelist, wrote, 'England has two books, the Bible and Shakespeare. England made Shakespeare, but the Bible made England.' Everyone agreed that it was a literary masterpiece, even in an era of William Shakespeare (1564–1616), Sir Francis Bacon (1561–1626), John Donne (1572–1631) and John Milton (1608–74).

The authorised Bible helped to transform the English language by adding new words, patterns and meters, and it enriched the language through its introduction of a new English prose style and its establishment of innumerable memorable passages, phrases and literary devices such as repetition, found in the opening images of Genesis:

In the beginning God created the heaven and the Earth. And the Earth was without form, and void; and darkness was upon the face of the deep. And the Spirit of God moved upon the face of the waters. And God said, Let there be light: and there was light. And God saw the light, that it was good: and God divided the light from the darkness. And God called the light Day, and the darkness he called Night.

Over time the work came to be known as the King James Bible in honour of its patron, and the standard of speech it established became one of the high points of English literature.

❧ TO THE MOST HIGH AND MIGHTIE

Prince, IAMES by the grace of God King of Great Britaine , France and Ireland, Defender of the Faith, &c.

THE TRANSLATORS OF THE *BIBLE*
with Grace, Mercie, and Peace, through I E S V S
C H R I S T our L O R D.

Reat and manifold were the bleſsings (moſt dread Soueraigne) which Almighty G O D, the Father of all Mercies, beſtowed vpon vs the people of E N G L A N D, when firſt hee ſent your Maieſties Royall perſon to rule and raigne ouer vs. For whereas it was the expectation of many, who wiſhed not well vnto our S I O N, that vpon the ſetting of that bright *Occidentall Starre* Queene E L I Z A B E T H of moſt happy memorie, ſome thicke and palpable cloudes of darkeneſse would ſo haue ouerſhadowed this land, that men ſhould haue been in doubt which way they were to walke, and that it ſhould hardly be knowen, who was to direct the vnſetled State: the appearance of your M A I E S T I E, as of the *Sunne* in his ſtrength, inſtantly diſpelled thoſe ſuppoſed and ſurmiſed miſts, and gaue vnto all that were well affected, exceeding cauſe of comfort, eſpecially when we beheld the gouernment eſtabliſhed in your H I G H N E S S E, and your hopefull Seede, by an vndoubted Title, and this alſo accompanied with Peace and tranquillitie, at home and abroad.

But amongſt all our Ioyes, there was no one that more filled our hearts, then the bleſſed continuance of the Preaching of G O D s ſacred word amongſt vs, which is that ineſtimable treaſure, which excelleth all the riches of the earth, becauſe the fruit thereof extendeth it ſelfe, not onely to the time ſpent in this tranſitory world, but directeth and diſpoſeth men vnto that Eternall happineſſe which is aboue in Heauen.

Then, not to ſuffer this to fall to the ground, but rather to take it vp, and to continue it in that State, wherein the famous predeceſſour of your H I G H N E S S E did leaue it ; Nay, to goe forward with the confidence and reſo-

A 2   lution

OPPOSITE AND ABOVE: The title page (opposite) and introduction (above) of the first edition. The King James Bible remains the most widely published text in the English language. It took around fifty scholars seven years to complete.

Mr. WILLIAM
SHAKESPEARES
COMEDIES,
HISTORIES, &
TRAGEDIES.

Published according to the True Originall Copies.

Martin Droeshout sculpsit London.

LONDON
Printed by Isaac Iaggard, and Ed. Blount. 1623.

ABOVE: Martin Droeshout's iconic engraving of Shakespeare met with the approval of Shakespeare's contemporary Ben Jonson, who wrote a short poem accompanying the portrait on the facing page.

OPPOSITE: The text was collated by two of Shakespeare's fellow actors and friends, John Heminges and Henry Condell, who appear in the list of 'Principall Actors' alongside Shakespeare himself.

Shakespeare's First Folio

(1623)

The publication of *Mr. William Shakespeares Comedies, Histories, and Tragedies*, seven years after his death, rescued some of his most iconic works from oblivion and established his reputation as the preeminent dramatist in the English language. Four hundred years later, his supremacy continues.

When William Shakespeare (1564–1616) died, some of his friends from the stage pooled their resources to compile and print an authorised collection of his work. Known as the First Folio, due to its large page size (indicating a work of special stature), the book included thirty-six comedies, histories and tragedies, including eighteen plays that had never been printed before: *All's Well That Ends Well, Antony and Cleopatra, As You Like It, Comedy of Errors, Coriolanus, Cymbeline, Henry VI, Henry VIII, Julius Caesar, King John, Macbeth, Measure for Measure, The Taming of the Shrew, The Tempest, Timon of Athens, Twelfth Night, Two Gentlemen of Verona* and *The Winter's Tale*.

Two fellow actors and friends from Shakespeare's theatre company, John Heminges and Henry Condell, laboured for two years to gather and edit the dramas, relying on handwritten scripts, promptbooks and other records. Assembling them was a complicated task and ultimately amounted to more than 900 double-columned pages. Among them were fourteen comedies (including *The Merchant of Venice, A Midsummer Night's Dream* and *Much Ado about Nothing*), ten histories (including *Richard II* and *Richard III*), and tragedies (including *Hamlet, King Lear* and *Romeo and Juliet*).

Although eighteen of the plays had previously been published in the smaller quarto size, the new corrected version was based on the most reliable source and edited to be in the most readable form for book readers. The volume also had on its title page a portrait of Shakespeare, which had been engraved by a young artist named Martin Droeshout, who had never met the playwright, though Shakespeare's friends attested to the likeness. The printing required meticulous care.

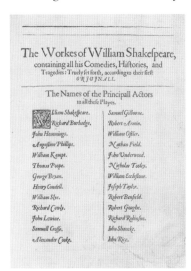

The book's original price was £1 (a substantial amount in those days) for an unbound copy; £2 or £3 for a bound version. Scholars generally believe that about 750 copies of the First Folio were printed in 1623.

The project was unusual from the start in that plays had never been published in folio before in England; they were not considered important or prestigious enough for such a large format. What most distinguished the book, however, was the quality of its contents. 'He was not of an age, but for all time!' Shakespeare's friend Ben Jonson (1573–1637) wrote in the preface.

Besides proving immensely popular with audiences of his day, many of Shakespeare's works have remained favourites of literature, stage and screen. The great modern stage and movie actor Laurence Olivier called Shakespeare's works 'the nearest thing in incarnation to the eye of God.'

Some of the stories are deeply psychological and dark. *Othello* explores themes of lust, jealousy and racial discrimination. *Macbeth* examines self-destructive ambition and paranoid regicide. *Romeo and Juliet* deals with the passionate tragedy of doomed love. And *Hamlet* plumbs the depths of revenge.

Some of the plots were later made into operas, musicals and symphonies, and the First Folio's influence extended beyond stage, screen and concert hall. Sigmund Freud acknowledged how his theories of the unconscious and other psychoanalytic ideas had been nurtured by his reading of Shakespeare and what it taught him about human emotions.

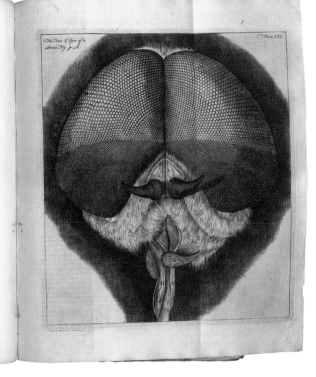

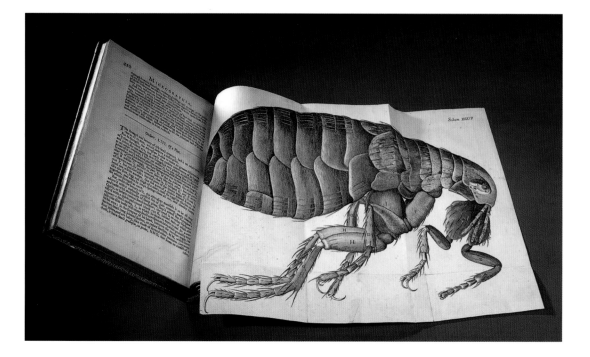

Micrographia
Robert Hooke

(1665)

In the 1660s, a brilliant young English polymath employed recent refinements of the microscope to explore a previously invisible world, then he shared his discoveries in an astonishing book showing huge magnified images of tiny organisms such as a louse, a mosquito and the minute living structures inside a slice of cork.

Samuel Pepys wrote in his diary that he had stayed up until 2 a.m. perusing Robert Hooke's *Micrographia: or Some Physiological Descriptions of Minute Bodies Made by Magnifying Glasses. With Observations and Inquiries Thereupon*, which he called 'the most ingenious book that ever I read in my life.' His opinion was widely shared, for the Dutch astronomer Christiaan Huygens rushed to congratulate the Royal Society on the amazing quality of the observations. The illustrated volume became a best-seller and a classic that opened up a whole new world to scientific investigation.

Hooke (1635–1703) had studied at Oxford and worked with such luminaries as John Wilkins, Thomas Willis and Robert Boyle, and he already had carried out an extraordinary range of scientific experiments and inventions. Hooke often designed and made his own instruments, such as vacuum pumps and telescopes, though for this project he used a magnificently crafted illuminated microscope that enabled him to inspect creatures and forms too minuscule to be detected by the naked eye. Then he used his drafting ability to capture what he saw through the lens in minutely detailed and painstakingly accurate drawings.

Hooke's illustrations revealed a miniature world that most readers had never imagined. 'By the help of microscopes,' he wrote, 'there is nothing so small, as to escape our inquiry; hence there is a new visible world.' His book opened up the wonders of parasites, insects and living cells.

On its oversized pages he presented a massive representation of a flea measuring 18 inches (45.7 cm) across, and the scene of a monster louse

LEFT: The head of a drone fly (top) and the foldout illustration of a flea (bottom) revealed a microscopic world that had never been seen before.

gripping a human hair was nearly 2 feet (62 cm) wide. Extraordinary sights that previously had been invisible to the naked eye were now exposed as the spectacular 'teeth of a snail' or 'the beard of a wild oat'. His was the first great coffee-table book.

In one entry, describing the inside view of a cork, he wrote:

> I could exceedingly plainly perceive it to be all perforated and porous, much like a Honey-comb, but that the pores of it were not regular … these pores, or cells … were indeed the first microscopical pores I ever saw, and perhaps, that were ever seen, for I had not met with any Writer or Person, that had made any mention of them before this.

His description became one of the most famous passages in the history of science, in part because the term he coined for the boxlike appearance of the plant's interior – 'cells' – would become the standard unit of life in biological science.

Hooke's text also included groundbreaking observations about the organic origin of fossils, descriptions of distant planets and other discoveries. As the first major publication of the Royal Society, *Micrographia* became one of the most important works in the history of science, inspiring wider public interest in microscopy, biology, palaeontology and astronomy.

Hooke has been called the greatest experimental scientist of the seventeenth century. He also was the Surveyor to the City of London, and as chief assistant to Christopher Wren, he helped supervise the rebuilding of the city after the Great Fire in 1666, and designed several landmark structures. He was not without his detractors in his own time, but today he is recognised as one of the great figures in the history of science.

Paradise Lost
John Milton

(1667)

Milton's epic poem, retelling the story of the expulsion of Adam and Eve from the Garden of Eden, is anchored in his profound Puritan faith. But people of all faiths and none admire the poetry of this masterful examination of good and evil.

John Milton (1608–74), born in London to a Protestant father, received a remarkably broad education in the classics, art and science. He spoke eight ancient and modern languages fluently, and through them had a commanding feel for the rhythm and phrasing of words, further refined by hearing his father's musical compositions. Milton's first published poem, 'Epitaph on the Admirable Dramatic Poet, W. Shakespeare', was included in the 1632 Second Folio of the Bard's works. He adopted Shakespeare's preferred metre of iambic pentameter for the epic poem that secures his reputation today.

Much of Milton's life and work can be seen in terms of hierarchy. In *Paradise Lost*, he considers the relative positions of heaven above, earth in the middle and hell down below. The dynamic between 'superior' man and 'inferior' woman is also a theme, although in this Milton was considerably less misogynistic than the prevailing attitude of his day. In his Christian faith he was a strict nonconformist, arguing against the hierarchical intervention of bishops and even ministers in the communication between an individual and God.

In his political beliefs he accepted that the ruling classes ruled because they had superior abilities to do so. But he was also dismayed at the inability of the Stuart kings Charles I and II to rule wisely, and supported the republican cause in the English Civil War. Consequently, his fortunes rose under the rule of Oliver Cromwell, but he lost favour upon the restoration of the monarchy following Cromwell's death in 1658.

Steeped in the Greek and Latin epics of Homer and Virgil, Milton had been determined since his student days to write such a work himself. In search of a suitably heroic English subject, he first considered the legendary King Arthur. Later, he contemplated a narrative about his very modern hero Oliver Cromwell.

In the end the choice of Adam and Eve was a departure from conventional military heroes. Milton's very domestic setting, the relationship between two ordinary people, is human and forgiving, informed by his own three marriages. His view of the battle between heaven and hell is coloured by his devout Christianity and by having lived through the English Civil War. Having been briefly imprisoned after the restoration of the English monarchy, Milton's idea of real heroism was being true to your faith and enduring the suffering that accompanied its persecution. *Paradise Lost* encompasses the experiences and beliefs that governed Milton's life.

He wrote it over at least ten years, and after he had lost his sight. The 10,000 lines of *Paradise Lost* were dictated to a secretary. The poem was intended to be read, not recited, but Milton's heightened language invoked the rhetoric spirit of the oral tradition of Greek and Roman epic poetry.

Despite Milton's own fall from grace under the restored monarchy, on its publication in 1667, *Paradise Lost* was recognised as a work of genius by both friends and enemies. Its influence on future authors (including William Blake and Mary Shelley) has confirmed its just claim to be among the greatest poetry ever written in the English language.

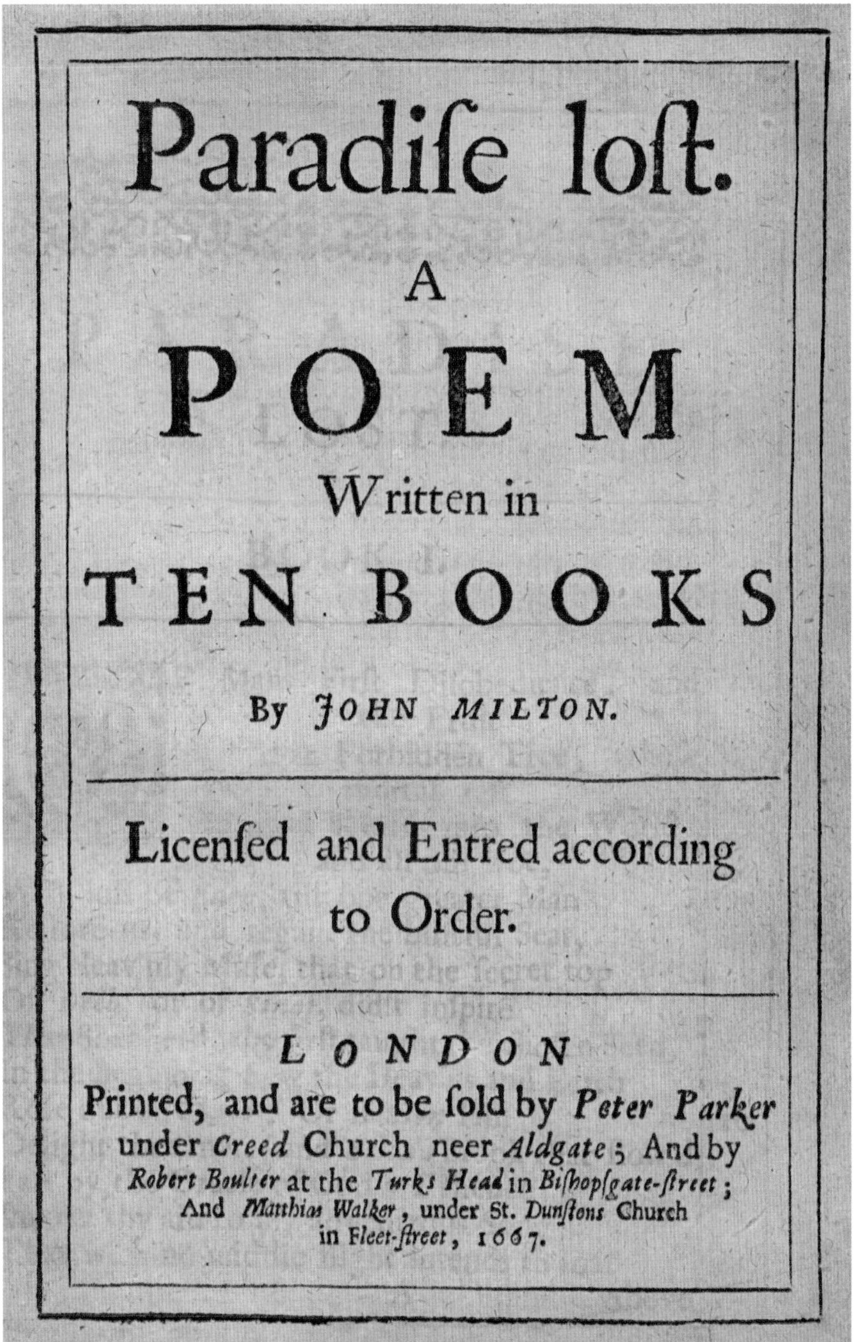

Paradise lost.

A

POEM

Written in

TEN BOOKS

By JOHN MILTON.

Licensed and Entred according to Order.

LONDON

Printed, and are to be sold by *Peter Parker*
under *Creed* Church neer *Aldgate*; And by
Robert Boulter at the *Turks Head* in *Bishopsgate-street*;
And *Matthias Walker*, under St. *Dunstons* Church
in Fleet-street, 1667.

*ABOVE AND OPPOSITE: The original 1667 title page (above) and the frontispiece from the
1669 edition (opposite). The portrait shows Milton as a young man, but he would have
been sixty-one and blind for fifteen years by the time this edition was published.*

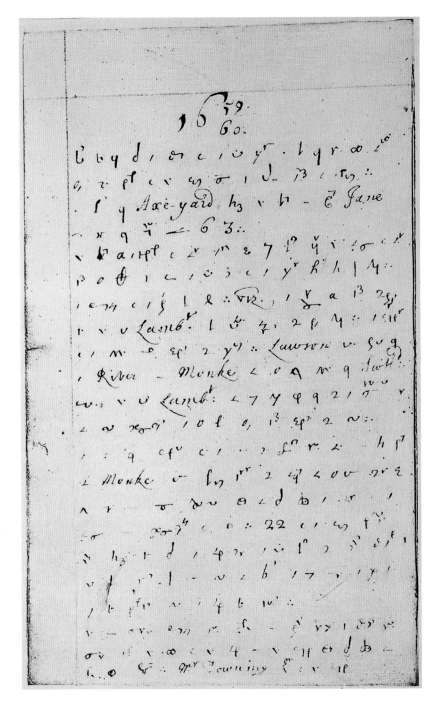

ABOVE: The first page from Pepys's diary, New Year's Day 1659/1660. Written in shorthand, Pepys continued his diary until 1669.

OPPOSITE: The six volumes of his handwritten journal were first published in two edited volumes in 1825.

Samuel Pepys's Diary

(1660–69)

A private daily diary, kept by a well-to-do Londoner during a dramatic period of English history, recorded in detail a number of important public events and mundane activities. His keen observations and elegant writing style have made it a notable work of literature and history that established the personal diary as a genre.

Samuel Pepys (1633–1703) was a Cambridge University–educated member of England's privileged class who kept a diary from January 1, 1660 to May 31, 1669, giving his eyewitness account of the coronation of Charles II, the Great Plague, and the Great Fire of London, as well as references to notable individuals he knew, including Sir Isaac Newton, who gave him gambling advice for dice games. His chronicle also included intimate details about his own sexual affairs, physical ailments, cultural observations and professional ambitions, providing a rare personal glimpse into everyday life in London during the Restoration period.

What made Pepys's version of history unique was that he offered a vivid, first-hand view of the world around him by including his own personal reflections on how it affected him. For example, on the subject of the Great Plague of London – an epidemic of bubonic fever that decimated London from 1665 to 1666, killing an estimated 100,000 people, or almost a quarter of the city's population, in just eighteen months – he noted in his diary on October 16, 1665:

> I walked to the Tower. But Lord, how
> empty the streets are, and melancholy,
> so many poor sick people in the streets,
> full of sores, and so many sad stories
> overheard as I walk, everybody talking of
> this dead, and that man sick, and so many
> in this place, and so many in that. And
> they tell me that in Westminster there is
> never a physitian, and but one apothecary
> left, all being dead – but that there are
> great hopes of a great decrease this week:
> God send it.

On September 2, 1666, he wrote of being woken by his servant, who had just spied a blaze in Billingsgate that turned out to become the Great Fire of London, which raged for four days in the city's medieval centre.

For ten years Pepys recorded details of his daily life. He wrote about his finances and business affairs. He recounted his domestic routines and problems with servants, and commented upon his fractious relationship with his wife, along with his pursuit of other women. He minutely described his tastes in books, music, theatre and science. He had a strong appetite for knowledge, as well as a weakness for women (to whom he said he stood in a 'strange slavery'). He wrote about foods he savoured and wines he drank. At times he confessed his jealousies and insecurities, sharing his innermost private thoughts.

On the one hand Pepys safeguarded his privacy by recording his entries in a form of shorthand, known as tachygraphy. But he also had the pages bound in six volumes and preserved and catalogued in his personal library as part of his estate. He also left a written key for the records to be deciphered, but the first person to do so, Reverend John Smith, hadn't discovered the guide, and yet, he laboured to make his transcription without it. First published in 1825 as *Memoirs and Correspondence of Samuel Pepys, Esq.*, Pepys's diary became celebrated as one of history's finest eyewitness accounts. The original manuscript and first transcription can be viewed at the Pepys Library at Magdalene College in Cambridge.

Philosophiae Naturalis Principia Mathematica
Isaac Newton

(1687)

A Cambridge mathematician's grand three-volume theoretical work applying mathematics to understanding the laws of nature and the universe may have been the greatest contribution in the history of science – what Albert Einstein would later call 'perhaps the greatest intellectual stride that it has ever been granted to any man to make.'

Isaac Newton (1642–1727) said his theory of universal gravitation began to take shape in his mind after an apple fell from a tree and struck him on the head. When his rival, Robert Hooke, later claimed credit for some of Newton's sweeping new ideas on universal gravitation, Newton became so distressed that he threatened not to publish his work and wrote to Hooke in a private letter, 'If I have been able to see further, it was only because I stood on the shoulders of giants.' Yet Newton never forgave Hooke for the slight, and he largely abandoned scientific research.

Luckily for the state of knowledge, Newton's book was published on July 5, 1687, and it ultimately became regarded as one of the most important works in applied mathematics, laying the foundations of classical mechanics, modern physics and astronomy, and helping to inspire many of the scientific and technological advances of the Scientific Revolution and the early Industrial Revolution.

Philosophiae Naturalis Principia Mathematica (*Mathematical Principles of Natural Philosophy*) is divided into three books, the first of which began with eight definitions and three axioms, the latter of which came to be known as Newton's laws of motion.

The first law states that objects continue to move at a constant velocity, which can be zero, unless acted upon by an external force. Inertia, as he called it, was the tendency of an object to resist change in motion.

The second law shows how an object in an inertial reference frame will be affected if an external force acts upon it, stating that the rate of change of momentum of a body is proportional to the resultant force acting on it, and will be in the same direction. In other words,

less force is needed to push something lighter; smaller objects have less inertia.

Newton's third law states that when one body exerts a force on a second body, the second body simultaneously exerts a force equal in magnitude, and opposite in direction on the first body: every action has an opposite and equal reaction.

Although Newton's *Principia* was mainly a description of the laws of planetary motion and showed that gravity caused a planet to move in an ellipse about the sun, his book provided many other revolutionary insights that helped to explain planetary motion, lunar motion, the ocean tides and many other phenomena.

The *Principia* established mathematics as the language of science and the key to knowing about the universe. Yet Newton continued to believe in God, writing, 'This most beautiful system of the sun, planets and comets, could only proceed from the counsel and dominion of an intelligent and powerful Being.'

Following *Principia*'s publication, Newton largely abandoned scientific research to devote his life to public service, taking a seat in the House of Commons and becoming Master of the Royal Mint. He was knighted in 1705 and died in 1727.

In 1747 the French physicist Alexis Clairaut declared that Newton's book 'marked the epoch of a great revolution in physics. The method followed by its illustrious author … spread the light of mathematics on a science which up to then had remained in the darkness of conjectures and hypotheses.'

In 2016 a first edition of *Philosophiae Naturalis Principia Mathematica* fetched the highest price – $3.7 million – for any scientific book ever sold.

PHILOSOPHIÆ

NATURALIS

PRINCIPIA

MATHEMATICA.

Autore *J*S. *NEWTON*, *Trin. Coll. Cantab. Soc.* Matheseos
Professore *Lucasiano*, & Societatis Regalis Sodali.

IMPRIMATUR·
S. P E P Y S, *Reg. Soc.* P R Æ S E S.
Julii 5. 1686.

L O N D I N I,

Jussu *Societatis Regiæ* ac Typis *Josephi Streater*. Prostat apud
plures Bibliopolas. *Anno* MDCLXXXVII.

ABOVE: The title page of the first edition. As president of the Royal Society,
Samuel Pepys gave his imprimatur to authorise the book for publication.

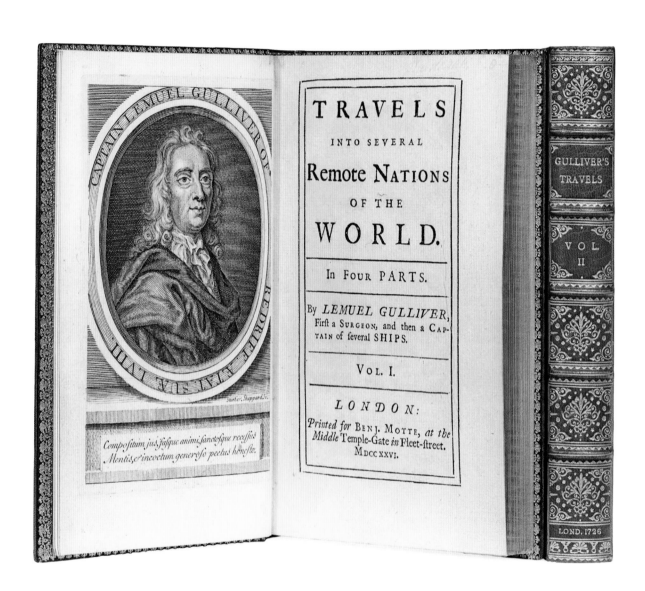

Gulliver's Travels
Jonathan Swift
(1726)

Jonathan Swift's masterpiece is a tale of misadventures for all ages. Children enjoy Gulliver's fantastical encounters, while adults recognise a sharp satire of human foibles and failings. Swift's deadpan descriptions of his experiences leave it to the reader to infer the absurdity of society's shortcomings.

Jonathan Swift (1667–1745) was born and educated in Dublin. He travelled to England as a young man and divided the rest of his life between Ireland and London. In London he was a founding member of the Scriblerus Club, along with Alexander Pope and other prominent authors of the day. They wrote collectively, under the pen name Martinus Scriblerus, satirising intellectual stupidity wherever they saw it. On one occasion he was assigned the task of parodying the new fashion for travel memoir – and the seeds of *Gulliver's Travels* were planted.

Gulliver's Travels was published, like all of Swift's work, under a pseudonym. It was purported to be written by Gulliver himself, and the frontispiece of the 1726 first edition even carried a portrait of the supposed author. Its full title was *Travels into Several Remote Nations of the World. In Four Parts. By Lemuel Gulliver, First a Surgeon, and then a Captain of Several Ships.*

Each part describes a different accident at sea, which results in Gulliver arriving in a strange country. The first two are the best known – Lilliput, where the people are tiny and Gulliver seems like a giant to them; and Brobdingnag, inhabited by giants beside whom he seems tiny. The third part, incorporating much of his Scriblerus Club travel satire, takes him to Laputa where the people despise all knowledge except science. The fourth is populated by the oafish humanoid Yahoos, but ruled by the Houyhnhnms, a race of wise horses.

The constant throughout is Gulliver himself, and Swift uses this to make the point that everything is relative. Gulliver, always the odd one out, seems relatively large beside the Lilliputians, small beside the Brobdingnagians, wise beside the Laputans and unsophisticated beside the Houyhnhnms. 'Nothing is great or little,' writes Swift, 'otherwise than by comparison.' His satire of course invites us to do just that – to compare with our own country the flawed people and regimes that he conjures up.

Small-mindedness is a recurrent theme. Kings and governments throughout the book are unable to accept any point of view but their own; so, for example, the Lilliputians go to war over the correct way to cut an egg. And there are a surprising number of jokes about bodily functions – Swift's way of reminding us that human beings are not perfectly spiritual; we all have our base sides.

The imaginary countries and author of *Gulliver's Travels* were both devices intended to insulate Swift from possible prosecution. He even had the finished version copied out by someone else to avoid his handwriting being recognised. In 1726, his London publisher, Benjamin Motte, was even more sensitive to the risks of criticising the British state; without consulting Swift, Motte not only deleted certain more risqué passages, but inserted text of his own in praise of the reigning monarch Queen Anne. Most of the original text was restored for the second edition in 1735, along with a letter from Gulliver complaining about the unauthorised editing of his adventures.

Gulliver's Travels had a direct influence on writers such as Voltaire and Dostoyevsky, and its inventive use of language has given us words that are still in use today. The *Oxford English Dictionary* defines 'lilliputian' as 'a diminutive person or thing' and 'yahoo' as 'a coarse, rude, or brutish person.'

Species Plantarum
Carl Linnaeus

(1753)

A Swedish botanist's love of nature, along with his keen eye and indefatigable research, resulted in a book entitled *Species Plantarum*, which offered a simplified binomial taxonomic ranking system to identify every known plant by its specific name (species), classified into its genus. Today his system is still in use, and Linnaeus is considered the father of both taxonomy and ecology.

As a precocious boy in a small southern Swedish town, Carl Linnaeus (1707–78) set about committing to memory the long Latin name of every plant he found on his family's land. It was no small feat, given the common wild briar rose, for example, was referred to by different botanists as *Rosa sylvestris inodora seu canina* or as *Rosa sylvestris alba cum rubore, folio glabro*.

His parents wanted him to enter the priesthood. But the devout Linnaeus made plants his obsession, and his encyclopaedic knowledge about their different types so impressed other naturalists that he ended up winning a scholarship to study medicine at the prestigious Uppsala University, where he focused on collecting and studying medicinal plants. After finishing his degree at the University of Harderwijk in the Netherlands, he continued his plant studies at the Leiden University. There he published a book, *Systema Naturae*, which presented the start of his groundbreaking classification of living things, which he thought would help reveal the divine order of God's creation in the universe. It presented his complete description of how he had classified more than 7,000 species of plants and 4,000 species of animals.

Based on years of collection and careful study, and close communication with many of Europe's leading botanists, in 1753 his book, *Species Plantarum*, was published by Laurentius Salvius in Stockholm, in two volumes.

The work described 5,940 plant species that were known at that time, which he had classified into approximately 1,000 genera, grouped into 24 classes.

It replaced existing cumbersome names with two-part terms, consisting of a single-word genus name and a single-word specific epithet or 'trivial name'. In addition to supplying the name, Linnaeus provided a brief and careful description of each species, and other names by which it had become known.

Linnaeus's plant taxonomy was based on its reproductive organs: its class was determined by its stamens (male organs), and its order by its pistils (female organs). His focus on plant sexuality and comparison to humans' sexuality was controversial in some quarters and prompted one critic, the botanist Johann Siegesbeck, to call Linnaeus's system 'loathsome harlotry'. But Linnaeus got his revenge by naming a small, insignificant European weed *Siegesbeckia*.

Linnaeus's hunger for finding and studying new plant species motivated many of his students to collect specimens on far-flung expeditions across the globe. One of them, Daniel Solander, served as naturalist for Captain James Cook's first round-the-world voyage; another, Pehr Kalm, collected species in the northeastern American colonies. Charles Darwin was also influenced by Linnaeus.

Some of Linnaeus's original plant specimens continue to be preserved at the Linnean Herbarium, the Swedish Museum of Natural History, and Linnaeus's botanical garden and manor home. His legacy is also kept alive by the Linnean Society of London and other botanical institutions.

In 1761 he was granted nobility and named Carl von Linné.

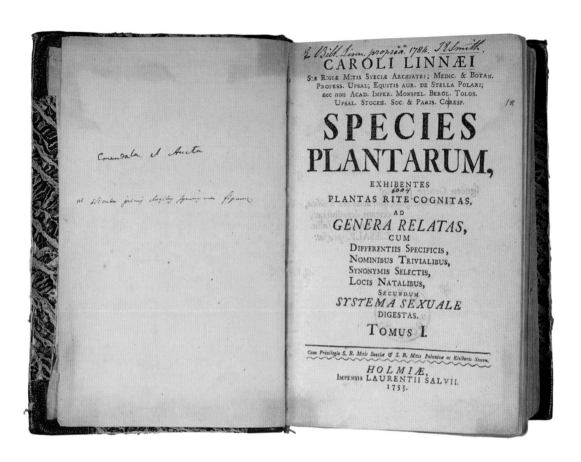

ABOVE AND LEFT: *Published in Stockholm, Sweden, in 1753,* Species Plantarum *was the first book to consistently use binomial names (genus followed by species within the genus) for plants. The second edition, published in 1762 (left), included an engraving of Linnaeus.*

A

DICTIONARY

OF THE

ENGLISH LANGUAGE:

IN WHICH

The WORDS are deduced from their ORIGINALS,

AND

ILLUSTRATED in their DIFFERENT SIGNIFICATIONS

BY

EXAMPLES from the beſt WRITERS.

TO WHICH ARE PREFIXED,

A HISTORY of the LANGUAGE,

AND

An ENGLISH GRAMMAR.

BY SAMUEL JOHNSON, A. M.

IN TWO VOLUMES.

VOL. I.

Cum tabulis animum cenſoris ſumet honeſti :
Audebit quæcunque parum ſplendoris habebunt,
Et ſine pondere erunt, et honore indigna ferentur,
Verba movere loco ; quamvis invita recedant,
Et verſentur adhuc intra penetralia Veſtæ :
Obſcurata diu populo bonus eruet, atque
Proferet in lucem ſpecioſa vocabula rerum,
Quæ priſcis memorata Catonibus atque Cethegis,
Nunc ſitus informis premit et deſerta vetuſtas.   Hor.

LONDON,
Printed by W. STRAHAN,
For J. and P. KNAPTON ; T. and T. LONGMAN ; C. HITCH and L. HAWES ;
A. MILLAR ; and R. and J. DODSLEY.
MDCCLV.

Samuel Johnson's Dictionary

(1755)

An eccentric genius toiled in a Fleet Street garret for eight years compiling a stupendous and highly literary dictionary that captured all of the richness and complexity of the English language in eighteenth-century London. The lexicographer's earthy witticisms delighted and irritated readers for many years to come.

In person, Samuel Johnson (1709–84) often made an unusual first impression. One close observer noted that 'he commonly held his head to one side … moving his body backwards and forwards, and rubbing his left knee in the same direction, with the palm of his hand … [and] made various sounds' like 'a half whistle' or 'as if clucking like a hen,' which was 'accompanied sometimes with a thoughtful look, but more frequently with a smile. Generally when he had concluded a period, in the course of a dispute, by which time he was a good deal exhausted by violence and vociferation, he used to blow out his breath like a whale.'

But beneath his odd mannerisms, Johnson showed a passionate genius for words. Adam Smith said, 'Johnson knew more books than any man alive.'

An omnivorous reader, whose modest means had prevented him from completing his education at Oxford, he struggled to support himself by writing poems, satire and criticism, until he hatched the idea of compiling 'a dictionary by which the pronunciation of our language may be fixed, and its attainment facilitated; by which its purity may be preserved, its use ascertained and its duration lengthened.'

Backed by a group of London booksellers, he laboured with six assistants to research and write a definitive compilation. *A Dictionary of the English Language: In Which the Words are Deduced from their Originals*, better known as *Samuel Johnson's Dictionary*, was published in 1755. The two-volume tome measured nearly 18 inches tall and 20 inches wide when opened, weighing in at roughly 20 pounds, and running 2,300 pages long.

The beautifully designed book contained entries for more than 42,000 words, complete with elegant definitions from every branch of learning, meticulous sense divisions, etymology and erudite literary quotations for each term. What most set the book apart, however, was its high literary quality and quirky, irrepressible wit.

Rust was defined as 'the red desquamation of old iron'; a cough is 'a convulsion of the lungs, vellicated by some sharp serosity'; rant as 'high sounding language unsupported by dignity of thought'; and network is 'any thing reticulated or decussated, at equal distances, with interstices between the intersections.' He was a staunch and outspoken conservative, and his commentary was peppered with such controversial political jibes as his definition of oats: 'Oats, which is defined quite simply as a grain commonly given to horses, but which in Scotland feeds the people.'

At first the book was priced at £4 10s (roughly equivalent to £350 today), but later abridged editions made it available to a mass audience at such a modest cost that it became a common fixture of many middle-class homes. A first-edition copy today sells for as much as £200,000. Prior to the completion of the *Oxford English Dictionary* in 1928, it was considered the favourite authority of the literary set.

Johnson became recognised as 'England's most distinguished man of letters', and was the subject of one of the greatest works of biographical art in literature, James Boswell's *Life of Samuel Johnson* (1791).

LEFT: *The first edition of Johnson's* A Dictionary of the English Language *took eight years to compile. Six assistants helped to define 40,000 words and add 114,000 illustrative quotations. When a miniature edition was published in 1796, the title page referred to it as* Johnson's Dictionary. *His friend and biographer Boswell wrote: 'The* Dictionary *was considered, from the moment of its inception, to be Johnson's, and from the time of its completion it was* Johnson's Dictionary – *his book and his property, his monument, his memorial.'*

The Castle of Otranto
Horace Walpole
(1764)

As the first Gothic novel, *The Castle of Otranto* allowed the polite reading public to delight in horror and revulsion for the first time. Horace Walpole's classic launched a literary style that would in turn launch the careers of Bram Stoker, Edgar Allan Poe and others.

Horace Walpole (1717–97) was a Member of Parliament and the son of Britain's first and longest serving Prime Minister, Sir Robert Walpole. He undertook the Grand Tour in 1739, a cultural voyage through Europe that was essential to the education of any son of a gentleman.

What he saw of medieval French architecture in particular gave him a taste for the Gothic, which he pursued both in word and in stone – Strawberry Hill, the home he built for himself in Twickenham in 1749, imitated medieval design and began the Gothic revival in architecture that reached its peak in Victorian England nearly a century later.

His fascination with the style gave him an obvious setting for his first novel, *The Castle of Otranto*. For content he drew his inspiration from old Germanic and British folk tales, with their supernatural elements and universal tropes – concealed identities, rightful heirs, tragic romances, heroes, villains and maidens. Walpole was reacting against the prevailing literary fashion of his day for realistic fiction, and he took pains to distance himself from it. He wrote in a deliberately archaic style of English; and he used a succession of framing devices to place it firmly in the past. He attributed the whole book to an imaginary author, William Marshal, who was supposed to have translated a sixteenth-century Italian text by one Onuphrio Muralto.

The Castle of Otranto starts with the extraordinary death of the son and heir of Manfred, owner of the castle, who is crushed when a giant supernatural helmet falls on him. It follows Manfred's evil efforts to father a new heir, and concludes with the identification of the rightful owner of Otranto. Walpole stocks his castle with a range of now-familiar Gothic elements – ghostly noises and apparitions, trapdoors, secret passages and doors that open by themselves. He heightens the drama, as Shakespeare would, by also including comic minor characters for light relief. The whole thing is a successfully chilling read, and became the template for a new genre of literature. Walpole's friend the poet Thomas Gray told him that *The Castle of Otranto* 'makes some of us cry a little, and all in general afraid to go to bed o'nights.'

Walpole himself first used the term 'a Gothic story' in the second edition, published in 1765, when he also wrote a new preface confessing that he was the true author. Although the revelation at first disappointed the reading public, the novel's impact and legacy are undeniable. Without it there might have been no *Northanger Abbey*, no *Dracula*, no *Fall of the House of Usher*, no *Hound of the Baskervilles*, no Tim Burton, no Twilight saga, no *Monty Python*, no *Game of Thrones*; perhaps no Wagner or Siouxsie and the Banshees. In *The Castle of Otranto* Horace Walpole invented Gothic culture as we know it today.

THE
CASTLE of OTRANTO,
A
STORY.

Translated by

WILLIAM MARSHAL, Gent.

From the Original ITALIAN of

ONUPHRIO MURALTO,

CANON of the Church of St. NICHOLAS
at OTRANTO.

LONDON:
Printed for THO. LOWNDS in Fleet-Street.
MDCCLXV.

ABOVE: The first edition (published December 24, 1764, but dated 1765)
claimed to be a translation of an Italian work from 1529, recently
discovered in the library of 'an ancient Catholic family in the north
of England.' In the second edition (published April 11, 1765),
Walpole acknowledged his authorship of the novel.

OPPOSITE: An early illustration (date unknown) of a scene from The
Castle of Otranto *by Susanna Duncombe (1725–1812).*

The History of the Decline and Fall of the Roman Empire
Edward Gibbon

(1776–88)

A groundbreaking description of the economic, cultural and political collapse of ancient Rome, The Decline and Fall of the Roman Empire is regarded as the first modern historical work. It consumed Gibbon's later life and continues to influence both the academic approach and the writing style of historians today.

Throughout the eighteenth century an essential part of any wealthy young Englishman's education was the Grand Tour – a voyage through Europe that exposed him to the finest art, music and architecture of the continent. Although travel was still difficult and often hazardous at this time, the Grand Tour followed a well-established and relatively safe route through France and Switzerland to Italy, considered the cradle of Western civilisation because of the Roman Empire. Grand Tourists returned to England through Austria, Germany and Holland. Travel, it was said, broadened the mind.

Edward Gibbon, twenty-six years old and with a formidable appetite for history, embarked on his Grand Tour in 1763. He reached Rome late the following year and was overwhelmed by the city. Gibbon was well read in Latin literature, and Rome's past came alive to him in the imperial ruins that surrounded him. He resolved there and then to write the story of the once all-powerful city's decline.

The first volume was published in 1776 and was instantly successful, running to three editions. It found a ready market among both classical scholars, armchair travellers and those on the Grand Tour, at a time when Britain saw itself as a modern-day Rome, building an empire of global trade and military might. Gibbon attributed Rome's fall to the influence of barbarians and Christians, and his criticism of the latter aroused some controversy in an empire-building country that believed in the strong foundations of the Church.

Gibbon's popularity came from his readable narrative style. He took the Roman point of view, with relatively little commentary beyond occasional opinionated asides. Above all he was not content simply to rehash the versions of earlier histories. Gibbon carefully drew his details from the contemporary Latin texts of the period. It is this use of primary sources that earns *The Decline and Fall of the Roman Empire* its reputation as the first modern, properly researched history book. What began as a history of Rome became an ambitious record of the entire Roman Empire, which at its height extended from southern Scotland to the Persian Gulf. The scale of Gibbon's output matched the scope of his research, which covered fifteen centuries and the many civilisations with which the empire came into contact. Produced over twelve years, it ran to six volumes and seventy-one chapters and brought Edward Gibbon considerable fame and fortune in his lifetime.

Perspectives on history change over the years, and some details of Gibbon's work have not stood the test of time and subsequent discovery. But it remains one of the most thorough accounts of its subject, nearly 250 years after it was first published. Its accuracy and clarity have made it the template for all modern historians. Winston Churchill, author of *A History of the English-Speaking Peoples*, styled himself on Edward Gibbon.

LEFT: Gibbon's monumental history of the Roman Empire was published in six volumes, between 1776 and 1788. Its objectivity and use of primary sources made it a template for later historians.

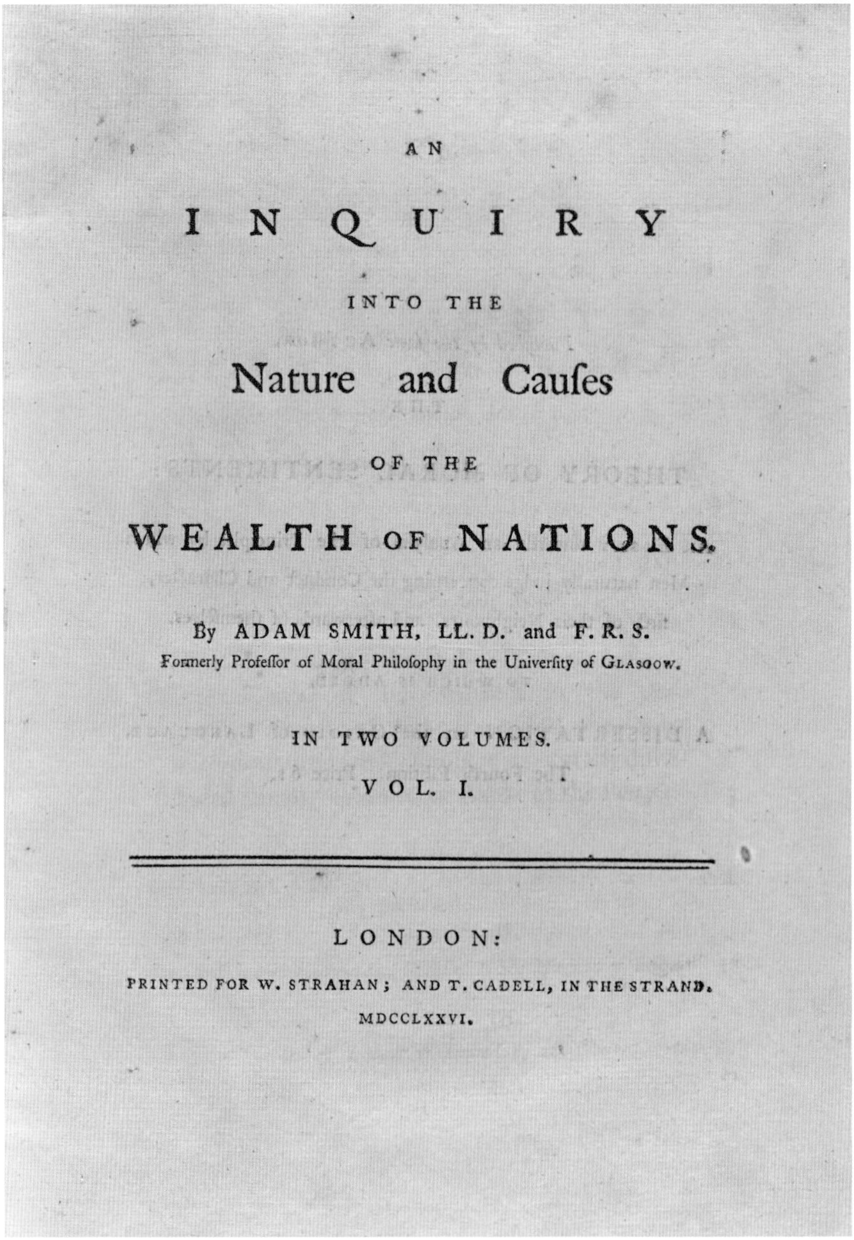

A N

I N Q U I R Y

INTO THE

Nature and Caufes

OF THE

WEALTH OF NATIONS.

By ADAM SMITH, LL. D. and F. R. S.

Formerly Profeffor of Moral Philofophy in the Univerfity of GLASGOW.

IN TWO VOLUMES.

VOL. I.

LONDON:

PRINTED FOR W. STRAHAN; AND T. CADELL, IN THE STRAND.

MDCCLXXVI.

ABOVE AND OPPOSITE: Adam Smith's 947-page magnum opus was published in two volumes in 1776. Smith's landmark treatise on political economy advocated free trade and paved the way for modern capitalism.

The Wealth of Nations
Adam Smith

(1776)

A Scottish moral philosopher's critique of Britain's outmoded mercantile model of trade, published shortly before the Declaration of Independence, provided a detailed rationale for a new approach to political economy based on labour and natural liberty – a system that would later become known as capitalism. The work immediately contributed to the spirit of revolution in the American colonies.

Adam Smith (1723–90) lectured on English literature, economics and logic at several leading universities in England and Scotland, which led to his publication of a distinguished work of the Enlightenment, *The Theory of Moral Sentiments*, which explored the natural principles of 'mutual sympathy' or empathy that govern morality.

For seventeen years, Smith laboured on a second book, which would be his magnum opus. After ten years of writing, *An Inquiry into the Nature and Causes of the Wealth of Nations* first appeared on March 9, 1776, at a time of great ferment, and its timing and message proved revolutionary.

For three centuries since the decay of feudalism, the governing economic theory in Britain had been mercantilism, which had required strict government regulation of trade in order to increase its power at the expense of rival colonies and nations. But Smith proposed a new model and ethos to replace the outworn system in the new age.

Not counting appendices and indices, his dense tome ran to 947 pages that were initially divided into five 'books'. Smith argued that free trade increases the wealth of nations by providing more occasion for labour and thus more occasion to create more wealth. Under his system, the more productively one labours, the more one earns. The resulting payment supplies individuals and the community

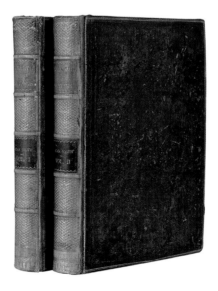

with their necessities, and with it can provide the opportunity to pursue additional revenue.

His central economic message was that if people are allowed to better themselves, it will produce economic prosperity for all. 'What improves the circumstances of the greater part can never be regarded as an inconveniency to the whole,' he wrote. 'No society can surely be flourishing and happy, of which the far greater part of the members are poor and miserable.' This led him to champion the doctrine of 'natural liberty', whereby the free market is allowed to operate without excessive state intervention.

In his view, the sovereign had only three duties: to protect the society from violence and invasion, to protect 'as far as possible, every member of the society from the injustice or oppression of every other member of it… [by] establishing an exact administration of justice', and to erect and maintain certain necessary public works and public institutions, which were beyond the interest of any individual or small group to create.

Few if any works in economics have had as much influence as *The Wealth of Nations*. His analysis of the division of labour and free trade, natural liberty, the limits on government intervention, and the general structure of the market, all heralded the shift to modern economics and helped to fuel revolutions in the American colonies, France and elsewhere.

Rights of Man
Thomas Paine

(1791)

Unlike other Founding Fathers of the American Revolution, Thomas Paine continued to support radical causes in the United States and elsewhere, penning the classic case for independence, human rights and political revolution. His rebellious ideas cost him dearly but helped to transform the world.

After emigrating from England to Philadelphia, Thomas Paine (1737–1809) quickly became famous as the author of the best-selling polemical tracts, *Common Sense* (1776) and *The American Crisis* (1776–83), which helped to fuel revolutionary fervour against the British Crown.

But when Frenchmen stormed the Bastille in 1789 and the revolt turned into another revolution, the conservative British statesman Edmund Burke, a former supporter of the American Revolution, issued a famous essay, *Reflections on the Revolution in France*, criticising the peasants' revolt and articulating the basic principles of his conservative philosophy.

Paine immediately fired off his rejoinder, *Rights of Man: Being an Answer to Mr. Burke's Attack on the French Revolution*, which he addressed to President George Washington. Paine's passionately argued book was published on March 16, 1791. Its appearance caused an international sensation and it sold as many as one million copies in just three weeks.

Rights of Man consisted of thirty-one articles, totalling 90,000 words. Writing in his trademark 'intellectual vernacular prose', Paine defended the Paris revolt and answered Burke's manifesto with an eloquent and detailed statement of his own political philosophy. Among his central points, he argued that civil government exists only through a social contract with the majority of men for the safeguarding of the individual, and that if government interferes with man's natural rights, revolution is permissible.

Paine rejected Burke's contempt for the French mob as the 'swinish multitude'. Paine responded: 'Whatever is my right as a man is also the right of another; and it becomes my duty to guarantee as well as to possess.' He regarded the French Revolution as a new beginning, whereby universal and natural rights were no longer denied by hereditary privilege, spurious argument premised on dubious history, bogus constitutionalism, invented tradition or common superstition.

Paine suggested reforms for British government, including a written constitution composed by a national assembly, the elimination of aristocratic titles and primogeniture, and a national budget without routine allotments for military and war expenses. He favoured a progressive income tax that was weighted against the rich; lower taxes and subsidised education for the poor; and a programme of public welfare, old-age pensions, marriage allowances and maternity benefits.

He opposed slavery and capital punishment, favoured universal brotherhood over nationalism and considered himself an atheist.

Wha WANTS ME

Paine paid a price for advocating natural rights. The book's publication sparked a furore in England. Having fled to France, he was tried and convicted in absentia for seditious libel but evaded hanging by never returning to the country. Paine also was imprisoned and nearly guillotined in France during the Terror, but he escaped punishment there as well.

His book shook the world, raising the idea of natural rights for all men everywhere.

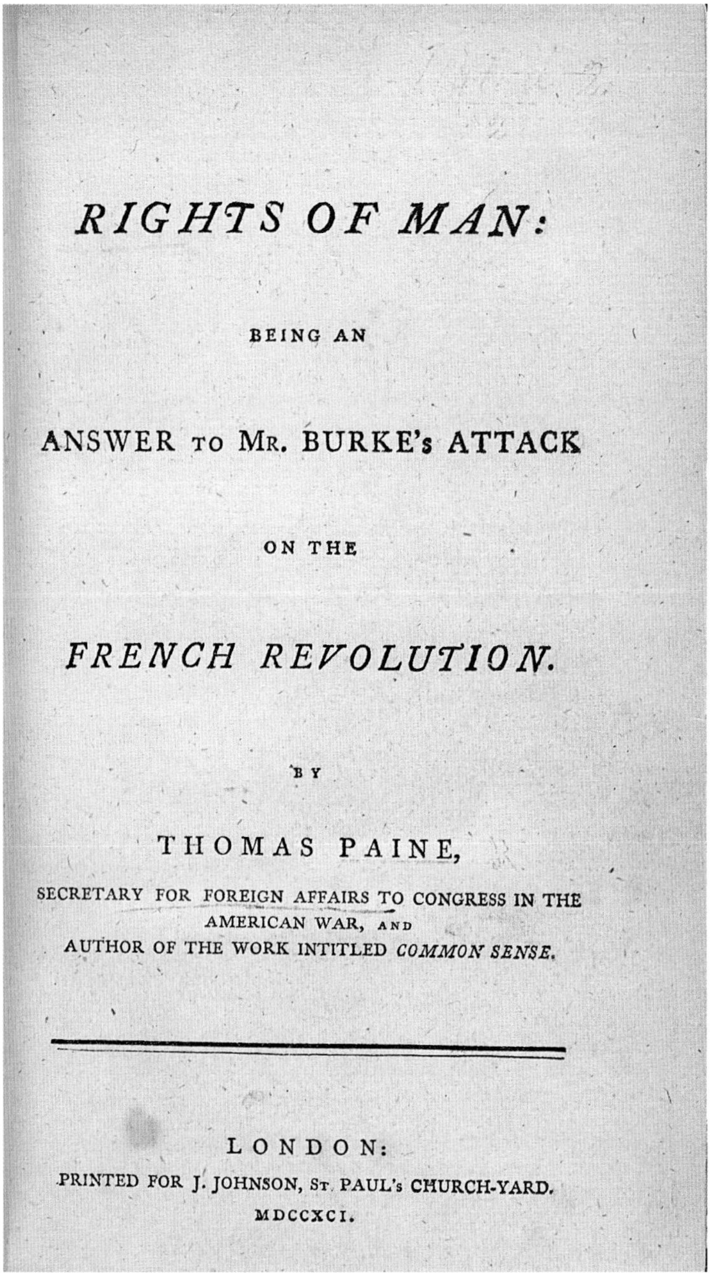

RIGHTS OF MAN:

BEING AN

ANSWER to Mr. BURKE's ATTACK

ON THE

FRENCH REVOLUTION.

BY

THOMAS PAINE,

SECRETARY FOR FOREIGN AFFAIRS TO CONGRESS IN THE
AMERICAN WAR, AND
AUTHOR OF THE WORK INTITLED *COMMON SENSE*.

LONDON:
PRINTED FOR J. JOHNSON, St. PAUL's CHURCH-YARD.
MDCCXCI.

ABOVE: This first edition, which was supposed to be published by Joseph Johnson on February 21, 1791, was withdrawn from circulation. The publishers feared that they would be prosecuted for sedition. It was eventually published by J.S. Jordan on March 16, 1791.

OPPOSITE: Isaac Cruikshank's 1792 caricature depicts Paine as a radical revolutionary for hire. The title – 'Wha Wants Me' – was a radical Scottish song of the period.

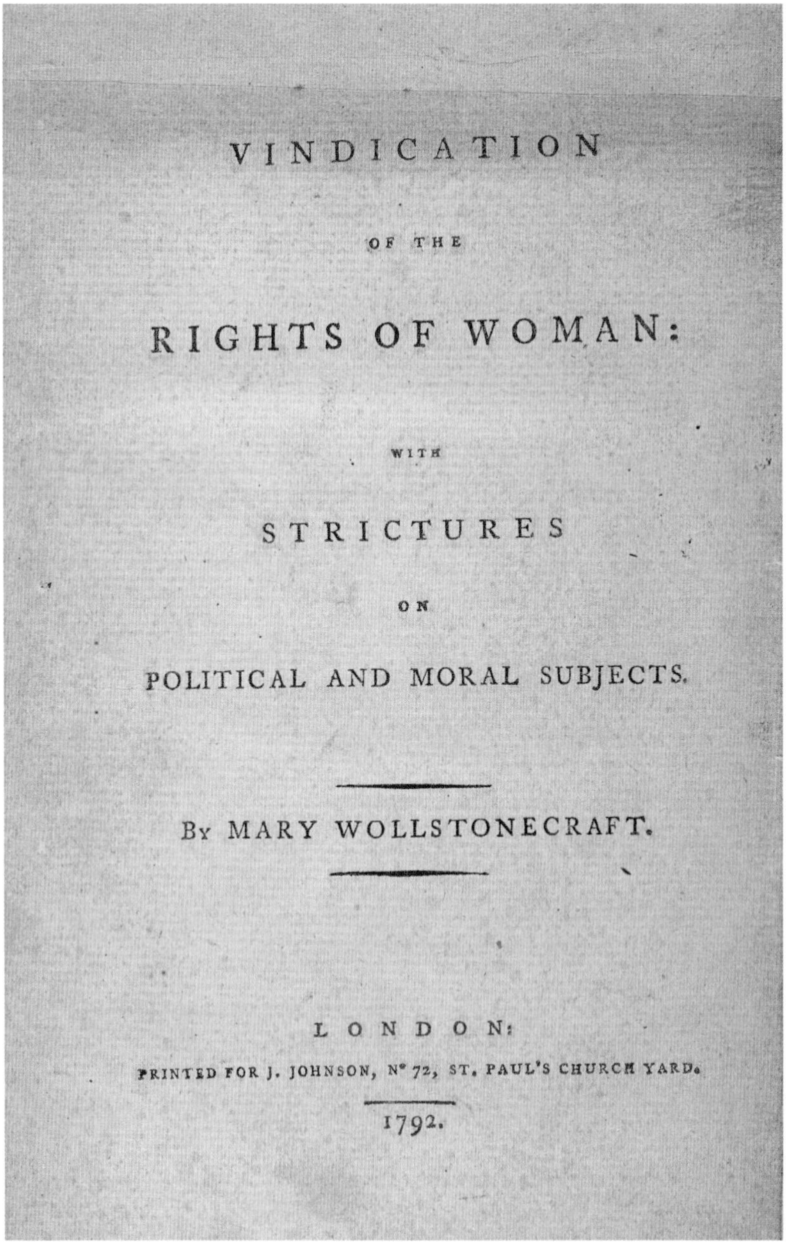

VINDICATION

OF THE

RIGHTS OF WOMAN:

WITH

STRICTURES

ON

POLITICAL AND MORAL SUBJECTS.

By MARY WOLLSTONECRAFT.

LONDON:

PRINTED FOR J. JOHNSON, N° 72, ST. PAUL'S CHURCH YARD.

1792.

ABOVE: *Wollstonecraft's groundbreaking work of literature – which advocated an equal education system for boys and girls and argued that women should be defined by their profession, not their husbands – established her as the mother of modern feminism.*

OPPOSITE: *John Opie's circa 1791 portrait of Mary Wollstonecraft shows her distracted momentarily from her studies. It is an unusual portrait for its period, when only wealthy men were depicted as intellectuals.*

A Vindication of the Rights of Woman
Mary Wollstonecraft

(1792)

Mary Wollstonecraft's manifesto for feminism – a groundbreaking challenge to both men and women – is still essential reading for any student of equality.

Mary Wollstonecraft (1759–97) saw firsthand the influence of abusive, domineering or unfaithful husbands upon their wives and children. Her observations shaped her critical view of the place of women in society, which she felt women were partly to blame for accepting. Women, according to the prevailing view, did not have the intellectual capacity to be anything other than beautiful objects, educated only in the accomplishments that might adorn a man's home – playing the piano and sewing, for example.

Wollstonecraft's religious beliefs could not accept such a distinction. If men and women were equal in the sight of God, she reasoned, then surely they were capable of the same spiritual virtue. And in that case, they must be given the same opportunities. She was convinced that a decent quality of education for women was the solution. Her first book, *Thoughts on the Education of Daughters* (1787), introduced some of these ideas in an otherwise straightforward primer for young ladies. Five years later they were more fully developed and expressed in *A Vindication of the Rights of Woman*.

In her 1790 pamphlet *A Vindication of the Rights of Men*, Wollstonecraft contributed to the debate about the value of the French Revolution. She argued that tradition – for example, the right of kings to govern – was not fixed but open to challenge by just and reasonable argument. In *The Rights of Woman* she extended that argument.

Educated womanhood benefits

everyone, Mary said. It was good for children, because it was a woman's job to educate them; it was good for the family, because it made husband and wife equal and therefore a more stable couple; and it was good for the nation because it allowed women to make intelligent contributions to social and political debates. On the subject of domestic equality, she attacked promiscuous, unfaithful husbands and insisted that they too should take some responsibility for chastity and fidelity in a marriage. She called on men, who held the power, to take steps to liberate their wives, and criticised women for spending their time in shallow pursuits such as vanity and gossip.

It was a radical publication, but a successful one, which very quickly went to a second edition. For the most part, reviewers admired those ideas whose impact was already being felt in society and ignored the more extreme suggestions such as representation in Parliament and coeducation.

After her death her husband wrote a biography of her, *Memoirs of the Author of A Vindication of the Rights of Woman*, which revealed the unconventional life she had led – an illegitimate child, cohabitation, association with artists and radical thinkers. In doing so he unwittingly damaged her reputation; for a century Mary Wollstonecraft was more notorious for her lifestyle than her proto-feminism. But from the twentieth century onwards she has been reassessed and hailed as a pioneer of liberation by women everywhere.

Grimm's Fairy Tales

(1812)

Two hundred years ago two young German brothers published a collection of folklorist fairy tales that would become – despite their dark, blunt, and often cruel and brutal themes – the standard children's book and one of the most influential and controversial literary works in Western culture.

Jacob Grimm (1785–1863) and Wilhelm Grimm (1786–1859) were born into a relatively prosperous middle-class household in Hanau near Frankfurt, but their father's death in 1796 plunged the family into poverty amid the turbulent period of the Napoleonic Wars. After their mother died in 1808, the brothers became fully responsible for the welfare of their three younger brothers and sister. Nevertheless, they persevered and found a way to support themselves and the others by drawing upon an interest they had acquired in childhood.

As boys, the pair had begun collecting traditional German folk tales and songs from their friends, and their fascination for the meanings and origins of such stories had led them to explore the new field of philology (the study of linguistics as the vehicle of literature and a representation of cultural history), which had sprouted in the fertile atmosphere of German Romanticism.

In 1812 they published a collection of eighty-six old German tales. The book was titled, *Kinder und Haus-Märchen* (*Children's and Household Tales*), which came to be known as *Grimm's Fairy Tales*.

Over the next forty years, the brothers brought out six subsequent editions, all of them extensively illustrated, first by Philipp Grot Johann, and later by Robert Leinweber. The stories introduced a host of immortal characters, including Rapunzel, Snow White and the Seven Dwarfs, Cinderella, Little Red Riding Hood, the Frog Prince, Hansel and Gretel, the Golden Goose, Rumpelstiltskin and many others. Most contained elements of cruelty, violence, fear, loss and death that reflected the grim and unvarnished reality conveyed in the tales.

Versions of the tales were widely published in many languages and editions. They also became the basis of many Walt Disney motion pictures, starting with *Snow White and the Seven Dwarfs* (1937). But the stories were controversial. The British poet W.H. Auden hailed them as 'among the few indispensable, common-property books upon which Western culture can be founded… It is hardly too much to say that these tales rank next to the Bible in importance.' But Adolf Hitler's embrace of the works as exemplifying his Nazi race theories led to their being banned in some quarters.

The tales' messages and meanings were the subject of *The Uses of Enchantment: The Meaning and Importance of Fairy Tales* (1976) by the Austrian-born psychoanalyst and Holocaust survivor, Bruno Bettelheim, who argued that the tales helped children deal with such existential problems as separation anxiety, Oedipal conflict, and sibling rivalries, and served other constructive purposes in their psychological development. But those interpretations as well have often generated debate.

Philip Pullman, who retold some of their tales in 2012, explains: 'Scholars of literature and folklore, of cultural and political history, theorists of a Freudian, Jungian, Christian, Marxist, structuralist, post-structuralist, feminist, postmodernist and every other kind of tendency have found immense riches for study in these tales.' However they are interpreted, *Kinder und Haus-Märchen* defined the fairy tale and forever changed children's literature.

RIGHT: The title page of the original 1812 edition of Kinder und Haus-Märchen *(*Children's and Household Tales*).*

TOP RIGHT: The 1819 edition with a frontispiece of 'Brother and Sister', showing an angel watching over the eponymous brother (transformed into a deer) and sister as they sleep.

FAR RIGHT: Portrait of Jacob and Wilhelm Grimm, by their younger brother Ludwig Emil Grimm.

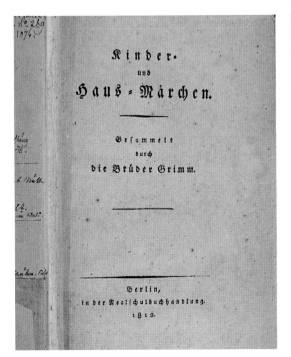

Pickering, pinx.^t   Greatbatch, sculp.^t

PRIDE AND PREJUDICE.

ABOVE AND OPPOSITE: The frontispiece of the 1833 edition (above) and title page of the 1813 edition (opposite). The frontispiece shows Elizabeth telling her father that Darcy was responsible for uniting Lydia and Wickham: 'She then told him what Mr. Darcy had voluntarily done for Lydia. He heard her with astonishment.'

Pride and Prejudice
Jane Austen
(1813)

Jane Austen's romantic comedy of manners pokes fun at some absurdities of English social life at the end of the eighteenth century, but the human foibles that she represents recur in every age.

Such is the universal popularity of *Pride and Prejudice* that even those who have never read it will recognise its opening line: 'It is a truth universally acknowledged that a single man in possession of a good fortune must be in want of a wife.' It's a teaser for the novel to come, setting out its themes of class, wealth, gender and matrimony with playful irony. An eighteenth-century man had many ways to advance in life besides marriage – through business or military service, for example – while a woman's only hope was a good marriage into money.

Jane Austen (1775–1817) was a parish rector's daughter and lived with her father for the first twenty-five years of her life. She first drafted *Pride and Prejudice*, under the title *First Impressions*, when she was just twenty-one. Her father submitted it to a publisher, but it was rejected, and she put it aside. When she returned to it, it was as a mature woman of thirty-five years, the published author of *Sense and Sensibility*. Reworked and retitled, *Pride and Prejudice* was well received and, like *Sense and Sensibility* before it, quickly sold out its first edition of 750 copies. It has sold an estimated twenty million copies since.

The novel chronicles the courtship of middle-class Elizabeth Bennet and upper-class Fitzwilliam Darcy, who form prejudiced and erroneous first impressions of each other – Elizabeth jumps to conclusions because she prides herself on making swift, accurate assessments of new acquaintances. Darcy's pride in his class leads him automatically to reject Elizabeth and hers. The stumbling blocks to

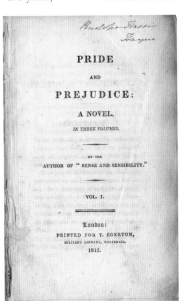

their love caused by these character flaws of prejudice and pride are compounded by others that Austen throws in their way. Love eventually overcomes almost all the false barriers of society, resulting in a plethora of marriages for Elizabeth and her sisters, only one of whom weds for money.

Austen uses several literary devices to tell her story. Events are often reported in the indirect speech of her characters. This creates a degree of distance from which to absorb the narrative, while also placing the reader at the heart of the action, as if eavesdropping on conversations.

Austen also relies heavily on letters as a way of moving the story on. It has been suggested that *First Impressions* may have been an entirely epistolary novel – that is, one that conveys its narrative through exchanges of correspondence. Letters allow characters and authors time for reflection, unlike the immediacy of conversation.

Finally, many scenes in *Pride and Prejudice* are set at large social gatherings of one sort or another, a perfect way to illustrate the absurdities of England's class-ridden society. Austen held a progressive view on class divisions and particularly on the place of women in society. Many of her characters are trapped in the roles that society has dictated for them. But Elizabeth and Darcy grow as they learn about themselves and each other, overcoming their pride and prejudice. In the end, love conquers all, and that's a story the world never tires of reading.

Frankenstein
Mary Shelley
(1818)

Frankenstein is the classic Gothic horror novel, and Shelley's monstrous creation has provided the premise for hundreds of books, plays and films. Her original story discusses nature, responsibility, isolation and the dangers of using powerful knowledge.

Frankenstein was originally written as a challenge. Three friends were stuck indoors reading ghost stories to one another one cold evening in 1816 and decided to see who could write the best tale of horror. The friends were the poet Lord Byron, his doctor John Polidori, and Mary Wollstonecraft Godwin, the daughter of the author of *A Vindication of the Rights of Woman*. The competition threw up two Gothic classics: Polidori's *The Vampyre*, the first-ever vampire novel; and Mary's *Frankenstein*.

Mary was there with her lover, the poet Percy Bysshe Shelley. The pair were married later that year, and Percy helped the new Mrs. Shelley (1797–1851) to expand her original short story into a novel over the following few months. Mary was inspired by the experiments of the Italian physicist Luigi Galvani, which proved that muscles could be animated with the application of an electric current – a phenomenon, christened Galvanism, that had been demonstrated publicly in 1803, on the body of a dead criminal in London.

Frankenstein was published in 1818, at a time when female novelists were still relatively rare. That fact, and the grisly subject matter, resulted in some mixed views from the critics of the day. But the book was an immediate success with the reading public, and within three years the first of many melodramatic versions of it appeared on the London stage.

The novel itself begins and ends with an epistolary framing device – the letters of an Arctic sea captain describing his meeting with Frankenstein, who has travelled to the frozen north to destroy the monster that he created. Shelley uses the icy wilderness to evoke the book's recurring motif of isolation. As Shelley relates the story that Frankenstein told the captain, we find that Frankenstein too is isolated, by his obsession with creating life and his ability to do so. And no one is more isolated than Frankenstein's monstrous creation, who is shunned, even by his creator.

The creature, although physically crude and brutish, is intellectually and emotionally mature – he reads Milton's *Paradise Lost*, for example. He hopes that Frankenstein will create a companion for him; and only when Frankenstein, horrified by what he has made, dashes that hope does the monster seek violent revenge. But when in the end he finds that Frankenstein has died in the Arctic of hypothermia, he grieves, aware that he is now more alone, more isolated, than ever.

In the twenty-first century the book still raises moral and psychological questions about man playing God. These ideas fascinate almost as much as the lurid possibility, closer than ever, of creating life from spare parts.

LEFT: A copy of the first edition from 1818, with handwritten amendments by Mary Shelley, some of which were incorporated into subsequent editions of the book.

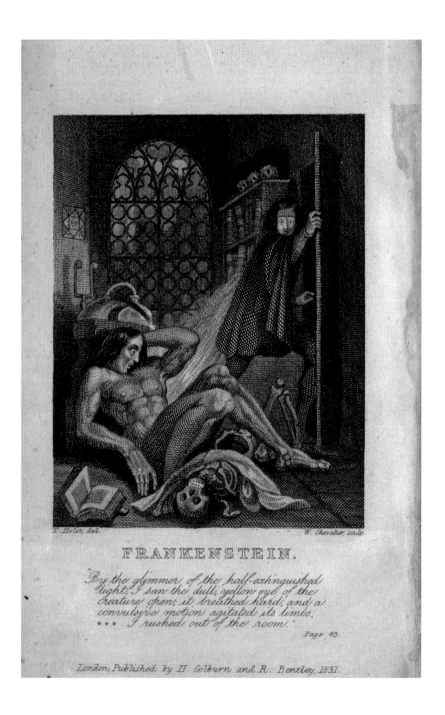

FRANKENSTEIN.

"By the glimmer of the half-extinguished
light, I saw the dull, yellow eye of the
creature open: it breathed hard, and a
convulsive motion agitated its limbs.
* * * I rushed out of the room."

Page 43.

London, Published by H. Colburn and R. Bentley, 1831.

ABOVE: *The frontispiece of the 1831 edition with an illustration by
Theodor von Holst, showing the creature awakening.*

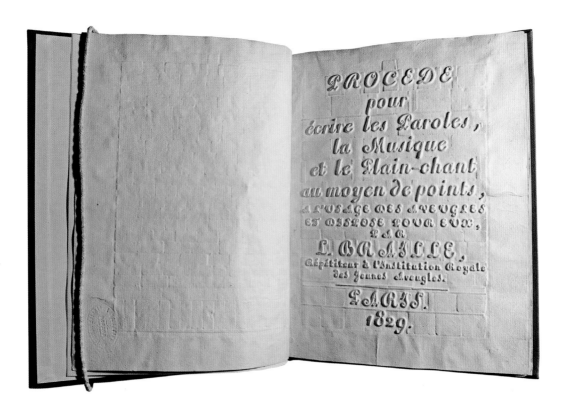

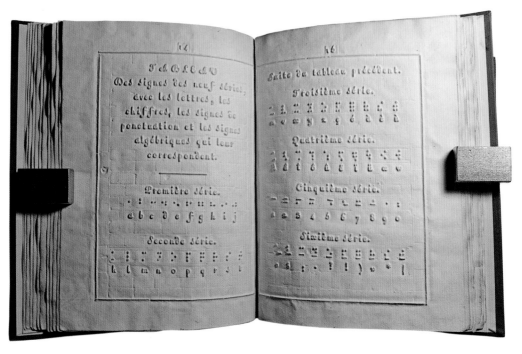

Procedure for Writing Words, Music and Plainsong in Dots
Louis Braille

(1829)

A blind boy invented an ingenious code of touch reading, which he shared with the world in the form of an unusual book with embossed pages, thereby bringing literacy to the blind, and with it, greater social inclusion, independence and productivity. Its symbols have spread to elevators and postage stamps.

Louis Braille (1809–52) was a bright and inquisitive three-year-old when he injured an eye with a sharp awl in his father's harness-making shop. The ensuing infections left the boy completely blind in both eyes – a curse which at that time normally doomed its sufferers to everlasting darkness and social isolation.

At his urging and the efforts of his family and a local priest, however, Louis was allowed to sit through classes with other school pupils, where he showed such remarkable academic ability that by the age of ten he received a scholarship to the Royal Institution for Blind Youth in Paris.

While studying there, he met a French army officer named Charles Barbier who had invented a basic tactile method of raised dots for enabling soldiers at night to compose and read messages without the benefit of illumination. Barbier's system consisted of sets of twelve dots on embossed paper that encoded thirty-six distinct sounds. But the military had rejected his method for being too hard for most soldiers to use.

Young Braille studied Barbier's code and identified its major defects. His solution was to develop a system of touch reading that would utilise cells containing six raised dots to represent each letter of the alphabet. His system also included symbols for punctuation marks and letter groupings.

Braille refined and expanded the idea to create a system of writing and reading for blind or visually impaired persons, which involved a new code for the French alphabet and musical notation. Within three years he had his work published in 1829 as *Procedure for Writing Words, Music and Plainsong in Dots*.

The new system became known as Braille, after its inventor. Both hands are usually involved, and the reading is done with the index fingers. The reader moves their hand from left to right over the line of raised dots to decipher the letters. With training, a skilled reader's speed can reach 150 words per minute.

Many famous musicians have attributed part of their success to their literacy. Ray Charles said, 'Learning how to read music in Braille and play by ear helped me develop a damn good memory.' Helen Keller said, 'We the blind are as indebted to Louis Braille as mankind is to Gutenberg.'

Through Braille, blind or visually impaired individuals have gained access to great literature, financial statements, legal contracts, restaurant menus and board games.

In Britain it's been estimated that only about 15,000 to 20,000 blind and low-vision persons out of 2 million now use Braille. Rates of use in the United States are not very different. In the age of the speaking smartphone, however, computer systems have been developed to assist the blind, and Braille is no longer the only lifeline available.

LEFT: The original French-language title page (above) and pages showing Braille's dots for letters of the alphabet, accents, numbers and punctuation (below).

Murray's Handbooks for Travellers

(1836)

As Britain proceeded in its age of empire, a London publisher launched a series of comprehensive, scholarly and detailed handbooks that were intended to educate, guide and comfort Britons on their movements abroad. Soon, a German contemporary also contributed to the genre, and the modern travel guide was born.

In the early 1830s John Murray III (1808–92), the son of an illustrious British publisher, began organising his detailed notes from his travels throughout Europe. What began as a personal project evolved into a new type of practical resource for travellers as he produced a book called *A Hand-Book for Travellers in Holland, Belgium, and along the Rhine, and throughout Northern Germany*, which appeared in 1836 and sold more than 10,000 copies in its first five years.

Where the writer had stayed, what he had eaten, and how he had utilised the local transportation were only a tiny fraction of the many subjects it covered. His handbook told about the local standards for the treatment of servants, where to look out for robbers, and what drugs to take to ward off local maladies. Murray organised his local descriptions and practical information along numbered routes, and he included a listing of useful local words for his refined English readers. The handbook included very detailed histories of the countries and cities being visited, with scholarly studies of their architecture, monuments, art, music and other cultural achievements. The Murray style exemplified the exhaustive and practical planning that would come to characterise the emerging tourist industry.

Murray's innovative book led to a successful, ongoing series, with titles that were continually updated by other contributors and readers who shared their latest informed impressions about diverse foreign places from a decidedly British perspective. He expanded his contributors to include several distinguished figures from his personal circle in London, who were fellow members of the Athenaeum Club, the Royal Geographical Society and other elite associations – all highly educated, sophisticated and extremely literate gentlemen. Their erudite and sometimes eccentric writing delighted and informed readers more than any other practical manuals had done. Murray's press kept replacing and inserting portions of the text as new accounts became available, and the series included an advertising section and endpapers announcing its most recent titles. After starting with destinations in Europe, it later expanded its coverage to Egypt, Algeria, India and Japan.

When viewed today, the nineteenth-century guidebooks provide a fascinating window into the mindset of the British Victorian tourist in a foreign land. Murray's correspondents' accounts are steeped in the perspectives of the British Empire.

One reader so admired the series that he began publishing his own version of travel guides that carried on the idea while incorporating some new features. Karl Baedeker (1801–59) acknowledged his friendship with Murray and appropriated several of Murray's approaches, even adopting a similar title. Baedeker's *Handbüchlein für Reisende* (*Handbooks for Travellers*) went on to set the standard for authoritative guidebooks for travellers – but without Murray, there would be no Baedeker.

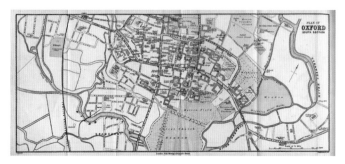

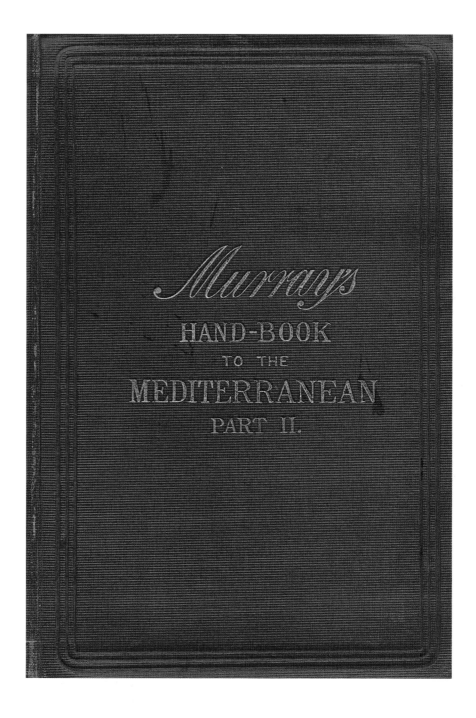

ABOVE AND OPPOSITE: Murray's travel guides, with their distinctive red covers and gold lettering, became famous for their comprehensive coverage and detailed information. They offered practical advice on hotels and transportation, made suggestions for cultural itineraries, and included foldout maps. These detailed and scholarly handbooks covered Britain, Europe, India, Japan and New Zealand.

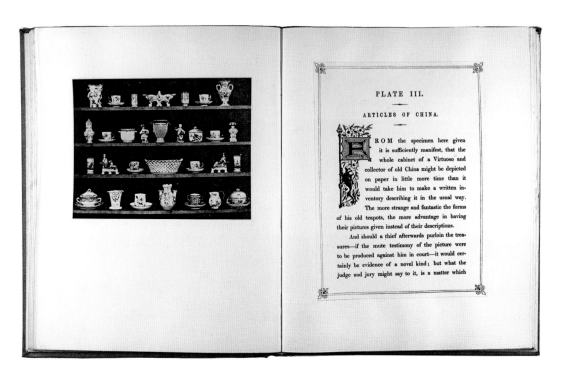

The Pencil of Nature
William Henry Fox Talbot

(1844–46)

Intended as a shop window for the process he had invented, Fox Talbot's book – the first commercially produced book of photography – illustrated the revolutionary possibilities that 'taking pictures' offered.

William Henry Fox Talbot (1800–77) had a brilliant mind. He published his first book, *The Flora and Fauna of Harrow*, at the age of twelve. He was as comfortable translating ancient Abyssinian cuneiform texts as he was developing ideas for electric motors. One thing he was not good at was drawing with a pencil, even with the help of a camera lucida – a device of lenses and mirrors that projected the artist's view onto paper so that it could be traced line by line. He wished there was a way of simply fixing the image he was seeing onto the page, and set about developing one.

Using his knowledge of chemistry, he conducted early experiments on paper soaked in salt and silver solutions in the 1830s. At the same time a Frenchman, Louis Daguerre, was working on a very different photographic process, capturing images on copper plates coated in silver nitrate. The two men publicly announced their processes within three weeks of each other, Daguerre first, in 1839.

The daguerreotype was a sharper image, but a fragile one, which had to be protected under glass in a box or frame. Talbot's calotype (from the Greek for 'beautiful impression') took on some of the graininess of the paper on which it was printed. Both processes produced only a single image, from which copies could be made with consequent loss of contrast. The calotype's great advantage was in the ease of reproduction – Daguerre's images could only be copied by re-daguerreotyping the first daguerreotype, while unlimited calotypes could be produced just by contact printing from the original.

Talbot refined his copying process until he was confident of consistent reproduction, and in 1844 he published the first part of *The Pencil of Nature*, a run of 285 copies, with five real calotypes stuck to the pages, each accompanied by Talbot's own very readable text. It was conceived as a series to be published in twelve monthly instalments.

Sales of the first part were sufficiently encouraging for Talbot to issue 150 copies of the second, this time with seven images. Thereafter, however, falling sales and problems with production meant that only six parts, and a total of twenty-four photographs, were issued. It is estimated that only fifty complete copies of the series survived.

Talbot chose his images carefully to illustrate a range of photographic uses. His subjects included architecture, landscape, still life and portraiture. Commenting on the latter, he felt he had to explain that it didn't take the camera any longer to draw three people than one. In the first part he included two images of collectible glass and china, pointing out that a photograph would be detailed enough to provide evidence in court following a theft – a commonplace event now but a startling idea back then. Part two included a photograph of a printed page, along with Talbot's suggestion that photography might eventually do away with the printing press, as indeed the photocopier eventually did a hundred years later.

Calotypes and daguerreotypes coexisted for some years. But having popularised the concept of photography, they were both overtaken in the 1850s by the new, cheaper collodion process, which combined the calotype's ease of copying with the daguerreotype's sharper picture. But *The Pencil of Nature* remains a brilliant manifesto for photographic possibility, and a landmark in the world of illustrated book publishing.

LEFT: The Pencil of Nature was published in six parts between 1844 and 1846 (above). The page showing 'Articles of China' (below) is from the first issue, with accompanying text describing how the photograph could replace a written inventory and might be used in a court of law as evidence of theft.

Narrative of the Life of Frederick Douglass

(1845)

A fugitive Maryland slave, who had learned to read and write, escaped to the North via the Underground Railroad and authored his own extraordinary narrative attacking slavery. Handsome and eloquent, he went on to become the most famous African-American of the nineteenth century.

On the balmy evening of August 16, 1841, a strikingly handsome young black man created a sensation when he spoke at an antislavery convention in Nantucket, Massachusetts.

His audience was thrilled to witness the first public oration of Frederick Douglass (1818–95) – a highly intelligent and articulate runaway slave – holding forth with powerful emotion about the evils of slavery.

Douglass further electrified abolitionists by writing a brief but searing literary autobiography, *Narrative of the Life of Frederick Douglass, An American Slave. Written by Himself*, which became one of the most important tracts of the antislavery movement.

'I was born in Tuckahoe, near Hillsborough, and about twelve miles from Easton, in Talbot county, Maryland,' he wrote.

> I have no accurate knowledge of my age, never having seen any authentic record containing it. By far the larger part of the slaves know as little of their ages as horses know of theirs, and it is the wish of most masters within my knowledge to keep their slaves thus ignorant… My father was a white man. He was admitted to be such by all I ever heard speak of my parentage. The opinion was also whispered that my master was my father; but of the correctness of this opinion, I know nothing; the means of knowing was withheld from me.

Douglass's narrative described in sharp, factual detail what it was like to grow up in slavery. Besides losing his mother at seven, he recalled watching his aunt Hester being whipped, and told how slaves were taught to remain silent about their masters' cruelties.

Yet Douglass named names. He also explained the sometimes smaller and more subtle cruelties that masters exhibited against their slaves when something didn't please them. Although he was allowed to learn to read and write, one of his masters disapproved of slaves becoming educated and took steps to prevent it.

Transferred from one master to another as a consequence of shifting estates, Douglass began to more actively resist and was whipped as a result. Finally, when a brutal overseer named Covey prepared to whip him again, Douglass fought back, and they struggled until Douglass finally won. Covey was so humiliated, he didn't try to whip him again and didn't reveal his failure for fear of losing face. After running away, Douglass was caught and jailed for two years. But he later ran away again, receiving help from the Underground Railroad, which enabled him to find sanctuary in New Bedford, Massachusetts, although he was careful not to reveal the network's workings.

Douglass's narrative sold 5,000 copies in its first four months and earned him such notoriety that he had to flee to England to avoid being apprehended as a fugitive slave. While in Britain and Ireland, a group of abolitionists purchased his freedom for $710.96, and he was able to return to the United States.

Douglass resumed his efforts on behalf of emancipation and published two more acclaimed autobiographies, *My Bondage and My Freedom* (1855) and *The Life and Times of Frederick Douglass* (1881, revised 1892). His writing and oratory earned great celebrity, and he was the second-most photographed American of the nineteenth century, after Abraham Lincoln. His work helped bring an end to slavery.

NARRATIVE

OF THE

LIFE

OF

FREDERICK DOUGLASS,

AN

AMERICAN SLAVE.

WRITTEN BY HIMSELF.

BOSTON:
PUBLISHED AT THE ANTI-SLAVERY OFFICE,
No. 25 CORNHILL
1845.

Frederick Douglass

ABOVE AND LEFT:

Frederick Douglass's portrait was included as a frontispiece to the first edition (above), and his image in photographs (left) became an important aspect of his public persona. He wanted to project an image of defiant respectability and was eager to control how he was portrayed. He wrote that 'Negroes can never have impartial portraits at the hands of white artists.'

JANE EYRE.

An Autobiography.

EDITED BY
CURRER BELL.

IN THREE VOLUMES.
VOL. III.

LONDON:
SMITH, ELDER AND CO., CORNHILL.
——
1847.

ABOVE: The title page of the first edition, which was published under the male pen name Currer Bell.
Charlotte Brontë suspected that female authors were 'liable to be looked upon with prejudice.'

OPPOSITE: Charlotte Brontë's handwritten manuscript is remarkably neat, with very few corrections. 'She would wait patiently,' her biographer Elizabeth Gaskell noted, 'searching for the right term, until it presented itself to her.'

Jane Eyre
Charlotte Brontë
(1847)

A vivid story of love and belonging, cruelty and class. The autobiographical nature of Charlotte Brontë's debut gives it a strength and wisdom that ring true for each new generation that reads it.

At its simplest level *Jane Eyre* is a well-told tale of the far-from-smooth course of true love. It owes its lasting success to its acute observation of a young woman growing up at a time when there were severe social limits on her life choices. It found immediate popularity with women, who recognised its protagonist's predicaments.

The Brontë sisters from West Yorkshire – Charlotte, Emily and Anne – are a formidable force in English literature. Emily gave us *Wuthering Heights*; Anne wrote *Agnes Grey* and *The Tenant of Wildfell Hall*. Charlotte Brontë (1816–55), the only one of the family to live beyond the age of thirty-one, wrote four novels, three of them published in her lifetime.

All three had their first novels published in 1847, but Charlotte beat the others by two months. Because writing fiction was still not considered a respectable activity for a woman, Charlotte was at pains to conceal her authorship and true identity: *Jane Eyre* was originally subtitled *An Autobiography*, ostensibly edited by one Currer Bell – the name Charlotte had used for her poetry.

Truth is a constant theme of the book, whether it be true love, real beauty or genuine religious faith. Several times Jane rejects relationships because she feels that love is absent. The difference between inner and outer beauty is expressed through several characters. Rochester's mistress, Céline Varens, is exceptionally beautiful but scheming, while the unassuming Jane has a spiritual beauty that shines

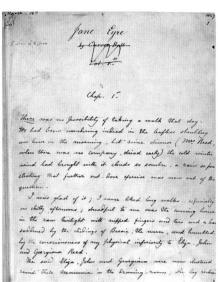

through in her moral decisions. By contrast, her teacher, Mr. Brocklehurst, is an outwardly Christian man who mistreats his pupils and embezzles the school funds for his own comfort.

Jane, like Charlotte, finds work as a governess, one of the few employment opportunities open to women in the early nineteenth century, and a socially ambiguous position. On the one hand, governesses were expected to be refined and educated; on the other, their status in the household was little more than a servant's. The duality often gave rise to tension in a household, and it gave both Charlotte and Jane the chance to observe and criticise English class. However, at no point does Charlotte challenge the social order. Her happy ending is only possible because she inherits a fortune that raises her position in society and makes her Rochester's equal.

Running throughout the novel is Jane's struggle to balance her instinct for independence with a longing for companionship, family and love. Jane's new equality with Rochester is further emphasised by his disfigurement after heroic actions in a house fire. The once handsome, rakish man is now ugly of hand and eye but noble of deed. Her inheritance guarantees her independence and his good heart assures her of true love and companionship. The assertive opening to the last chapter – 'Reader, I married him.' – is now one of the most famous lines in English literature.

David Copperfield
Charles Dickens
(1850)

David Copperfield charts the passage from youth to maturity, for both the protagonist and its author. Copperfield survives loss and cruelty to find love and a new family. Dickens rated this his best novel.

Charles Dickens (1812–70) was the very popular author of seven novels when he began to write his autobiography. Finding it too difficult to write so directly about his past, he decided instead to fictionalise it, and *David Copperfield* was the result.

The story is in the form of a bildungsroman – the German for 'novel of education' – a coming-of-age tale that follows a character's journey, generally from oppressive childhood to adult happiness. It need not be autobiographical, although Charlotte Brontë's *Jane Eyre*, which appeared only three years before *David Copperfield*, is another example of a bildungsroman that blends fiction and real life.

Copperfield's 'education' is at the hands of cruel men and with the loss throughout the book of those dearest to him. His father dies before he is born, his mother later in his youth; his beloved nurse, Peggotty, leaves to get married; Mr. Micawber is imprisoned; his wife, Dora, and his lifelong friends Steerforth and Ham all die. Cruelty comes from his stepfather, his teacher, and his employer, and David sees other examples of abuse all around him as he grows up. Some, like Steerforth and Uriah Heep, conceal their wicked natures at first but are unmasked.

David Copperfield contains some of Dickens's most memorable and well-drawn characters, including the very ''umble' Uriah Heep, eccentric Betsy Trotwood, the affectionate Micawbers and kite-flying Mr. Dick. Among them are many mother and father figures to whom the young Copperfield turns in the absence of his own. We are

each our parent's child, and one of the strengths of *David Copperfield* is to provoke our thoughts about our own childhood circumstances.

The novel marks a turning point in Dickens's output. Earlier works had taken aim at the injustices of Victorian society. With *David Copperfield*, Dickens becomes much more interested in the characters and motives of his creations, laying the ground for his later, darker novels, such as *Bleak House, Hard Times* and *Great Expectations* (the latter another bildungsroman).

Dickens the great social commentator is more personal in *David Copperfield*, but his interest in Victorian conditions persists. The migration from country to town in the wake of the industrial revolution brought overpopulation, poverty and crime, and David Copperfield witnesses all of these in school, factory, prison and office. Dickens experienced all of these too, having worked, as he makes David do, in a bottle factory, as a journalist and for a law firm, and having seen his own family thrown into debtors' prison.

David Copperfield was first published in nineteen monthly parts costing a shilling each over 1849 and 1850. Its publication in book form, illustrated like many of his novels by Phiz (the pen name of Hablot Knight Browne), coincided with the final instalment. It has never been out of print since. For a new edition just three years before his death, Dickens included a new preface, in which he wrote, 'like many fond parents, I have in my heart of hearts a favourite child. And his name is David Copperfield.'

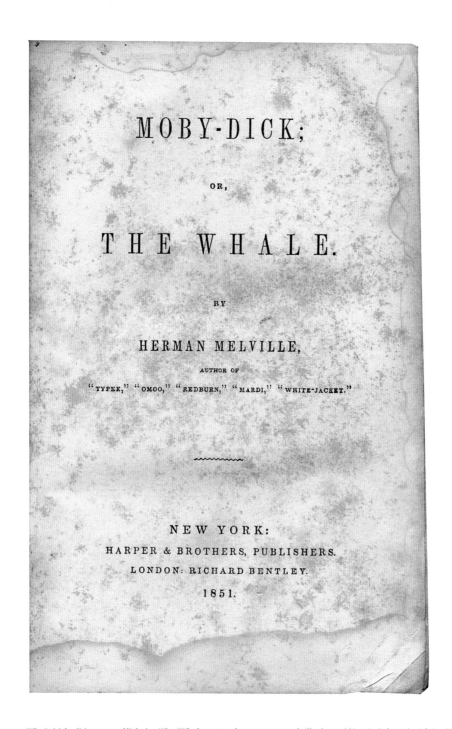

MOBY-DICK;

OR,

THE WHALE.

BY

HERMAN MELVILLE,

AUTHOR OF

"TYPEE," "OMOO," "REDBURN," "MARDI," "WHITE-JACKET."

NEW YORK:
HARPER & BROTHERS, PUBLISHERS.
LONDON: RICHARD BENTLEY.
1851.

ABOVE: The British edition was published as The Whale *on October 18, 1851. Melville changed his mind about the title in time for the American edition (shown here), which was published on November 14, 1851, as* Moby-Dick; or, The Whale.

OPPOSITE: This illustration, showing 'The Voyage of the Pequod *from the Book* Moby Dick *by Herman Melville', was one of twelve literary maps produced by the Harris-Seybold Company of Cleveland between 1953 and 1964.*

Moby-Dick
Herman Melville
(1851)

A former mariner's epic tale about Captain Ahab's obsessive pursuit of a ferocious white whale is revered as one of the great novels in English literature. Yet some of its most enduring qualities may have come from a hike up Monument Mountain with America's leading symbolic novelist.

Herman Melville (1819–91) had spent eighteen months roaming the oceans as an ordinary seaman aboard the whaling ship *Acushnet*. His experiences were to find outlet in his greatest novel, which was first published in London in October 1851 as *The Whale* and a month later in New York as *Moby-Dick; or, The Whale.*

Melville had gathered an enormous body of research and oral history about whaling, yet as he toiled over his novel, he longed to produce something more profound and original. On August 5, 1850, Melville took a break from his labours to go on an outing with a friend, Oliver Wendell Holmes Sr., and the celebrated author Nathaniel Hawthorne, who had recently published his great allegorical novel, *The Scarlet Letter.* Together they climbed Monument Mountain in Great Barrington, Massachusetts, in what was for the younger writer Melville a life-altering exchange. Hawthorne's influence on the scope of *The Whale* was profound, and Melville dedicates the book to him, 'in token of my admiration for his genius.'

Melville's narrator, Ishmael, tells the story of Captain Ahab's obsessive quest for the white whale that had wrenched off his leg on a previous whaling expedition and left him with a peg leg carved from a whale's jawbone. As the voyage progresses, Ishmael realises that the voyage is less of a commercial whaling trip and more about Ahab's revenge. Their ship, the *Pequod*, encounters many other ships, always ending with an inquiry about the whereabouts of the white whale, Moby-Dick. At the conclusion, the whale ends

up destroying the *Pequod*, and all those aboard, a similar fate to the whaler *Essex* out of Nantucket, which was sunk by a sperm whale in the Southern Ocean in 1820, of which seven crew members survived thanks only to cannibalism.

Melville had read an account of the *Essex* written by its first mate, Owen Chase, and was also aware of the story of Mocha Dick, a white sperm whale killed in the late 1830s in waters off the Chilean island of Mocha, which was said to attack ships with premeditated ferocity.

Moby-Dick is both a gripping narrative on the perils of harpooning from a flimsy whaleboat and the tensions that arise from one man's secretive monomania. Interspersed are essays on whales and whale hunting, and Melville uses many different literary styles and devices, including songs, poetry, stage directions and soliloquies. The book's many asides are used in the exploration of social status, good and evil, and the existence of God.

Although the book's opening line – 'Call me Ishmael' – would become one of the most famous in literature, the book was not a commercial success in Melville's lifetime. When he died in 1891, the book had sold 3,200 copies and long been out of print.

The book's revival began at the centenary of his birth in 1919. E.M. Forster and D.H. Lawrence both became champions of the novel, and it has been reevaluated throughout the twentieth century and steadily gained its place in the canon of great American literary works.

Roget's Thesaurus

(1852)

Roget was a brilliant British physician and polymath who obsessively compiled lists of synonyms. When his 'catalogue of words' was eventually published, it became an indispensable reference work.

Peter Mark Roget (1779–1869) was an accomplished author of scientific papers on a variety of subjects, but like other writers, he often struggled to find the right word. As a boy trying to escape from an overbearing mother, he'd use private notebooks to compile lists of things he had learned. The note-taking became a compulsion.

As he later explained, at the age of twenty-six, he completed a 'classed catalogue of words on a small scale', modelled on Carl Linnaeus's zoological classification system, to aid him with his 'deficiencies'. For years the makeshift system helped him with his literary compositions.

After retiring as secretary of London's fabled Royal Society, the hyperactive Roget found himself with too much leisure time, and his daughter suggested that he publish the document as an aid to others, in order that they might enjoy some of the same benefits. He laboured on it incessantly for four years until publishing it in 1852 as *The Thesaurus of English Words and Phrases Classified and Arranged so as to Facilitate the Expression of Ideas and Assist in Literary Composition* – now known as *Roget's Thesaurus* – having taken the word 'thesaurus' from the Greek term for 'treasury or storehouse'.

Roget's original listing featured 1,000 categories and 15,000 words. His approach was to group words according to ideas rather than alphabetically, as in a dictionary.

His was not the first work to attempt to furnish synonyms. One earlier example was *British Synonymy; or, an Attempt at Regulating the Choice of Words in Familiar Conversation*, published in 1794, by Hester Lynch Piozzi, a friend of the great English lexicographer Samuel Johnson. 'Synonymy,' she wrote, 'has more to do with elegance than truth.'

Roget didn't consider words to have synonyms; he believed every word is unique. He recognised that his listing was inherently imperfect.

Over time, however, the name Roget would become virtually synonymous with 'synonym', prompting some writers to dismiss the compendium as a tool for the linguistically lazy. Writing in *The Atlantic*, Simon Winchester, the author of a work about the making of the *Oxford English Dictionary* and other books, said: 'To put it more forcefully: *Roget's Thesaurus* no longer merits the unvarnished adoration it has over the years almost invariably received. It should be roundly condemned as a crucial part of the engine work that has transported us to our current state of linguistic and intellectual mediocrity.'

Despite more recent criticism, the reference work became so popular that it was published in a second edition in 1853, and many more editions after that. His son, Dr. John Lewis Roget, in 1879 compiled an expanded version that has gone on to become a standard part of every reference library. The 1992 edition contains more than 250,000 words. More than 30 million copies have been sold since 1852, and millions of copies remain in use.

Although its use may be disdained by serious writers, it has proved to be useful for students preparing term papers and has become, in the words of Winchester, 'a vade mecum for the crossword cheat.'

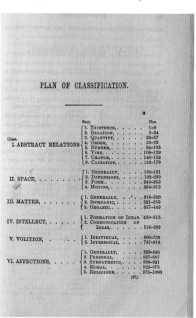

PLAN OF CLASSIFICATION.

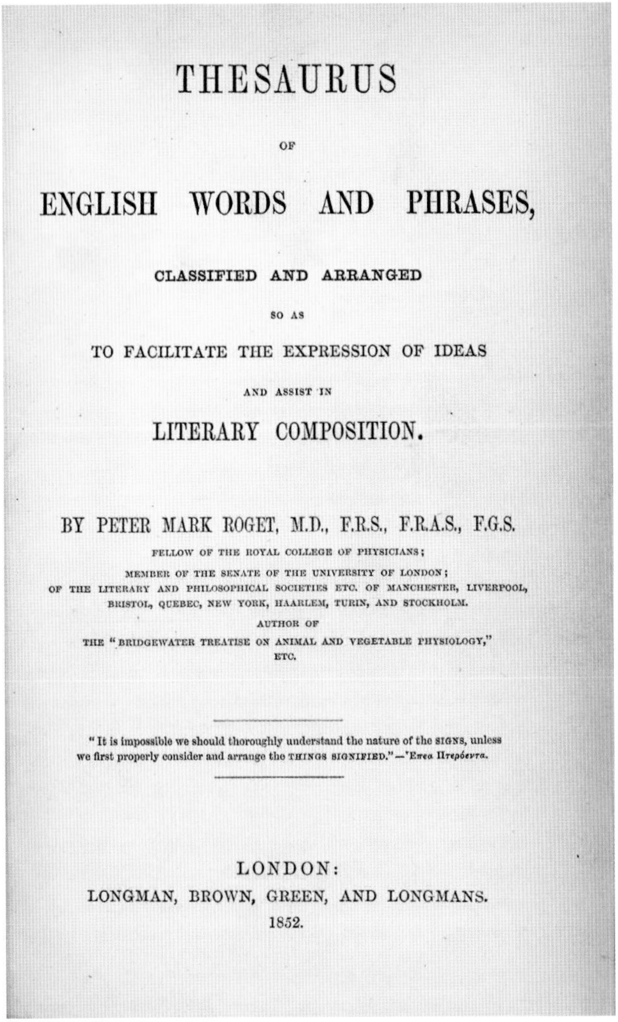

THESAURUS

OF

ENGLISH WORDS AND PHRASES,

CLASSIFIED AND ARRANGED

SO AS

TO FACILITATE THE EXPRESSION OF IDEAS

AND ASSIST IN

LITERARY COMPOSITION.

BY PETER MARK ROGET, M.D., F.R.S., F.R.A.S., F.G.S.

FELLOW OF THE ROYAL COLLEGE OF PHYSICIANS;

MEMBER OF THE SENATE OF THE UNIVERSITY OF LONDON;

OF THE LITERARY AND PHILOSOPHICAL SOCIETIES ETC. OF MANCHESTER, LIVERPOOL,
BRISTOL, QUEBEC, NEW YORK, HAARLEM, TURIN, AND STOCKHOLM.

AUTHOR OF

THE "BRIDGEWATER TREATISE ON ANIMAL AND VEGETABLE PHYSIOLOGY,"
ETC.

" It is impossible we should thoroughly understand the nature of the SIGNS, unless
we first properly consider and arrange the THINGS SIGNIFIED."—'Επεα Πτερόεντα.

LONDON:

LONGMAN, BROWN, GREEN, AND LONGMANS.

1852.

ABOVE: The first edition of the Thesaurus of English Words and Phrases *was published in 1852, almost fifty years after Roget had started compiling words to 'facilitate the expression of ideas'. The word 'thesaurus' came from the Greek for 'storehouse', or 'treasury of knowledge'.*

OPPOSITE: Roget used a system of verbal classification that he divided into six parts: Abstract Relations, Space, Matter, Intellect, Volition, Affections. Each class was then broken down into smaller groups to form clusters of linked words.

WALDEN;

OR,

LIFE IN THE WOODS.

By HENRY D. THOREAU,

AUTHOR OF "A WEEK ON THE CONCORD AND MERRIMACK RIVERS."

I do not propose to write an ode to dejection, but to brag as lustily as chanticleer in the morning, standing on his roost, if only to wake my neighbors up. — Page 92.

BOSTON:
TICKNOR AND FIELDS.
M DCCC LIV.

ABOVE: The title page of the first edition included Sophia Thoreau's drawing of her brother's cabin.

OPPOSITE: A bronze statue of Thoreau stands next to a replica of his one-room cabin close to Walden Pond.

Walden
Henry David Thoreau
(1854)

Thoreau's two years in the wilderness by Walden Pond brought him closer to God. What began life as a simple memoir ended up as a manual for spiritual and practical self-reliance in nature.

Henry David Thoreau (1817–62) lived in Concord, Massachusetts, where one of his neighbours was Ralph Waldo Emerson, the philosophical poet and proponent of individualism. Emerson headed the transcendentalist movement, which believed in the fundamental goodness of nature and people, and the corrupting influence of industrial society.

Society, Thoreau felt, had broken with nature through industrialisation; by breaking from society to live in nature, he hoped not only to develop his spirituality but to get a better perspective of what he had left behind. While transcendentalists thought that God was symbolised by nature, Thoreau went further and believed that God was actually present in all the elements of nature, from a rabbit scampering through the woods to the bubbles forming in ice on the pond.

On July 4, 1845, Thoreau moved into a wooden shack that he had built beside Walden Pond, in woodlands owned by Emerson, and declared his intention of staying there for two years, two months, and two days. It was a statement of individualism, a declaration of independence from Concord society, and a personal experiment in what Thoreau called 'living deliberately' – looking for God in all things.

Thoreau's philosophical position raised many moral conflicts. Although he rejected society, he needed it. He travelled several times a week into Concord, where he sold his crop of beans. He praised the solitude, but although he did not seek human company, he happily met other users of the pond and woods – children, women, fishermen, squatters. He revelled in his simple, hand-to-mouth, animalistic existence, yet

for pleasure read ancient Latin and Greek, the products of sophisticated, cultured societies.

Thoreau argued that since God was in all men, all men must be equal. Consequently, he was arrested on one visit to Concord and jailed for nonpayment of taxes, which he withheld on the grounds that they supported a state that supported slavery. The experience of imprisonment, although only for one night, led him to write an essay, 'Civil Disobedience' (1849), in which he argued that people should look to themselves and not civic society for their moral values.

He returned to civilisation exactly on schedule, on September 6, 1847, showing no inclination to prolong the experiment. It took him seven years to order his thoughts on his pond-side experiences. On its eventual publication in 1854, the radical ideas in *Walden* were broadly well-received by critics. But sales to the public were slow, and the book was not reprinted in Thoreau's lifetime.

After his death, criticism of it damaged his reputation until the end of the century, when some reassessment of his ideas was made. A new biography in the 1930s brought his political thinking to a new generation, and his individualistic philosophy inspired civil-rights leaders like Gandhi and Martin Luther King Jr. Although *Walden* was driven by Thoreau's spiritual beliefs, it found a new sphere of influence in the 1960s with the hippie movement and rising concerns about the environment.

Environmental, spiritual, political, philosophical – *Walden* is a complex, impassioned work that was ahead of its time but now strikes a chord on many levels with each new generation.

Madame Bovary
Gustave Flaubert
(1857)

Now considered the first great novel of literary realism, Flaubert's first novel was also his masterpiece. The modern novel starts with this one. But in 1857 it saw him taken to court on charges of immorality.

Romanticism, the artistic fashion that dominated the first half of the nineteenth century, had little to do with reality. It dealt with high emotion, individual idealism and an imagined lost utopia – the past, and unspoiled nature, rather than the imperfect present and the ugly sprawl of the industrial age.

Gustave Flaubert (1821–80) turned all that on its head. *Madame Bovary* was given an almost-contemporary time frame, starting in the 1820s and ending in the late 1840s. Although the novel is set in rural French villages and towns, its characters are drawn from the bourgeoisie; the dull French social and commercial classes that emerged only after the French Revolution of 1789. They lead petty, unimaginative lives and are mostly happy that way. Ten years before the publication of *Madame Bovary*, Flaubert had written: 'To be stupid, and selfish, and to have good health are the three requirements for happiness; though if stupidity is lacking, the others are useless.'

The exception is Madame Bovary – Emma – whose head is full of the impossible ideals in the romantic novels she reads. Reality bores her, and to escape it she embarks on a series of affairs, and lives well beyond her means. Emma incurs huge debts for herself and her country doctor husband. When her lovers reject her and her debts are called in, the real world crashes in on her, and Madame Bovary seeks another escape. Even the romantic act of taking poison is not what it seems, and she dies a slow, painful death.

It's a striking, tragic story, but what marks it out as a masterpiece is Flaubert's use of language. He depicts the remarkable and mundane details of his modern world with precision and extraordinary care, but more than that, his text reflects the pace and emotion of his scenes. He describes Emma's boredom, for example, in slow sentences; and her illicit love-making in a rush of excited syllables. Vladimir Nabokov, the author of *Lolita*, wrote of *Madame Bovary*: 'it is prose doing what poetry is supposed to do.'

The tale was first published in instalments in the magazine *La Revue de Paris* in the autumn of 1856, and Flaubert's relatively frank and passionate descriptions of Emma's acts of sexual infidelity scandalised the French capital. In January 1857, he and the magazine's publisher were prosecuted for breaches of public decency. There's no such thing as bad publicity, however, and when they were both acquitted and *Madame Bovary* was published in book form in April that year, it sold extremely well.

Since then, *Madame Bovary* has been recognised as a landmark in the development of the novel. Its influence on authors throughout the twentieth century has been profound. It is said that Flaubert agonised over every word he used, sometimes taking a week to write a single page. If so, it was worth it: from Henry James and Marcel Proust to Milan Kundera and Julian Barnes, novelists have described it as a perfectly structured literary masterpiece.

RIGHT: Flaubert was put on trial for obscenity between the novel's serialisation in La Revue de Paris *in 1856 and its book publication in two paperback volumes the following year.*

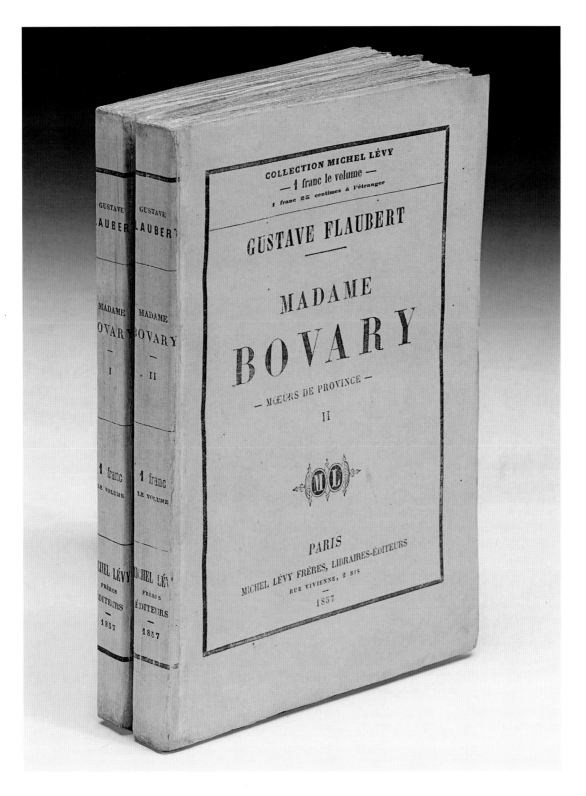

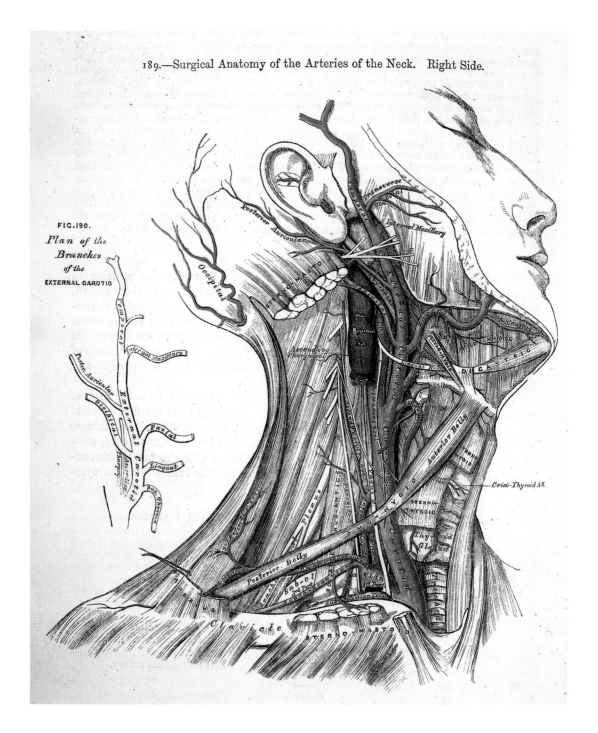

189.—Surgical Anatomy of the Arteries of the Neck. Right Side.

FIG. 190.

Plan of the
Branches
of the
EXTERNAL CAROTID

ABOVE: The first edition of 1858 was published in black and white under the title Anatomy, Descriptive and Surgical. *Henry Gray wrote the text, Henry Vandyke Carter created the illustrations, and the dissections were undertaken jointly. Colour illustrations were introduced for the eleventh edition in 1887.*

Gray's Anatomy

(1858)

In mid-Victorian London, a pair of brilliant young hospital staffers – an upper-class anatomy lecturer and a lower-status surgeon-in-training – teamed up to produce an illustrated anatomical study of the human body. But the work was bloody: it required them to dissect countless cadavers of the poor, and record what lay under the skin.

Henry Gray (1827–61) and Henry Vandyke Carter (1831–97) were both in their twenties and working at St. George's Hospital in London when they decided to collaborate on the production of an anatomy textbook for medical students. Gray was a well-connected anatomist, surgeon and fellow of the Royal Society; Carter was a younger, less wellborn medical student who was also a gifted artist.

In order to produce their comprehensive study – despite a lack of refrigeration, photography and other advantages – they needed a steady supply of fresh corpses, which came from paupers who had died in institutions or perished in the city without leaving any means to pay for their burial.

The pair worked together for eighteen months under the watchful eyes of other physicians and medical students. As the scalpel and forceps revealed what they found beneath, Carter sketched his drawings to accompany what Gray was writing in his notes:

> showing behind, above, below, concave, smooth, passes through, arises from, and lies along; and at the same time telling trapezius, clavicle, sternum, hyoid, sterno-thyroid… Oblique section of the articulations of the tarsus and metatarsus. Showing the six synovial membranes.

Gray's prose was a model of lucidity, and Carter's images an achievement of remarkable concision – in the tradition of Andreas Vesalius, but also resembling a precisely drafted engineering blueprint and an exact map of human geography. Together, they presented students and practitioners with an accurate and accessible guide to the body, in words and pictures that perfectly fit together to show and explain each realm.

Anatomy, Descriptive and Surgical – later known as *Gray's Anatomy* – with text by Henry Gray and wood engravings by Henry Vandyke Carter, appeared in 1858, during a golden age of medicine and at a time when new advances in printing had suddenly allowed such a work to be published. The engraver, Butterworth and Heath, did a magnificent job.

The response to it was resoundingly positive. *The British Medical Journal* called the book 'far superior to all other treatises on anatomy' and marvelled that 'the woodcuts… are excellent – so clear and large that there is never any doubt as to what is intended to be represented.' The medical reviewers often commented on the book's ability to present needed practical information in an accessible form. The detailed drawings were executed from fresh dissections, and the text was easy to read.

Its initial printing of 2,000 copies was quickly sold out, and more printings and editions followed. The latest edition, the forty-first, was published in September 2015 as *Gray's Anatomy: The Anatomical Basis of Clinical Practice*. The publisher describes it as nearly 1,600 pages long, with an index of 108 pages, and it is about two and a half inches thick. Its 2,000 colour illustrations reflect the latest developments in digital wizardry, including new diagnostic and clinical imagery in photography, X-ray, CT, MR and ultrasonic images. The work also features enhanced online content, including anatomical videos and a bonus imaging library.

Gray's Anatomy is the most widely used medical text ever written and one of the standard reference works for general medical readers. Its name is a household phrase. Gray, however, didn't live long enough to fully enjoy his success. He died from smallpox at the age of thirty-four.

On the Origin of Species
Charles Darwin
(1859)

Decades after returning home from a lengthy scientific expedition across the globe, a distinguished English naturalist, geologist and biologist unveiled his new theory of evolutionary biology, which many historians agree remains the most important academic book ever published – 'the book that changed everything.'

During a five-year voyage of discovery on board the HMS *Beagle*, Charles Darwin (1809–82) travelled to the remote Galápagos, a small barren cluster of volcanic islands that lie on the equator about sixty miles off the coast of Ecuador. Spanish explorers had named them for the giant tortoises that inhabited them, and each island seemed to have its own distinctive type. After discovering fossils of creatures resembling huge armadillos, Darwin made notes about the geographical distribution of the modern species in hope of finding the species' 'centre of creation'. His notebooks from the expedition show him beginning to speculate about the possibility that 'one species does change into another'; on one page he has sketched a sort of genealogical tree showing how successive forms may have evolved – a sketch that would become the most famous diagram in science.

Carefully studying the birds he encountered in his empirical research, he observed: 'One might really fancy that from an original paucity of birds in this archipelago, one species had been taken and modified for different ends.' He began to wonder if the different birds had become transformed by their struggle for existence on their little islands into a series of types particularly suited to their particular niches.

After returning home in 1837, he continued to work up his findings. By December 1838, he had formulated his basic theory, realising that populations gradually evolve over generations through a process he called 'natural selection'. 'These facts,' he would later conclude, 'seemed to me to throw some light on the origin of species – that mystery of mysteries, as it has been called by one of our greatest philosophers.'

Yet it would not be until June 1858, when he delivered a paper with Alfred Russel Wallace to the Linnean Society of London, that Darwin began to go public with his discoveries. On November 24, 1859, John Murray published Darwin's book, *On the Origin of Species by Means of Natural Selection, or the Preservation of Favoured Races in the Struggle for Life*, intended for general readers. It immediately attracted intense interest in scientific circles and beyond.

Darwin's theory of evolution by natural selection, with its treelike model of branching common descent and environmental adaptation, and branching speciation, became the founding document of evolutionary biology, presenting the unifying concepts of the modern life sciences. The theory explained the diversity of living organisms and their adaptation to the environment, showing how species evolved. It also shed light on many other scientific questions, explaining the world's geologic record and a host of other mysteries.

His theory generated intense controversy in religious and scientific quarters, in part because it challenged reigning biblical doctrines of creationism and catastrophism. His proposal that human beings were descended from common ancestors, and not independently created, continues to draw religious objections to this day. Sir Francis Galton, the Victorian polymath, commented in 1908: 'Its effect was to demolish a multitude of dogmatic barriers by a single stroke, and to arouse a spirit of rebellion against all ancient authorities whose positive and unauthenticated statements were contradicted by modern science.'

Surveys have consistently voted *On the Origin of Species* the most influential book ever written.

RIGHT: The title page of the first edition (above) and the only illustration included in the book (below), showing what Darwin called 'the great Tree of life ... with its ever branching and beautiful ramifications.'

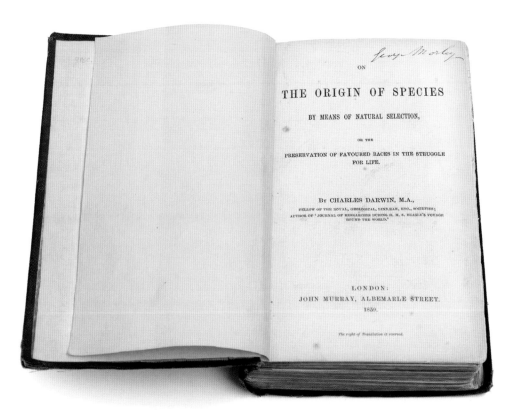

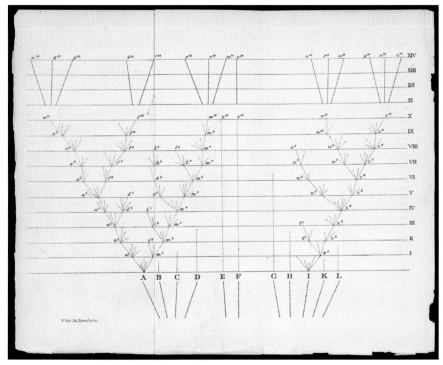

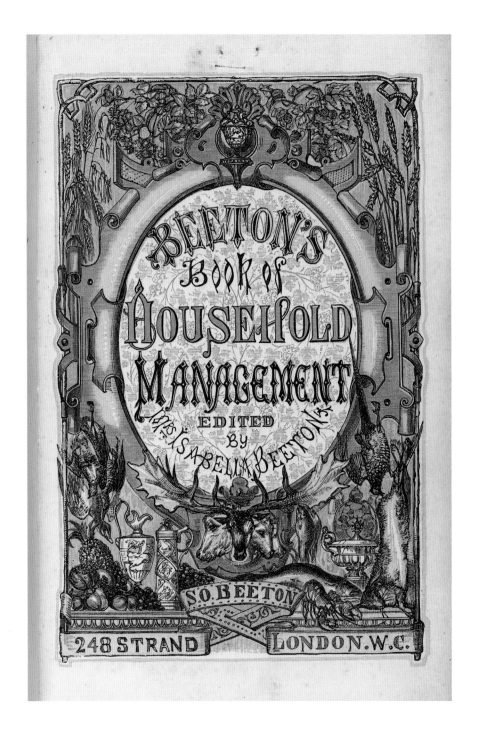

Mrs. Beeton's Book of Household Management

(1861)

A book so successful that its author's name is a byword for efficient housekeeping. Isabella Beeton's guide for middle-class homes had sold more than two million copies by the time of her death, despite her lack of personal experience in cooking and cleaning. It has never been out of print.

In 1852, a go-ahead young publisher called Samuel Beeton launched a new monthly periodical called *The Englishwoman's Domestic Magazine*, aimed at the lady of the middle-class house. The rise of the middle classes was a phenomenon of the Industrial Revolution and the Railway Age. New wealth and increased mobility meant that many women no longer learned practical skills from their mothers or lived near enough to turn to them for advice.

Beeton's magazine contained fiction, fashion tips and household advice. It was designed to improve the home lives of women for whom a working and social life outside the home was not considered respectable. In 1856, his cookery correspondent left the magazine, and the following year he asked his new young wife, Isabella, to write for him. Mrs. Beeton (1836–65) began by translating French short stories, but was soon persuaded to take over the cookery column. It is a measure of her culinary inexperience that her first recipe, for a sponge cake, forgot to mention eggs or to say how much flour was required.

Nevertheless, she persevered, inviting recipes from readers or copying them from existing cookbooks. According to her sister Henrietta, Isabella tested all the recipes herself, so her cooking skills must have improved. One would hope so: in the harsh winter of Christmas 1858, she regularly made soup for the poor.

The column became very popular, and in 1859, Sam launched a supplement to the magazine, to

JELLIES, CREAMS and SWEET DISHES.

be collected in twenty-four parts, called *Beeton's Book of Household Management*. It included not only recipes but useful sections on social etiquette, first aid and the duties of servants. Beeton Publishing first issued it as a single volume in 1861. It was an immediate success, selling 60,000 copies in its first year alone.

Although she is now sometimes accused of plagiarism, her book was seen in its time as an invaluable compilation of good advice. Mrs. Beeton revised and expanded her *Book of Household Management* frequently, covering more and more areas of domestic concern, including legal issues and tips on thrift. She died of puerperal fever, four years after the first edition, but by then the Mrs. Beeton brand was so strong that subsequent editions implied that she was still alive and contributing. By 1907, the book had swollen to more than 2,000 pages and was an essential presence in any British middle-class home.

Central to its success were the recipes, and in particular the way Mrs. Beeton presented them. She was the first to list ingredients separately and include timings for the various cooking processes. Having drawn her material from so many sources, she standardised their format so that they were all equally easy to use.

Mrs. Beeton, the original domestic goddess, has long been a household name in Britain, and her encyclopaedic book, which offers a fascinating glimpse into middle-class Victorian domesticity, has never been out of print.

Les Misérables
Victor Hugo
(1862)

A romantic novel on an operatic scale. It's no wonder that Victor Hugo's tragic tale of compassion and redemption made such a successful adaptation to the musical stage. The book's emotional scenes and detailed historical background are pure drama.

When Victor Hugo (1802–85) died, the crowd that attended his state funeral in Paris was larger than the entire population of the city. He was revered as a political philosopher as much as an author, having helped to shape France's Third Republic. In France today, he is remembered for his poetry and plays as well as his novels; in the wider world his fame rests on *The Hunchback of Notre-Dame* and *Les Misérables.*

While *The Hunchback of Notre-Dame* evokes medieval Paris, *Les Misérables* is set in the France of Hugo's childhood, its climax the failed Paris Uprising of 1832. Against this impoverished, violent background, Hugo tells the story of escaped petty thief Jean Valjean, constantly at risk of recapture and imprisonment by determined police inspector Javert.

Forgiven by a compassionate bishop for stealing silver candlesticks, Valjean is determined to turn over a new leaf. Under a false name he becomes a successful businessman. He takes pity on Fantine, a poor single mother fired from one of his factories, and when she dies he becomes a guardian to her daughter, Cosette.

Valjean and Javert cross paths repeatedly, and repeatedly find their moral beliefs at odds with either their self-interest or their sworn duty. Ultimately, each must be true to themselves, and on different occasions, each shows clemency to the other. For Javert the conflict is too great, and he kills himself. Valjean is driven to reveal his true identity as a former convict, which offends Cosette's new husband, Marius. Marius severs all contact between his wife and Valjean, who

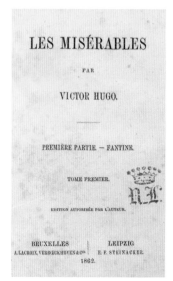

has become a loving father figure to her. Valjean and the young couple are reunited only on Valjean's deathbed.

Hidden identity is a recurring theme of Hugo's book. Valjean and other characters frequently take on false names to conceal their pasts. Cosette's former guardians, the Thénardiers, adopt a new surname when they start a new life in Paris, and Inspector Javert conceals his identity when he acts as a royalist spy behind the republican barricades. All such deceptions are doomed to failure in the novel.

Moral actions, however, are rewarded. When another man is falsely identified as Jean Valjean and arrested, the real Valjean reveals himself to prevent injustice. Valjean saves the unmasked spy Javert from a firing squad, an act which leads later to Javert not arresting Valjean when he could have. *Les Misérables* is a highly moral story in which compassion is the greatest virtue, leading always to redemption. It is a landmark of literary Romanticism.

Victor Hugo was already a celebrated author when *Les Misérables* was published in 1862. Critics objected to the politics, sentimentality, immorality and poverty illustrated by some of its characters, and the Catholic Church banned it outright. The reading public, however, loved it. The first English translation of it was published in New York only two months after the original French edition; the first British version appeared only four months after the American one. Both sold well. Anxious for news of its progress, Hugo telegraphed his London publisher with the briefest of messages: '?' The publisher telegraphed back: '!'

ABOVE AND OPPOSITE: Émile Bayard's illustration, 'Cosette Sweeping' (above) –
drawn for the first edition and still used to promote film, television and theatre
adaptations – and the title page of the first edition (opposite).

Ouvrage couronné par l'Académie française.

JULES VERNE

VOYAGE AU CENTRE

DE

LA TERRE

VIGNETTES PAR RIOU

BIBLIOTHÈQUE
D'ÉDUCATION ET DE RÉCRÉATION
J. HETZEL ET Cⁱᵉ, 18, RUE JACOB

PARIS

—

Tous droits de traduction et de reproduction réservés.

ABOVE AND OPPOSITE: The first edition included detailed illustrations by Édouard Riou, which helped readers visualise the prehistoric animals and plants described.

Journey to the Centre of the Earth
Jules Verne
(1864)

This extraordinary story from the grandfather of science fiction has continued to grow in popularity. Jules Verne's underground adventure was based on the cutting-edge scientific discoveries of his day.

Often dismissed in Britain and America as a genre writer and source of plots for B movies, Jules Verne (1828–1905) is held in higher literary regard in Europe. He has been more widely translated than any other author in the world except Agatha Christie.

Verne was born in the French river-port of Nantes. His mother came from a family of sailors and boat builders, which may account for his fascination with geography and exploration. He lived in an age of scientific discovery and of adventurers who travelled to the furthest corners of the world.

From 1863, Verne began to write a series of books under the title *Voyages Extraordinaires* (*Extraordinary Voyages*). They included fiction and non-fiction works, and his aim was to convey to readers his own sense of wonder at mankind's rapidly expanding scientific knowledge of the planet. Although not trained in science, Verne was meticulous in checking his facts. It is said that he read fifteen newspapers every day, and his clear understanding of scientific theory fed his imagination. By his death he had written fifty-four *Extraordinary Voyages*, and after it his son, Michel, added a further eight to the series.

For the first two voyages Verne conjured journeys by ship and balloon to the unexplored lands of the Arctic and central Africa. In the third, *Journey to the Centre of the Earth*, he moved for the first time into science fiction. The novel described not only possible geographies but an entire imagined subterranean world that was consistent with the latest geological theories, inhabited, for example, by prehistoric animals becoming known at the time through fossils.

The journey of the title is made by a German scientist and his young, unadventurous nephew after they decipher an old coded manuscript. Verne's choice of characters allows him to write conversations in which one explains scientific theory to the other (and to the reader), while both marvel at the wonders and terrors around them.

Journey to the Centre of the Earth has been the subject of considerable political revision. In English editions, which followed the Franco-Prussian War of 1871, for example, the central characters were renamed to sound less German, and some passages were omitted for being anti-British or over-scientific.

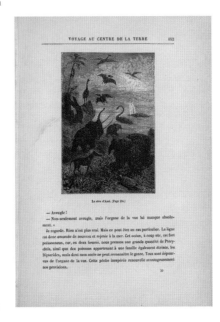

Jules Verne was not the first author to invoke an underground landscape – among others, Dante depicted Hell as one in his fourteenth-century *Inferno*. But Verne was the first to approach the subject with scientific integrity. Although much of the science on which he based his vision has been overtaken by later discoveries, his underworld adventure still fascinates today. Verne's engaging enthusiasm has inspired a whole literary genre – steampunk – which applies anachronistic science to nineteenth-century adventures. He is regarded by many as the grandfather of modern science fiction.

Alice's Adventures in Wonderland
Lewis Carroll
(1865)

Lewis Carroll was the pseudonym of an eccentric English mathematician and church deacon who made up a very strange fantasy tale for a ten-year-old girl. It became one of the most popular works of Victorian children's literature and triggered all kinds of prurient theories and psychedelic dramatisations.

Charles Lutwidge Dodgson (1832–98) was a reclusive stammerer, yet he taught mathematics at Oxford. He was also a devout deacon of the Anglican Church, who was unmarried and formed friendships with young girls, some of whom he liked to photograph and take on short trips.

On July 4, 1862, Dodgson and a friend, Reverend Robinson Duckworth, rowed a boat up the Isis (the River Thames) carrying three young daughters of Oxford University's Vice-Chancellor and Dean of Christ Church, Henry Liddell. They included Lorina (aged thirteen), Alice (ten), and Edith (eight). During their outing, Dodgson told them a fantastical story he had invented, about a make-believe girl named Alice. The girls liked it so much that Alice asked him to give her a written version in order that she might have it to enjoy. A month later he took them on another trip and continued telling more of the story. Dodgson wrote down his tale, adding some illustrations on the manuscript pages. In November 1864, he gave Alice a bound copy of the manuscript, but as his relationship with the Liddell family had cooled, he sought out other children to get their response.

The manuscript went over so well that he hired a professional illustrator, John Tenniel, to work with him on an expanded version that was doubled in length to 27,500 words and included new episodes about a Cheshire Cat and a Mad Tea Party.

Published in 1865 as *Alice's Adventures in Wonderland*, it became so popular that Lewis Carroll published a sequel, *Through the Looking-Glass, and What Alice Found There* (1871).

Although the novel was intended for children, *Alice's Adventures in Wonderland* also appealed to adult readers. It tells the story of a girl named Alice, who falls down a rabbit hole that takes her into a fantasy world populated with strange creatures. The narrative is filled with fascinating anthropomorphic characters, nonsensical situations and memorable phrases that have become commonplace: 'Off with their heads!'; 'Curiouser and curiouser!'; 'It's no use going back to yesterday, because I was a different person then.'

Alice follows the White Rabbit wearing a waistcoat and pocket watch. She drinks an elixir from a bottle that causes her to shrink, until she eats a cake that makes her fall asleep. She meets the Mouse and the Cat, and the blue Caterpillar smoking a hookah. Other characters include the March Hare, the Hatter and the Dormouse, the King of Hearts and the Queen of Hearts.

Alice's Adventures in Wonderland has been translated into at least 174 languages, with more than a hundred English-language editions alone. The book has also generated countless adaptations in theatre and film. Critics have argued over the book's symbolism and whether the narrator was under the influence of opium or magic mushrooms. Biographers have titillated their readers with salacious details about the author. But the book remains an icon of children's literature.

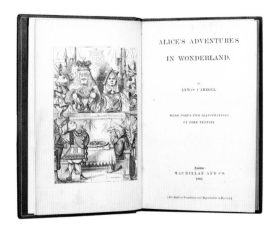

At this the whole pack rose up into the air, and came flying down upon her; she gave a

ABOVE AND LEFT: Although dated 1866, this first official edition of Alice's Adventures in Wonderland *went on sale in November 1865. There had been an earlier printing, published in July 1865, which was withdrawn from circulation. John Tenniel, whose illustrations came to define Alice, had been unhappy with the reproduction of his drawings in the first edition and donated the entire print run to children's hospitals and institutions.*

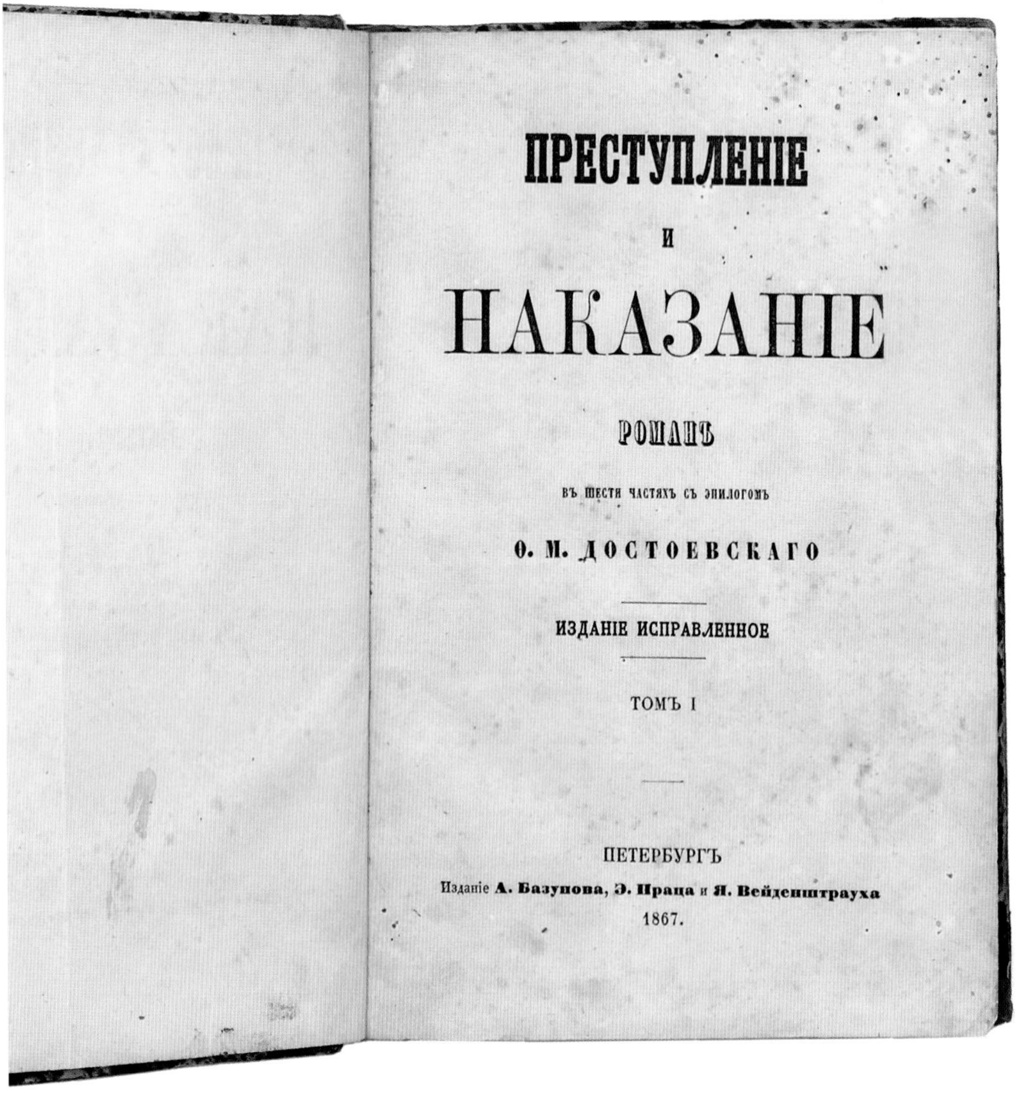

ПРЕСТУПЛЕНІЕ

И

НАКАЗАНІЕ

РОМАНЪ

ВЪ ШЕСТИ ЧАСТЯХЪ СЪ ЭПИЛОГОМЪ

О. М. ДОСТОЕВСКАГО

ИЗДАНІЕ ИСПРАВЛЕННОЕ

ТОМЪ I

ПЕТЕРБУРГЪ

Изданіе А. Базунова, Э. Праца и Я. Вейденштрауха

1867.

ABOVE: Crime and Punishment *first appeared in the literary journal* The Russian Messenger, *published in monthly instalments throughout 1866. This is the title page of the first book publication from 1867.*
OPPOSITE: The Heritage Press edition from 1938, featuring wood engravings by Fritz Eichenberg.

Crime and Punishment
Fyodor Dostoyevsky

(1867)

A former prisoner's traumatic experiences in poverty, crime and punishment helped to shape his classic story of a tormented murderer and his redemption. Dostoyevsky's haunting novel put him in the first rank of Russian writers and influenced the course of modern literature.

For the crime of belonging to a literary group that discussed banned books critical of tsarist Russia, Fyodor Mikhailovich Dostoyevsky (1821–81) was sentenced to death, but the punishment was commuted at the last moment with a mock execution, and he spent four years in a Siberian prison camp, followed by six years of compulsory military service in exile.

At the time of his arrest in 1849, Dostoyevsky already had published a novel, *Poor Folk*, but the trauma of his imprisonment left deep scars. The experience may have brought on epileptic seizures and a lifelong preoccupation with religion and psychology, which would mark his later literary works. After his release in 1854, he resumed his writing, and in 1861, published a book about his prison experiences, *The House of the Dead*.

He appears to have conceived the idea for *Crime and Punishment* out of economic desperation, having amassed considerable debts from his chronic gambling, and he was also trying to aid the family of his late brother. Dostoyevsky initially offered the work to the prestigious literary journal *The Russian Messenger* as a story or novella about a young man who gives in to 'certain strange, "unfinished" ideas, yet floating in the air', which change his life forever. With his lover serving as his stenographer, he began dictating the story in frenzied bursts. *Crime and Punishment* appeared in the journal in instalments, from January 1866 to December 1866, and was published in a single volume the following year.

Crime and Punishment tells the story of Rodion Raskolnikov, an impoverished former student in St. Petersburg who plots and carries out the murder of a detestable pawnbroker to steal her cash in order to perform good deeds with the money, telling himself that he is following a higher purpose. He is eventually suspected and caught, mainly by his conscience, and realises what he has done is wrong. Dostoyevsky's account of Raskolnikov's inner turmoil includes descriptions of his dreams, which appear to carry a deeper symbolic meaning. The book is also filled with Dostoyevsky's philosophical statements, such as: 'To go wrong in one's own way is better than to go right in someone else's…. The darker the night, the brighter the stars, The deeper the grief, the closer is God!' and 'A hundred suspicions don't make a proof.'

As one Russian critic put it: 'He was one of ourselves, a man of our blood and our bone, but as one who has suffered and has seen so much more deeply than we have, his insight impresses us as wisdom.' Franz Kafka called him his 'blood-relative' and James Joyce paid tribute to him as 'the man more than any other who has created modern prose, and intensified it to its present-day pitch.' Sigmund Freud and Albert Einstein also acknowledged his influence on their work. *Crime and Punishment* remains one of the best-selling novels, and there have been no fewer than twenty-five film adaptations.

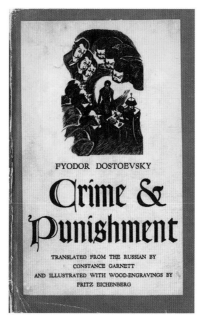

FYODOR DOSTOEVSKY

Crime & Punishment

TRANSLATED FROM THE RUSSIAN BY
CONSTANCE GARNETT
AND ILLUSTRATED WITH WOOD-ENGRAVINGS BY
FRITZ EICHENBERG

Das Kapital
Karl Marx

(1867)

A German political economist's sweeping critique of 'capitalism' was a towering achievement in literary persuasion as well as economic theory – one that established a coherent new system for understanding the exploitative economic basis of industrial society. No other theorist would influence the world in the century to come as much as Marx.

By 1867, Karl Marx (1818–83) already had spent forty-five years as a journalist, writing commentary for newspapers in Germany, England and Horace Greeley's *New-York Tribune*. No English translation of his and fellow German intellectual Friedrich Engels's revolutionary call to arms, *The Communist Manifesto*, had yet been published, so many of his readers didn't know the full extent of his contempt for the established order. His experience as a professional writer had sharpened his knowledge of world events, refined his persuasive powers and done much to shape his trenchant political analysis.

His projected master work, which he intended to publish in several volumes, reflected his lifelong study of literature, as evidenced by his ample quotations from Homer, Plato, Dante, Cervantes, Shakespeare, Milton and other classic authors, as well as allusions to popular ballads and melodrama of his time. He saw himself as a 'poet of dialectics'.

In the course of writing it, he confided to Engels: 'Whatever shortcomings they may have, the advantage of my writings is that they are an artistic whole.' He also revealed: 'For two months I have been living solely on the pawnshop, which means that a queue of creditors has been hammering on my door, becoming more and more unendurable every day … It is truly soul-destroying to be dependent for half one's life.'

The first volume of *Das Kapital: Kritik der politischen Oekonomie* (*Capital: Critique of Political Economy*) was published in September 1867, in German. Marx said his purpose was to lay a scientific foundation for the politics of the modern labour movement, showing how the economic system promoted by Adam Smith, David Ricardo and other leading political economists was built on exploitation of labour. He wanted to do for economic thinking what Darwin had done for understanding the natural order.

Marx described the structural contradictions of a capitalist economy, in particular the class struggle between labour and capital, the wage labourer, and the owner of the means of production. 'Capital,' he wrote, 'is dead labour, that vampire-like, only lives by sucking living labour, and lives the more, the more labour it sucks.'

Marx argued that the economic basis of society determines its social structure and psychology of the people within it. Class struggle is the normal and inevitable condition in a capitalist society. Material misery of the workers will increase, and with it, their alienation. The laws of capitalism will eventually bring about its destruction. Viewed today, many of his observations about globalisation and other future trends in capitalism seem remarkably prescient.

Marx did not live long enough to complete his projected series, and the first English translation would not appear until 1887, along with other volumes in the series that were written by Engels. So he would never know how much influence his work would have on world affairs.

The book laid the theoretical foundation for all subsequent communist philosophy, economics, and politics, providing a new way to analyse social structures. Marx's theories led to the creation of communist states in Russia, Eastern Europe, China, Korea and parts of Latin America. It remains required reading in universities throughout the world and continues to provide the bone of contention in economics, historiography, sociology and political science.

Das Kapital.

Kritik der politischen Oekonomie.

Von

Karl Marx.

Erster Band.

Buch I: Der Produktionsprocess des Kapitals.

Das Recht der Uebersetzung wird vorbehalten.

Hamburg

Verlag von Otto Meissner.

1867.

New-York: L. W. Schmidt. 24 Barclay-Street.

ABOVE: The surprisingly modern-looking font chosen for the title is fitting for a book that would go on to inspire revolutions in Russia, China and many other countries around the world in the twentieth century.

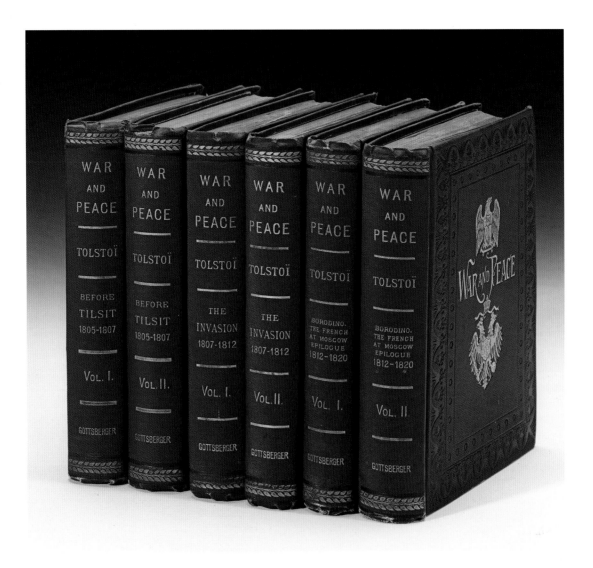

ABOVE: The first English-language edition was translated from the French by Clara Bell and published in New York by William S. Gottsberger. The six volumes appeared between 1885 and 1886.

OPPOSITE: A page from Tolstoy's manuscript, which was painstakingly transcribed by his wife Sophia.

War and Peace
Leo Tolstoy
(1869)

Although Leo Tolstoy's epic Russian novel is best known for its sheer length, there were many distinctive features that set it apart from previous literary works and insured its towering reputation as one of the greatest books in world literature.

Born into an aristocratic family, Count Lev Nikolayevich Tolstoy (1828–1910) grew up to become a farmer and served in the army in the Crimean War, an experience that planted the seeds of his subsequent pacifism. He later became a moral philosopher, anarchist and writer, and lived with his wife Sophia Tolstaya (1844–1919) and their children at Yasnaya Polyana, his estate 100 miles south of Moscow.

It was a trip to France and Belgium in 1860–61 that shaped Tolstoy's political and literary destiny. In Paris he met Victor Hugo, whose battle scenes in *Les Misérables* had a profound influence on *War and Peace*. Tolstoy's political philosophy was also engaged by a visit to French anarchist Pierre-Joseph Proudhon, then exiled in Brussels. Tolstoy reviewed Proudhon's 1861 publication *La Guerre et la Paix* (*War and Peace*), whose title he would eventually borrow for his masterpiece.

The product of herculean labour, both by Tolstoy and his wife – who served as his copyist and editor through more than seven drafts – *War and Peace* was first serialised between 1865 and 1867 in *The Russian Messenger* magazine under the title *The Year 1805*. His story was based upon prodigious and painstaking research and his own experience in the Crimean War. After its magazine publication, Tolstoy continued to revise and expand his novel, until it was published in its entirety, at nearly a million words long, in 1869.

War and Peace is an elaborate historical fiction that starts during the reign of Tsar Alexander I and ends in 1813, shortly after Napoléon Bonaparte's ill-fated march on Moscow – a period a generation before Tolstoy's birth. The book follows the fortunes of the aristocratic Bolkonsky and Rostov families, who are caught up in this turbulent period of war and peace. The narrative mixes vivid descriptions of real and fictional events with philosophical commentary.

Some critics initially downplayed the work due to its melding of fact and fiction, philosophical commentary, and alternate use of Russian and French in various passages. But all the leading writers of the day, especially the major Russian, French, and English novelists, hailed it as a masterpiece.

When the French translation was published in 1879, Gustave Flaubert exclaimed, 'What an artist, and what a psychologist!' Later admirers included Ernest Hemingway, who confessed that Tolstoy had taught him to 'write about war in the most straightforward, honest, objective and stark way.' The South African novelist J.M. Coetzee called Tolstoy 'the exemplary master of authority', saying he was the most trustworthy storyteller. Others have remarked upon Tolstoy's use of countless, memorable idiosyncratic details, such as the description of the doomed man who fiddles with his blindfold just before his death.

Tolstoy denied that *War and Peace* was a novel as such and maintained that the best Russian literature did not conform to standards. He regarded *Anna Karenina* as his first true novel.

Despite Tolstoy's own doubts, *War and Peace* is a staggering achievement. Capturing the grand sweep of history and the private experiences of individuals, this vast novel changed literature and captured the Russian soul.

The Adventures of Huckleberry Finn
Mark Twain

(1884)

Some purists blanched when a popular humorist published a colourful, fictional narrative full of vulgar, vernacular language, involving two rebellious teens and a slave, but Mark Twain's masterpiece is still regarded as the great American novel and a classic study of Southern antebellum race relationships.

Samuel Langhorne Clemens (1835–1910) took his pen name of Mark Twain from the call a Mississippi River boatman made when his vessel was in safe water – a depth of two fathoms (12 feet, or 3.7 metres). But that was not all he carried from his youthful experience on the 'monstrous big' river. Some of its sounds and smells remained with him decades later as he crafted stories about the adventures of two imaginary characters as they rafted down the great muddy with a runaway slave named Jim.

The Adventures of Huckleberry Finn was first published in London in December 1884 and in New York in February 1885, as a direct sequel to *The Adventures of Tom Sawyer*. It's told in the first person by a young teen named Huckleberry 'Huck' Finn, who was the best friend of Tom Sawyer and later would be the narrator of two other Twain novels (*Tom Sawyer Abroad* and *Tom Sawyer, Detective*).

'You don't know about me, without you have read a book by the name of "The Adventures of Tom Sawyer,"' the book began, 'but that ain't no matter. That book was made by Mr. Mark Twain, and he told the truth, mainly. There was things which he stretched, but mainly he told the truth.'

The narrator conveys their encounters from his point of view and in his authentic voice, saying, 'We said there warn't no home like a raft, after all. Other places do seem so cramped up and smothery, but a raft don't. You feel mighty free and easy and comfortable on a raft.' He also delivers many witticisms such as: 'Hain't we got all the fools in town on our side? And ain't that a big enough majority in any town?'

On a deeper level, Huck is caught in a moral conflict between the values that proper society and some of his adult antagonists seek to impose and enforce, versus his own values of friendship and Jim's human worth. In the end Huck follows his heart and rejects the hypocrisy of Christian slaveholder culture.

From the time of its first appearance to today, the book has occupied a special place in American literature, being both beloved and exalted as a classic, but also as a work that some social arbiters have always found offensive – supposedly, for its crude language, such as its use of the word 'nigger', but more often because its message of racial amity is deemed as taboo and threatening.

Packed with a large cast of colourful characters and vivid details about regional life along the Mississippi in the 1840s, the novel unleashes scathing satire against the entrenched attitudes and hegemony of the Tidewater South. It also taps into adolescent feelings of inner conflict and alienation.

The book's original pen-and-ink illustrations by E.W. Kemble proved a perfect match for Twain's word visions, capturing the rambunctious characters' spirits and the dramatic situations with equal skill.

In 1935, Ernest Hemingway summed up its significance: 'All modern American literature comes from one book by Mark Twain called *Huckleberry Finn* … it's the best book we've had. All American writing comes from that. There was nothing before. There has been nothing as good since.'

RIGHT: The red cover (below left), and frontispiece and title page (above) of the first edition, published in the UK by Chatto & Windus on December 10, 1884. The first American edition (below right) was published on February 18, 1885, by Charles L. Webster and Company.

Frontispiece

HUCKLEBERRY FINN

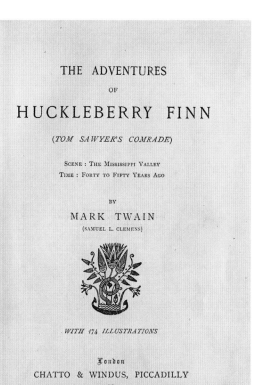

THE ADVENTURES

OF

HUCKLEBERRY FINN

(TOM SAWYER'S COMRADE)

SCENE : THE MISSISSIPPI VALLEY
TIME : FORTY TO FIFTY YEARS AGO

BY

MARK TWAIN

(SAMUEL L. CLEMENS)

WITH 174 ILLUSTRATIONS

London
CHATTO & WINDUS, PICCADILLY
1884

[All rights reserved]

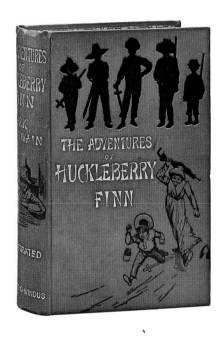

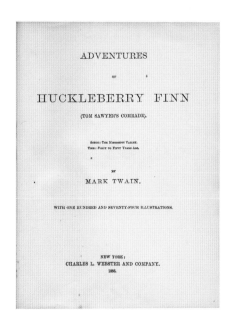

ADVENTURES

OF

HUCKLEBERRY FINN

(TOM SAWYER'S COMRADE).

SCENE: THE MISSISSIPPI VALLEY.
TIME: FORTY TO FIFTY YEARS AGO.

BY

MARK TWAIN.

WITH ONE HUNDRED AND SEVENTY-FOUR ILLUSTRATIONS.

NEW YORK:
CHARLES L. WEBSTER AND COMPANY.
1885.

THIS NUMBER CONTAINS

The Picture of Dorian Gray.

By OSCAR WILDE.

COMPLETE.

JULY, 1890

LIPPINCOTT'S

MONTHLY MAGAZINE

CONTENTS

PRICE TWENTY-FIVE CENTS

J:B:LIPPINCOTT:Cọ:PHILADELPHIA:

LONDON: WARD, LOCK & CO.

PARIS: BRENTANO'S, 17 AVENUE DE L'OPÉRA.

The Picture of Dorian Gray
Oscar Wilde

(1891)

Oscar Wilde's only novel, a complex story of morality and duality, scandalised Victorian literary critics; but Wilde's impassioned defence of it and the passage of time have led to its recognition as a masterpiece.

In the 1880s Oscar Wilde (1854–1900) had yet to make his name as a playwright of witty comedies like *Lady Windermere's Fan* and *The Importance of Being Earnest*. His chief claim to fame, beside a small volume of poetry, was his yearlong lecture tour of America, during which he promoted the philosophy and art of Aestheticism. This movement insisted that art should exist for its own sake and not be the servant of morality or money. It and Wilde were roundly mocked for the idea at the time.

After a period of writing short pieces of journalism and fiction, Wilde wrote his first and only novel in 1890 and it was published in full in the July edition of a monthly magazine. It scandalised reviewers with its decadent storyline, although unknown to Wilde his editor had already removed some of the most sensational material.

In Wilde's tale, Dorian Gray is an incredibly beautiful young man who, upon seeing his portrait painted by the artist Basil Hallward, mourns the inevitable loss of his youthful beauty. He wishes that the portrait would age, and not he. Later, he is encouraged by Hallward's friend Lord Henry Wotton to make the most of his youth by leading a life of debauchery and promiscuity. Gray finds that over the course of two decades he keeps his good looks, but the portrait gradually changes to show the wear and tear that his years of hedonism should have wrought on his face and body.

It was the depiction of Gray's pleasure-seeking immorality, with its homoerotic overtones, which so shocked the nation's literary critics.

Wilde defended it stoutly in terms of his allegiance to Aestheticism. When the novel appeared in book form the following year, he added a preface of epigrams in defence of art for art's sake, which has become almost as famous as the novel itself.

The book was poorly received, published as it was at the height of strait-laced Victorian puritanism. It was seen as a corrupting work not fit for reading by impressionable young minds. In fact, the book ends with the restoration of a moral order: driven by guilt at the consequences of his hedonism, Gray tries to destroy the portrait but is found dead beside it the following morning. The portrait has reverted to its original youthful image, while Gray's body is withered and disfigured. Art and morality have triumphed.

The eternal conflict between public and private behaviour at the heart of *The Picture of Dorian Gray* insures its continuing popularity. It is also fascinating because of the reflection in it of its flamboyant author: Wilde's imprisonment only five years later for homosexual acts with a beautiful young man broke him utterly. Of his only novel, Oscar Wilde remarked: 'Basil Hallward is what I think I am: Lord Henry is what the world thinks of me: Dorian is what I would like to be – in other ages, perhaps.'

OPPOSITE AND LEFT: The Picture of Dorian Gray *first appeared in the July 1890 edition of* Lippincott's *(opposite). The magazine's editor, J.M. Stoddart, removed passages that he thought would offend his readers' moral sensibilities. A longer, revised edition of the novel was published in book format (left) by Ward Lock and Co. the following year.*

The Time Machine
H.G. Wells

(1895)

With his debut novel – a dystopian vision of the world in the year 802,701 – H.G. Wells popularised the fantasy of time travel and established his reputation as the father of science fiction.

The notion of time travel is infinitely attractive. Who doesn't want to know how things turn out? Who wouldn't like to put right the mistakes of the past? H.G. Wells (1866–1946) was not the first author to play with the idea. Samuel Madden's *Memoirs of the Twentieth Century* was published in 1733; and closer to Wells's own lifetime, Charles Dickens transported Scrooge to Christmases past and future in 1843's *A Christmas Carol*. But at a time when science was moving from an amateur pursuit to a professional occupation, Wells was the first to consider time travel from a scientific perspective.

Science was H.G. Wells's subject. He studied it at the Royal College of Science, where the college magazine published his short story 'The Chronic Argonauts', a first attempt at time-travel fiction. He worked for a time as a teacher, and his first book was *A Textbook of Biology*. After a period of writing humorous articles for magazines, he wrote his first full-length work of fiction, *The Time Machine*.

In it, an unnamed inventor travels to the future. Most of the book describes his adventures in a futuristic world inhabited by two humanoid species: the idle, childlike Eloi and the predatory, subterranean Morlocks. The actions of these two groups make *The Time Machine* not only a fantastical adventure but a powerful, political allegory.

H.G. Wells was a committed socialist, critical of the way class in Victorian society was diverging. The Morlocks are the descendants of the working classes, locked away for so long in dark factories that in the future they live underground. The Eloi have evolved from the capitalist elite, dominant for so long that they have lost their intellect and interest in the world. In *The Time Machine*, the workers have turned against the ruling classes and prey on them at night.

If you have criticisms to make of the society in which you live, it sometimes helps to relocate your story to a distant time or place. *Gulliver's Travels* successfully satirised Jonathan Swift's times by inventing strange lands; *The Time Machine* does so with strange times.

The book is a pessimistic view of the future, a commentary on both capitalism and communism. It ends with the time traveller going thirty million years into the future to find that the planet itself is dying. Wells's fiction imagines how both scientific and social trends of his age might develop if left unchecked.

The Time Machine has spawned some twenty sequels by other authors and inspired countless other works of time-bending science fiction. The appeal of travel to the past and the future remains timeless.

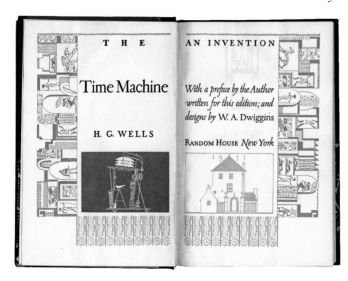

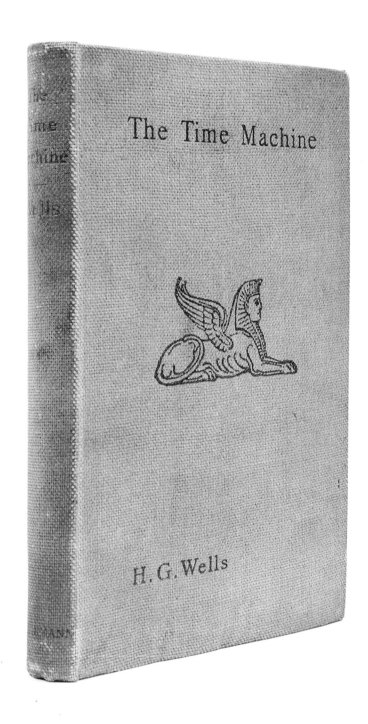

The Time Machine

H. G. Wells

DIE

TRAUMDEUTUNG

VON

DR· SIGM. FREUD.

»FLECTERE SI NEQUEO SUPEROS, ACHERONTA MOVEBO.«

LEIPZIG UND WIEN.

FRANZ DEUTICKE.

1900.

Verlags-Nr. 676.

ABOVE AND OPPOSITE: Although dated 1900, the first edition (above) was published in November 1899. Only 600 copies were printed and it took eight years to sell out. The first English edition (opposite), translated by the Austrian-born psychiatrist A.A. Brill, was published in 1913.

The Interpretation of Dreams
Sigmund Freud

(1899)

A Viennese neurologist's long-standing interest in dreams led him to develop a new theory about dimensions of a hidden human unconscious as revealed through the interpretation of dreams. Making sense of his patients' confusing dreams was one way he carried out his study of the human mind, which he called 'psychoanalysis'.

The physician Sigmund Freud (1856–1939) was keenly interested in strange and confusing dreams. Reflecting on one he had following the death of his father in 1889, he wrote in his notes: 'The dream thus stems from the inclination to self-reproach that regularly sets in among survivors.' He also began encouraging his patients to speak about their dreams, asking them to tell him, without censoring, whatever associations came into their minds about what they had dreamed. He began to see dreams as important, hidden clues to a person's deepest fears, hopes and fantasies.

While on a summer retreat, he decided to do a formal study of the subject, and in 1897, he began to pull together his thoughts and observations that he had gleaned from some of his case studies.

Two years later he published a sixty-two-page monograph, *Die Traumdeutung* (*The Interpretation of Dreams*), in which he laid down a new theory arguing that dreams are a form of wish fulfilment, often precipitated by the events of the previous day, which he called the 'day residue'.

'In the pages that follow,' he wrote, 'I shall bring forward proof that there is a psychological technique which makes it possible to interpret dreams, and that, if that procedure is employed, every dream reveals itself as a psychical structure which has a meaning and which can be inserted at an assignable point in the mental activities of waking life.'

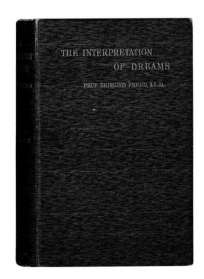

Freud asserted that dreams have a double level of meaning: its manifest content and its deeper, truer, hidden meaning, which he called its 'latent content'. Freud theorized that a part of the mind he called the 'censor' edits our dreams and disguises the true content in order to allow us to remain asleep. Dreams function as 'guardians of sleep'. This 'dream-work' occurs by means of a set of various, unconscious processes.

By means of 'displacement', a dream object's emotional significance is separated from its real object or content and attached to an entirely different one that won't raise the censor's suspicions. Condensation enables a dream object to stand for several associations and ideas. Symbolisation substitutes a symbol to replace an action, person or idea. And representation translates a thought into visual images.

He explained dreams as wish fulfilment and outlined a new framework by which they might be properly interpreted. For Freud, an unanalysed dream was like an unopened letter.

Freud's monograph initially attracted little attention, and the first printing, amounting to 600 copies, didn't sell out for eight years. But it was Freud's own favourite, and he continued to revise and expand it with each new edition – the last being published in 1930. By the 1920s it had started to be recognised as the seminal work on psychoanalysis, and today it is widely regarded as one of Freud's most significant works.

Remembrance of Things Past
Marcel Proust

(1913–27)

A sprawling novel spanning several volumes, or a memoir about lost memories? Proust's experimental masterpiece is now recognised as one of the most important works of fiction of the early twentieth century.

Born in a rural suburb of Paris, Marcel Proust (1871–1922) suffered from ill health throughout his life. It interrupted his education, his employment and his writing – as his early novel *Jean Santeuil*, left unfinished, can testify. Biographers have described him as a dilettante: someone who, thanks to wealthy parents, was able to dabble in many things without dedicating himself to anything in particular. But no one can doubt his commitment to *Remembrance of Things Past*, all one and a quarter million words of it.

The death of his parents in 1903 and 1905 seems to have spurred him to take writing more seriously. In 1904, he published a well-received translation of a work by the English art critic John Ruskin. Armed with Ruskin's view of art in society, Proust revisited the themes of *Jean Santeuil*, and from 1909 onwards a new novel began to emerge from his pen, titled *À la Recherche du Temps Perdu*. It consumed him for the rest of his life, and he died before the publication of the last three volumes.

The title translates more accurately as *In Search of Lost Time*. 'Remembrance of things past', a phrase from a sonnet by Shakespeare about memory and loss, was the title chosen by C.K. Scott Moncrieff, who first translated the book into English in the 1920s.

Memory and loss are indeed the main themes of Proust's book. In it, an unnamed narrator, a would-be writer, describes his uneventful life in minute detail, regretting time wasted and enjoying times won back by the power of memories – memories that can be triggered accidentally by the most unexpected and mundane events. The most famous of these occurs in *Swann's Way*, the first volume: the narrator dips a madeleine – a small cake – into his tea, and the taste transports him back to childhood madeleines fed to him by his aunt.

Very little of consequence happens to the narrator. He falls in and out of love, gossips about other affairs and contemplates art; there is no drama, no conventional plot. For this reason academics still debate whether it is a traditional novel at all. But nor is it a true memoir. Although there are many similarities between the narrator and Proust, and between the narrator's acquaintances and Proust's, it is certainly a work of fiction.

More than anything it is, in its discussion of its themes and its descriptive passages, a work of the finest writing, a work of art that earns it the accolade of being the first modern novel. This is the Ruskinian approach: by his evocative writing, Proust and his narrator become not only authors but artists.

RIGHT AND BELOW: Proust's masterpiece was published in thirteen volumes between 1913 and 1927. After being turned down by several publishers, including Gallimard, Proust paid for the publication of the first volume. Realising their error, Gallimard wooed Proust with dinner at the Ritz and went on to publish all subsequent volumes of his epic novel.

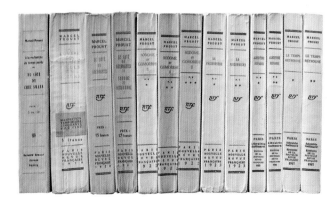

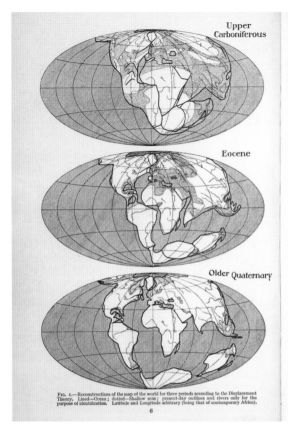

FIG. 1.—Reconstructions of the map of the world for three periods according to the Displacement Theory. Lined—Ocean; dotted—Shallow seas; present-day outlines and rivers only for the purpose of identification. Latitude and Longitude arbitrary (being that of contemporary Africa).

6

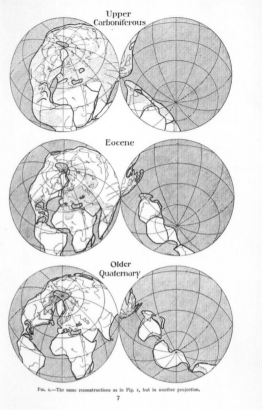

FIG. 2.—The same reconstructions as in Fig. 1, but in another projection.

7

ABOVE: Diagrams from the book showing continental drift in three geological periods: Carboniferous (358.9–298.9 million years ago), Eocene (56–33.9 million years ago) and Older Quaternary (2.58–1 million years ago).

LEFT: Wegener on his second expedition to Greenland in 1913, where he achieved the first-ever overwintering on the inland ice sheet.

OPPOSITE: The first edition, published in 1915, was followed by expanded editions in 1920, 1922 and 1929.

The Origin of Continents and Oceans
Alfred Wegener
(1915)

The Origin of Continents and Oceans forever changed the way we understand our planet, but it took fifty years for geologists to move from ridicule to acceptance of Alfred Wegener's theories of plate tectonics.

Alfred Wegener (1880–1930) studied astronomy but maintained an interest in geophysics, climatology and meteorology. His first book, *The Thermodynamics of the Atmosphere*, was written after an expedition to Greenland in 1906–08, where he set up a weather station and pioneered the use of weather balloons to track polar air circulation.

Wegener had noticed on a map how well the coastlines of western Africa and eastern South America fit together. As he did further research, he found that geological features, such as mountain ranges and coal deposits, occurred at the same place on both continents, as if they had once been joined. For example, the sequences of rock strata of Santa Catarina in Brazil matched those of Karoo in South Africa. He likened it to aligning the lines of print on the two halves of a torn sheet of newspaper.

Wegener also observed that identical fossil species could be found on continents on either side of an ocean hundreds of miles wide. Other fossils were being found in locations far removed from their preferred climates, such as the fossilised tropical ferns discovered in Spitsbergen, Norway.

Conventional geological theory at the time held that the continents were fixed in their places. The appearance of the same features on both sides of an ocean was explained by the existence of land bridges, now sunk or eroded, which once connected continents and enabled species to cross between the two. Wegener could not reconcile this explanation with the fact that continents rise and fall over time, a

phenomenon known as isostasy. He began to develop the idea that the continents themselves were slowly moving across the surface of the earth, separating and colliding, having once been joined together as one supercontinent, which he named Pangaea – the Greek for 'all lands'.

At the outbreak of war in 1914, he enlisted in the German army, and while recovering from wounds in 1915, he first published his theory of continental drift as *Die Entstehung der Kontinente und Ozeane* (*The Origin of Continents and Oceans*). But in the middle of a global conflict it attracted little attention. Second and third editions of the book appeared after the war, in 1920 and 1922 respectively, the latter being widely translated for the first time. With each he included more and more supporting evidence for his theories.

However, Wegener's proposals were broadly mocked by the geological establishment, simply because he was not himself a geologist, and his theories broke conventional geological rules.

Wegener published an updated fourth edition of *The Origin of Continents and Oceans* in 1929, before setting off in 1930 on another expedition to Greenland, during which he died. In 1953, the emerging new science of paleomagnetism proved that India had once been in the southern hemisphere, supporting Wegener's claim nearly forty years earlier. Studies of the Mid-Atlantic Ridge, where two plates meet, also backed him up; and by 1964, when the Royal Society held a symposium on plate tectonics, Wegener's inspired insight was finally recognised.

Relativity: The Special and General Theory
Albert Einstein
(1917)

Following more than a decade of calculations and writing, a German physicist published his complete theory of relativity, which subsequent experiments would prove correct and which many scholars have since called 'the biggest leap of the scientific imagination in history' – ideas that continue to fuel inventions and dreams.

The German theoretical physicist Albert Einstein (1879–1955) first published his theory of special relativity in 1905, holding that the speed of light in a vacuum is independent of the motion of all observers, and the laws of physics are the same for all observers who are not moving or accelerating.

For the next ten years he worked on a related general theory of relativity that was published in a paper in 1915.

He later presented the two theories together in a book, *Relativity: The Special and General Theory,* which was first published in 1917. Within three years, it had run through fourteen German editions, totalling 65,000 copies. But it took more time for the gravity of Einstein's revolutionary ideas to become widely accepted as law.

Relativity is a method for two people to agree on what they are seeing if one of them is moving. Einstein's equivalence principle holds that gravity pulling in one direction is completely equivalent to an acceleration in the opposite direction. Thus, a rider on an elevator accelerating upwards feels like gravity is pushing them into the floor.

Einstein's relativity theory introduced a new framework for all of physics, proposing new concepts of space and time, relativity of simultaneity, and kinetic and gravitational time dilation. Einstein posited that every time you measure an object's speed, its momentum – or how it experiences time – will always be measured in relation to something else: it is relative. The speed of light remains the same no matter who measures it or how fast the person measuring it is going, and nothing can travel faster than the speed of light. Einstein not only pronounced his theory – he also said it was provable.

In November of 1919, he became an overnight celebrity throughout the world when a solar eclipse provided the first accepted confirmation of his theory of general relativity. Headlines everywhere hailed him as the greatest scientific genius since Isaac Newton.

The theory of special relativity was also confirmed in numerous other tests, and the physics community generally understood and accepted it by the 1920s. Special relativity rapidly became a significant and necessary tool for theorists and experimentalists in the new fields of atomic physics, nuclear physics and quantum mechanics.

The full significance of general relativity wasn't as widely recognised until the 1960s, when it became central to such discoveries as quasars, microwave background radiation, pulsars, black hole candidates and Big Bang theories. Its practical applications have included the development of global positioning systems and high-precision time measurement.

Unlike most other scientific breakthroughs, general relativity was largely a product of Einstein's unique thinking and not a further contribution to other work that was going on at that time. No one else was thinking of gravity as equivalent to acceleration, as a geometrical phenomenon, as a bending of time and space. Consequently, his surprising theory vastly expanded scientific knowledge and altered the course of history.

RIGHT: The first edition of 1916 (below) and the first English translation of 1920 (above). Along with quantum mechanics, Einstein's theory of relativity is one of the key pillars of modern physics. His publication rewrote Newton's physical laws and introduced a new way of understanding the universe.

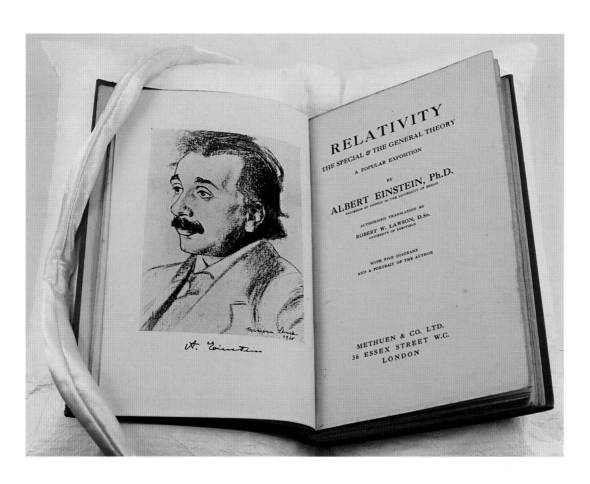

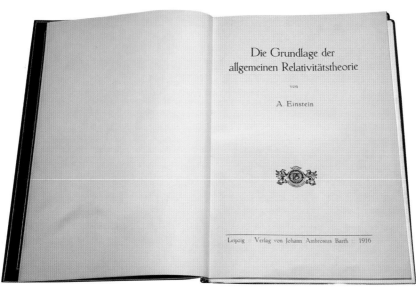

Ulysses
James Joyce
(1922)

An Irish lyricist battled his Catholic upbringing, literary conventions and censorship to fully capture in words a complete human life in a single place on a single date – June 16, 1904. Modelled on Homer's epic *Ulysses*, the author's vast, timeless, highly symbolic and soulful account raised the bar for literary fiction.

James Joyce (1882–1941) was a young Irish fiction writer whose collection of exquisite short stories, *Dubliners* (1914), and a novella, *The Portrait of the Artist as a Young Man* (1916), amounted to slender but deeply evocative masterpieces that introduced characters and themes that he decided to develop in a sequel. The colossal result, *Ulysses*, began with parts that were serialised in 1918 through 1920 in an American journal, *The Little Review*. But in 1921, the United States Post Office seized copies of the publication and refused to distribute them on grounds that they were 'obscene'. After a trial, the journal was forbidden to publish more copies of *Ulysses*.

Working in Paris, Joyce met Sylvia Beach, an American expatriate who operated the small Shakespeare and Company bookshop, and she volunteered to publish the entire suppressed and still-not-completed book. Beach shepherded the immense manuscript through an all-consuming editorial process to its publication on February 2, 1922, Joyce's birthday. The story of the book's publishing, along with many other details surrounding the work and its author, became a fabled part of modern literary history.

The 730-page novel chronicled the activities of Leopold Bloom in Dublin on an ordinary day – now called Bloomsday – though as the critic Edmund Wilson observed, Joyce's enormous task was to render 'as precisely and as directly as it is possible in words to do, what our participation in life is like – or rather, what it seems to us like as from moment to moment we live.' Joyce's work was no ordinary achievement.

Joyce's vast account dealt with every aspect of Bloom's life and human existence, from birth to death, including sexual fantasies and bodily functions, mood changes, and a wide range of thoughts and emotions. It was told with a level of lyricism and stylistic virtuosity rarely achieved in writing, and he devised a number of innovative techniques such as stream of consciousness and interior monologue to penetrate deeper than any author had gone before. His combination of realism with symbolism or expressionism mystified readers. Regarded as one of the richest books ever written, it brims with tragicomedy, puns, parodies and literary allusions, all of which add up to a passionate affirmation of life. Thus, the term 'Joycean' was born.

One of the most famous passages occurs in the final episode when Leopold's wife, Molly, lies in bed next to her husband, dreaming in detail about the day's events and some of her life's most memorable moments, which Joyce delivers in unpunctuated stream-of-consciousness fashion: 'he asked me would I yes to say yes my mountain flower and first I put my arms around him yes and drew him down to me so he could feel my breasts all perfume yes and his heart was going like mad and yes I said yes I will Yes.'

Not every critic embraced the book as a great literary masterpiece. Karl Radek called it 'a heap of dung, crawling with worms, photographed by a cinema camera through a microscope.' But a legal ban against it was finally overturned in *United States v. One Book Called Ulysses* in 1933, wherein the judge essentially found it was too great a work of art to be banned as obscene.

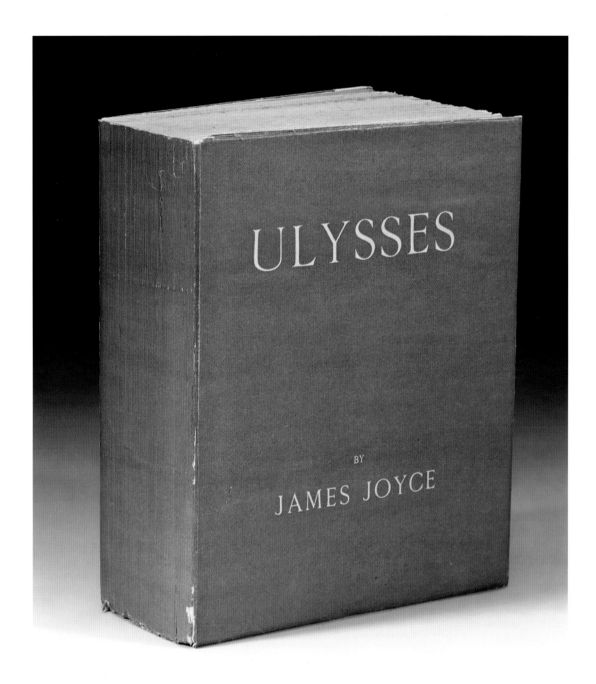

ABOVE: The first edition of Ulysses *was published in 1922, in Paris by Shakespeare and Company.*

OPPOSITE: Sylvia Beach and Joyce in her Shakespeare and Company bookstore. The Sporting Times *review, shown on the wall behind, described the novel as the writings of a 'perverted lunatic who has made a speciality of the literature of the latrine …'*

Penguin Modern Classics   3/6

Franz Kafka
The Trial

ABOVE AND OPPOSITE: *A Penguin paperback edition (above) from 1965, with a cover illustration by André François,
and the first English-language edition (opposite), published in New York by Alfred A. Knopf in 1937.*

The Trial
Franz Kafka
(1925)

Composed during the early months of a dehumanising war, Kafka's meditation on the alienating effects of modern society is still relevant almost a century later. This haunting classic of existentialism offers a bleak but compelling vision of what it is to be human.

Much is made of Franz Kafka's sense of alienation from the world in which he lived. Born in Prague, he was a Czech in the Austrian Empire, a German speaker among Czechs, a Jew among Germans, a lapsed Jew among Jews, a vegetarian. In 1914, when he started to write *Der Prozess* (*The Trial*), he had just moved out of the family home and was living alone.

In *The Trial*, Kafka (1883–1924) presents all the elements of a perfect nightmare – a bewildering situation, an unfamiliar location, a maze of corridors and rooms, a nameless threat, powerlessness to act, all leading inevitably to disaster. His protagonist Josef K. is arrested, although neither K. nor the reader knows what crime he is supposed to have committed. Much of the book is taken up with K.'s more or less futile efforts to take control of his situation and deal with the court of law that will try him. In the end he accepts his unavoidable fate, which is death. He cannot overcome destiny or human weakness.

The Trial can be understood on many levels. Superficially, it is a satire on the impenetrable bureaucracy of the state machine. It is easier just to go along with the dictates of government than to challenge them. In the original German, the title *Der Prozess* carries the double meaning of both a legal trial and a process. K.'s search for explanations can also be seen as a metaphor for life, the process of living, and thereby proceeding inevitably towards death. It's a hopeless, dystopian view, but K.'s efforts to get clarification about

his situation reflect the existentialists' attempts to find freedom and meaning in an absurd, illogical world.

K. seeks help and comfort from various sources: from the rule of law, in the person of the lawyer Huld; from the arts, in the painter Titorelli; from sex and companionship, with Leni and other women; from religion, embodied in the prison chaplain; and from the family circle, in the form of his uncle Karl. None of them are much use, and K. must accept, like the existentialists, that he alone is responsible for living an authentic, meaningful life. Instead, he goes meekly to his death in the final chapter, tamed and subject to the will of the court, as he says with his dying breath, 'like a dog'.

On a deeper level, the judicial system in *The Trial* can be seen to represent spirituality. K.'s arrest is a calling to a more spiritual existence that pulls him out of his mundane routine as a bank official. His encounters in the course of the book are opportunities to take control of his spiritual life. But there is little doubt that he is guilty, having sinned: perhaps his crime is simply to have lost faith in his spiritual self.

The Trial is a complex, dark book, which remained unfinished in Kafka's lifetime. His friend Max Brod edited it for publication in 1925, a year after Kafka's death. It was not published in English until 1937. But existentialism grew in popularity in the wake of World War II, influencing art, literature, and psychology. In an absurd, alienating world, Kafka's story of individual responsibility is now seen as an early milestone of existentialist philosophy.

The Tibetan Book of the Dead
Walter Y. Evans-Wentz

(1927)

Translated in the 1920s and popularised since the 1960s, *The Tibetan Book of the Dead* is actually a collection of writings that describe the process of dying as a natural transition, according to Tibetan Buddhist concepts of death and rebirth.

In 1927, Oxford University Press published *The Tibetan Book of the Dead* by Walter Y. Evans-Wentz (1878–1968), which purported to be selections from a rediscovered Tibetan work known as the *Bardo Thödol* (*Liberation through Hearing in the Intermediate State*). The work had been attributed to the eighth-century Buddhist teacher Padmasambhava, whose writings in Sanskrit were later recovered by a 'treasure revealer', Karma Lingpa (1326–86).

In essence the *Bardo Thödol* is a funerary manual that can be used to guide the nearly departed to recognise the signs of impending death and impart advice on how they should pass through the intermediate state (*bardo*) between death and rebirth. There are descriptions given of the visions and other sensory experiences the dying and dead will encounter as their consciousness is guided towards a favourable next life.

Once dead, the texts of the *Bardo Thödol* are read aloud to the deceased by the living to encourage the consciousness of their loved one to realise the illusory or dreamlike nature of life experiences, and thus to attain liberation through this recognition. The text centres around the fundamental notions of death and impermanence that are key to Tibetan Buddhist philosophy; however, this particular book, or set of writings, is by no means the only reference work used as part of the Tibetan or Himalayan funerary tradition. The *Bardo Thödol* succeeded in capturing the attention of the West through the popularity of Evans-Wentz's translation, which has had the greatest influence on the Western view of Buddhism.

Evans-Wentz chose his title based

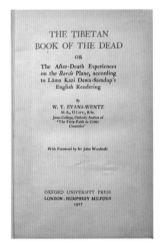

THE TIBETAN
BOOK OF THE DEAD
OR
The After-Death Experiences
on the *Bardo* Plane, according
to Lāma Kazi Dawa-Samdup's
English Rendering

By
W. Y. EVANS-WENTZ
M.A., D.Litt., B.Sc.
Jesus College, Oxford; Author of
'The Fairy-Faith in Celtic
Countries'

With Foreword by Sir John Woodroffe

OXFORD UNIVERSITY PRESS
LONDON: HUMPHREY MILFORD
1927

on interest in *The Egyptian Book of the Dead*, and his introduction and annotations reflected his study of theosophy, not Buddhism. In fact, he was a wealthy American realtor and amateur folklorist who didn't speak Tibetan or read Sanskrit, but while travelling in India, he acquired some old Tibetan manuscripts from a British military officer.

Evans-Wentz was so intrigued by the text, he hired a translator, Lama Kazi Dawa-Samdup, and the pair spent two months together, transcribing and discussing the documents, although Evans-Wentz never credited the translator when he submitted the book for publication.

Shortly after it appeared, the work caught the attention of the famous psychologist Carl Jung (1875–1961), who referred to it in some of his writings. In 1964, Timothy Leary, Ralph Metzner and Richard Alpert recast the book in *The Psychedelic Experience*, offering a shortcut to enlightenment via hallucinogenic drugs. The surrounding lore also influenced musical performers, including John Lennon, Leonard Cohen and David Bowie.

Since the 1960s there have been a number of new editions and translations published by Tibetan scholars, including the Italian, Giuseppe Tucci (1894–1984), and Chögyam Trungpa (1939–87), a Tibetan lama. Other highly regarded English translations have been produced by Robert Thurman and Gyurme Dorje.

The Tibetan Book of the Dead is a cornerstone of Buddhist wisdom that continues to offer insight into the process of dying. Its ultimate message is that the art of dying is as important as the art of living.

ABOVE AND OPPOSITE: The traditional colour print shown above illustrates the 100 peaceful and wrathful deities described in the book, which are believed to visit the deceased between death and rebirth. The title The Tibetan Book of the Dead *was coined by Walter Y. Evans-Wentz. When his book was published in 1927 (opposite), it became the primary source for Western understanding of the Tibetan Buddhist view of death and the afterlife.*

ABOVE AND OPPOSITE: *The privately printed first edition from 1928 (above) was published in Florence, Italy. The first uncensored edition (opposite), published by Penguin in 1960, became the subject of a watershed obscenity trial that turned it into an overnight best-seller. Penguin's second edition in 1961 included a note from the publisher: 'For having published this book, Penguin Books was prosecuted under the Obscene Publications Act, 1959 at the Old Bailey in London from 20 October to 2 November 1960. This edition is therefore dedicated to the twelve jurors, three women and nine men, who returned a verdict of "not guilty" and thus made D.H. Lawrence's last novel available for the first time to the public in the United Kingdom.'*

Lady Chatterley's Lover
D.H. Lawrence
(1928)

A highly charged tale of class, intellect and, inescapably, sex, D.H. Lawrence's last novel is famed as much for pushing publishable boundaries as for exploring social and intellectual divisions.

Lady Chatterley's Lover is notoriously the first book to have been prosecuted under Britain's 1959 Obscene Publications Act. The coarse language and detailed, explicit descriptions of Lady Chatterley's lovemaking with her gamekeeper, Mellors, had caused the book to be banned in Japan, Australia, the United States and Britain.

In 1928, Lawrence (1885–1930) had to have it privately printed in Florence after his own publishers refused. In many countries only censored or black-market editions of the book were available, until Penguin Books published an unexpurgated edition in 1960, challenging Britain's new law. Penguin was brought to court, but the book was cleared of the charge of obscenity. The landmark decision cleared the way for sexually explicit material of all kinds, and helped to usher in the sexual revolution of the 1960s. But its reputation as a piece of posh pornography was sealed by the trial that not only boosted sales to the tune of three million copies but obscured the novel's true literary merit.

The plot follows Lady Constance Chatterley's dissatisfaction with her loveless marriage to impotent, arrogant businessman Sir Clifford Chatterley. Constance is an intelligent, sensual woman, and she finds her equal in Mellors. Their passionate encounters in a woodland hut on Chatterley's estate are in marked contrast with Clifford's passive, childlike dependence on his nurse, Mrs. Bolton. Constance eventually becomes pregnant by Mellors, but there is to be no completely happy ending for any of the characters. Clifford, informed of her affair, refuses to divorce his wife, who nevertheless leaves him. Mellors is sacked and waits for a divorce from his estranged wife. Lady Chatterley lives with her sister, not her lover, and she too must wait and hope.

The rather downbeat conclusion undercuts the book's overall more positive themes. Love, Lawrence contends, is the complete union of both mind and body. It depends on equality of passion in both respects, and it does *not* depend on social equality. Furthermore, Clifford represents cold, hard industrial modernity, which destroys the environment and dehumanises man. Constance and Mellors, on the other hand, stand for nature, human and wild, whether it is in their appreciation of the natural landscape or their sexual encounters on the forest floor.

D.H. Lawrence wrote only four full-length novels, all of which are concerned with the possibilities for human relationships in the Industrial Age. He was a Realist, without equal as a detailed chronicler of the working classes' lives and emotions. But he was also a Romanticist; the tension between industry and nature is a theme of romantic novels throughout the nineteenth century. For his fearless portrayals of the sex act, he was unfortunately dismissed as a mere pornographer in many obituaries at the time of his death. With the passage of time he has been reassessed. His works fit comfortably in the great British literary tradition alongside Austen, Dickens, the Brontës and Hardy.

All Quiet on the Western Front
Erich Maria Remarque
(1929)

All Quiet on the Western Front is a brutal account of the effects of war on young soldiers at the front. It has sold more than fifty million copies since its publication, but was one of the first books declared 'decadent' by the Nazis and burned in public bonfires in 1933.

When he turned eighteen in 1916, German-born Erich Maria Remarque (1898–1970) enlisted in the army and was posted to the Western Front in northern France. Much of *All Quiet on the Western Front* is autobiographical, and certainly based on firsthand experiences. It is narrated by its central character, Paul Bäumer, who enlists with several of his classmates at the age of nineteen.

The book describes life on the front line, and the often violent deaths, one by one, of Paul's comrades. It is unflinching in its depiction of horrific injuries, and although Remarque insists in his preface that he is not making political points, his characters repeatedly question the nationalism that drives the conflict. The soldiers' real enemies are not 'the enemy', but the men in power, far behind the lines of battle. Soldiers kill each other not out of any ideological purpose but purely to avoid being killed. One of the book's key passages is the moment when Paul stabs a French infantryman for the first time in hand-to-hand combat. He bitterly regrets his instinctive action and nurses the man as he slowly dies. In another passage he is similarly sympathetic to 'enemy' Russian prisoners.

Traditional war novels glorified heroism and patriotism. Remarque presents the grim reality of modern warfare, where killing is made easier by machines – guns, tanks and airplanes. More than earlier wars, World War I dehumanised those who fought it, both by the means of killing and by the sheer scale of it.

All Quiet on the Western Front chronicles the soldiers' emotional disconnection in the face of such slaughter. You might die at any moment, so you live only in the moment. 'Goodbye' becomes the hardest word. The men cut themselves off from family and friends, from memories of the past and from hope for the future. The only shreds of humanity that survive are the intense bonds between brothers in arms.

Remarque found that publishers were hesitant about printing his book, fearing that ten years after his country's defeat in World War I, there would be little appetite for stirring up memories of it again. Instead, it was serialised in the Berlin daily newspaper the *Vossische Zeitung* in the last two months of 1928, where the response was encouraging enough to publish it in book form the following year. *All Quiet on the Western Front* was at once an international success, translated into more than twenty languages and selling two and a half million copies in the first eighteen months. An American film production of it was released as early as 1930 and was nominated for five Oscars and won three, including Best Picture and Best Director.

One of the most remarkable things about *All Quiet on the Western Front* is its success in countries such as America and Great Britain, which might not have been expected to sympathise with the traumas of enemy soldiers. Remarque's masterpiece succeeded, and endures, because of its universal message: war is hell for all combatants, and at heart all men are brothers.

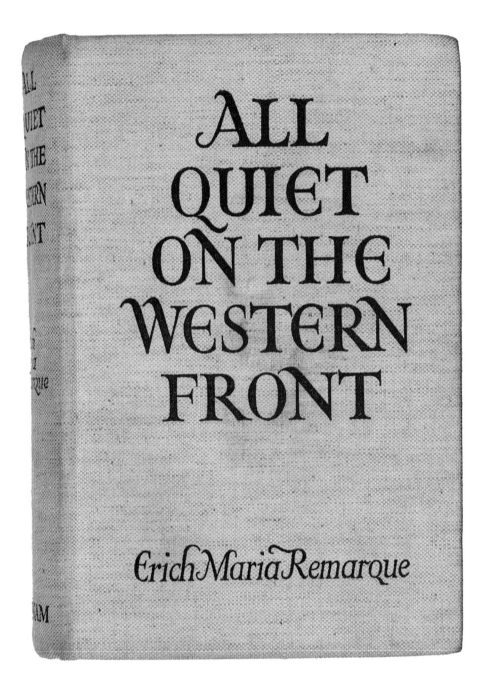

*ABOVE AND OPPOSITE: The first UK edition (above), published in 1929 by Putnam.
The Grosset & Dunlap edition (opposite) was published in 1930 in New York. It is
described as 'unexpurgated' because it included a scene of a battalion's visit to a latrine
that Little, Brown (the original US publisher) removed for fear of offending its readers.*

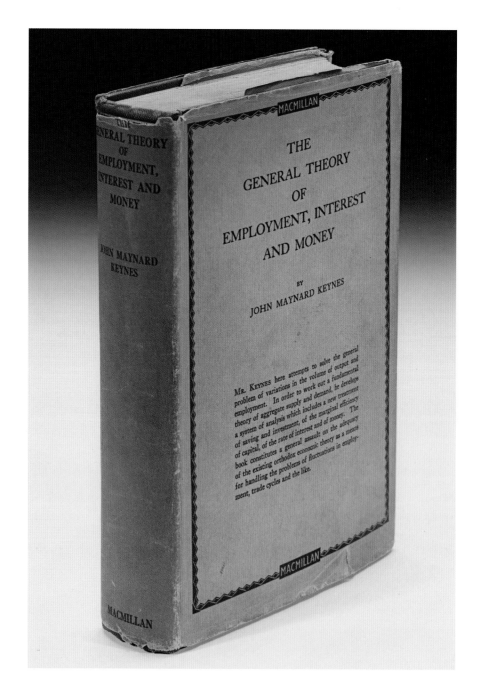

ABOVE AND OPPOSITE: The first edition (above) and a photo of Keynes (opposite) from the late 1920s. In a letter to George Bernard Shaw, Keynes claimed that The General Theory of Employment *would revolutionise the way the world thought about its economic problems. Bertrand Russell described Keynes as having the sharpest intellect that he'd ever encountered: 'When I argued with him, I felt that I took my life in my hands, and I seldom emerged without feeling something of a fool.'*

156_____100 Books that Changed the World

The General Theory of Employment, Interest and Money
John Maynard Keynes

(1936)

Writing during the depths of the Great Depression, when mass unemployment was threatening the survival of the capitalist system, a distinguished English economist offered a bold new theory: the government needed to take on more public works and deficit spending. His book challenged earlier approaches and changed modern economics for decades to come.

Although the world was plunging into a depression, Professor John Maynard Keynes (1883–1946) of Cambridge University remained optimistic, writing in 1930 that instead of nationalising the means of production, the solution was for the system to get 'a new alternator, not a whole new car.' Based on his studies of the relationship between unemployment, money and prices, he wrote a book, which he told his friend George Bernard Shaw would 'change the way the world thinks about its economic problems.'

His magnum opus, *The General Theory of Employment, Interest and Money*, was published in February 1936 in English, German, Japanese and French.

'I have called this book *The General Theory of Employment, Interest and Money*,' he wrote:

> placing the emphasis on the prefix *general*. The object of such a title is to contrast the character of my arguments and conclusions with those of the classical theory of the subject, upon which I was brought up … I shall argue that the postulates of the *classical* theory are applicable to a special case only and not to the general case … the characteristics of the special case assumed by the classical theory happen not to be those of the economic society in which we actually live, with the result that its teaching is misleading and disastrous if we attempt to apply it to the facts of experience.

Keynes suggested a new approach for managing the unemployment problems spawned by an economic depression. He argued that the level of employment is determined, not by the price of labour, but by the spending of money, and that it was wrong to assume that competitive markets would produce full employment. Instead, government needed to undertake more public works programmes and more deficit spending until the crisis abated. He also favoured the reduction of long-term interest rates and the reform of the international monetary system as structural measures to encourage investment and consumption by the private sector.

World War II began a few years after the book was published. When the war was over, many analysts concluded that Keynes's theory had been borne out by the role of governments' public works and military spending in helping to curb the depression. Keynesian economics was widely embraced by Western governments.

Paul Krugman, the Nobel Prize–winning economist and columnist for the *New York Times*, ranked Keynes's book with only a handful of other works in economics that have transformed the way people view the world. *Time* magazine, which included Keynes in its list of the most important people of the twentieth century, said that 'his radical idea that governments should spend money they don't have may have saved capitalism.'

How to Win Friends and Influence People
Dale Carnegie
(1936)

The original self-help book. Dale Carnegie's homespun philosophical guide to achieving the American Dream is the template for hundreds of others since its publication. It has won millions of friends and influenced millions of people.

Dale Carnegie (1888–1955) was born on a dirt farm in Missouri. Between the morning and evening milking of the cows, he studied at his local college and began to work as a travelling salesman for a meat company in Chicago, for whom he became its top rep. Recognising his powers of verbal persuasion, he dreamed first of being a lecturer, then an actor, for which he trained at the American Academy of Dramatic Arts. Unable to find stage work, he began in 1912 to teach public speaking at the YMCA in New York. It became clear that there was an untapped market for boosting people's confidence.

YMCAs in other cities started hosting Carnegie and his courses, and he was eventually delivering sold-out lectures on public speaking in New York's Carnegie Hall – named after the massively successful Scottish immigrant Andrew Carnegie. Dale Carnegie, like his namesake, understood how to motivate people – specifically, how to do business with them – and he set up the Dale Carnegie Institute to deliver training courses based on his ideas. When a stenographer from the publishers Simon & Schuster presented him with a transcript of one of his Carnegie Hall talks, he realised he had the makings of a book.

How to Win Friends and Influence People was published in October 1936 and at once became a best-seller. The initial marketing ploy – sending five hundred copies of it to graduates of Carnegie Institute courses – resulted in sales of 5,000 copies. Its fame spread quickly, and in the first three months sales passed the quarter-million mark. In its first year the book went through dozens of reprints and seventeen new editions as Carnegie constantly revised his text. To this day, it still sells 300,000 copies annually.

Carnegie's advice was originally divided into six parts: how to handle people, how to make them like you, how to bring them around to your way of thinking, how to lead them, how to write letters and, finally, how to have a happier home life. Across these headings he proclaimed some forty simple principles for improving your chances of success. They were all down-home, folksy tips, such as remembering people's names. Smile. Be a good listener. Give honest appreciation, not negative criticism. Admit your mistakes; don't point out theirs. Look at it from their point of view. Be encouraging and respectful. Avoid arguments.

Carnegie was effectively selling human nature at its best, the Forrest Gump wisdom of a farmer's son. These are the principles for living that everyone had learned at their mother's or father's knee but which, perhaps in the desperate years of the Great Depression, they had forgotten. By applying them to business practice, Carnegie was tapping into the American Dream – prosperity, success, and freedom through good manners and hard work.

To date, it has been translated into thirty languages and sold more than thirty million copies. It is said that in the ten years following the fall of communism, around seventy editions of *How to Win Friends and Influence People* were published in Russian as the country embraced entrepreneurism. The book has spawned an entire genre of publishing and influenced hundreds of books in the same style.

RIGHT: Copies of 'the most popular work of non-fiction of our time' were stamped with issue numbers. (This reprint from 1937 is number 469,143.) It sold 250,000 copies in its first three months and is estimated to have sold more than thirty million copies to date.

THIS IS COPY No 469143

THE MOST POPULAR WORK OF NON-FICTION OF OUR TIME

HOW TO WIN FRIENDS AND INFLUENCE PEOPLE

BY DALE CARNEGIE

1. What are the six ways of making people like you?
   See pages 75-133.

2. What are the twelve ways of winning people to your
   way of thinking? *See pages 137-217.*

3. What are the nine ways to change people without giving
   offense or arousing resentment? *See pages 221-253.*

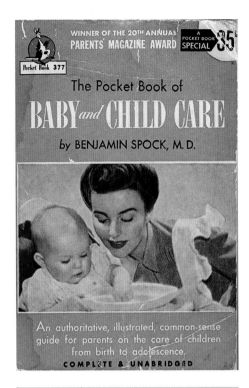

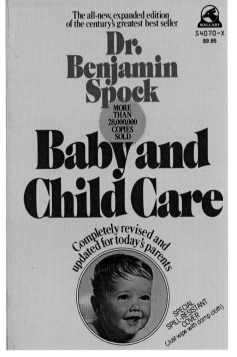

Dr. Spock's Baby and Child Care

(1946)

A sensitive but common sense manual for baby and child care, timed to appear at just the right moment, became one of the best-selling books in American history and transformed society for generations to come.

The end of World War II in the United States triggered a historic 'baby boom', as Americans who had postponed getting married and having children were no longer bound by the economic depression, age and military service. But postwar changes in social morays called for a modernised guide to child-rearing.

Benjamin McLane Spock (1903–98) was an American paediatrician who had been educated at Yale and New York, where he graduated first in his class at Columbia University College of Physicians and Surgeons in 1929. He won an Olympic medal in rowing and showed an affinity for literature and Freudian theory, becoming the first paediatrician to seriously study psychoanalysis and apply it to children and parents.

In 1927 he married Jane Cheney, who assisted him in his research and writing of the book that was published in 1946 by Duell, Sloan & Pearce as *The Common Sense Book of Baby and Child Care* and later called *Dr. Spock's Baby and Child Care.*

Going against his own old-fashioned upbringing, Spock began his book with a reassuring message: 'Trust yourself, you know more than you think you do.' His comprehensive and practical advice suggested how to deal with everything from colic and toilet training, to temper tantrums and sibling rivalry. 'It's best to keep stuffed animals out of your baby's crib or cradle,' he wrote, 'little babies don't care much about them, and they may pose a suffocation.'

Instead of demanding conformity, regimentation and punishment, he advocated tolerance and expressions of affection and support for young children – ideas that some critics considered radical and out of the mainstream at that time.

He called for young mothers to be loving, attentive and optimistic,

recommending: 'Make out a schedule for yourself, on paper if necessary, that requires you to be busy with housework or anything else while your baby is awake. Go at it with a great bustle – to impress your baby and to impress yourself.'

He believed that a child who is appreciated 'for what they are, even if they are homely, or clumsy, or slow, will grow up with confidences in themselves … They will have a spirit that will make the best of all the capacities that they have, and of all the opportunities that come their way. They will make light of any handicaps.'

Spock emerged as a prominent political activist in the 1960s and '70s when he participated in the civil rights and anti-war movements, leading demonstrations against nuclear weapons, the military draft during the Vietnam War, and other causes. 'It isn't enough to bring up children happy and secure,' he said, 'you need to provide a decent world for them.'

As a result of his outspokenness, he was assailed by traditional moralists such as Dr. Norman Vincent Peale and Reverend Billy Graham, and reviled by politicians, including Vice President Spiro Agnew, who accused him of being too 'permissive', spawning a rebellious generation.

Despite these criticisms, *Baby and Child Care* is now thought to have sold more than fifty million copies in forty-two languages, making it one of the best-selling books of all time. Many parents considered it their family bible, and it continues to be published in new editions today.

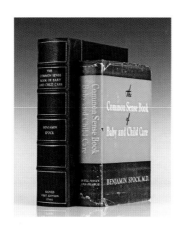

LEFT AND OPPOSITE: The original hardback edition (left) and four paperback reissues (opposite). Baby and Child Care *is the best-selling non-fiction book of the twentieth century in America.*

The Diary of a Young Girl
Anne Frank

(1947)

While forced to hide in an attic with her family and four other fugitives, a Jewish girl poured out her most intimate thoughts in a personal diary that was later recovered and read by millions.

Anne Frank (1929–44) and her relatives had fled for their lives from Germany to Amsterdam during World War II. They tried to remain concealed in a secret attic space that had been created behind a bookcase in her father's office building, where they would remain for two terrifying years.

The attic was cramped and stuffy, devoid of adolescent entertainment or schoolhouse activities. One of the girl's only diversions began on June 14, 1942, when she wrote her first entry in a small red-and-white-checkered autograph book she had received for her thirteenth birthday. She confided her feelings to several imaginary friends, sharing a cauldron of emotions about her fellow fugitives and their accomplices, ever careful not to reveal anyone's true identity.

Like other youths her age, Anne longed for approval while struggling to separate herself from her parents and trying to become her own person. Writing with great honesty, she expressed her conflicted feelings about her family, and shared secrets about a possible romantic interest, as well as her developing thoughts about life. Her diary showed extraordinary emotional depth and literary ability, coupled with a remarkable optimism, given what she was experiencing.

'It's a wonder I haven't abandoned all my ideals,' she wrote shortly before her arrest, 'they seem so absurd and impractical. Yet I cling to them because I still believe, in spite of everything, that people are truly good at heart.'

Two years and one month into their captivity, the fugitives were betrayed and sent off to concentration camps. Of the eight persons, only her father would survive. Anne succumbed to typhus in Bergen-Belsen in 1945. She was fifteen.

Two of their former friends found the girl's manuscript, written on loose sheets of paper, strewn on the attic floor, and gave them to Otto Frank after the war. He later recalled how he felt when reading his daughter's diary for the first time, saying, 'For me, it was a revelation. There, was revealed a completely different Anne to the child that I had lost. I had no idea of the depths of her thoughts and feelings.' He later got the work published.

A version of the diary first appeared in Amsterdam in 1947. In 1952, it was published in the United States and the United Kingdom as *Anne Frank: The Diary of a Young Girl*. In the 1960s it became a huge international best-seller and inspired award-winning stage and movie versions, contributing to greater awareness about the fate of the Jews in the Holocaust. Many critics have included it on their lists of the most important books of the twentieth century.

Anne Frank's story personalised the Nazi persecution of Jews during the war, and valorised the human spirit. 'I don't want to have lived in vain like most people,' she wrote. 'I want to be useful or bring enjoyment to all people, even those I've never met. I want to go on living even after my death!'

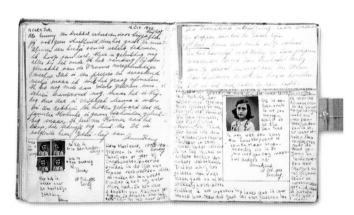

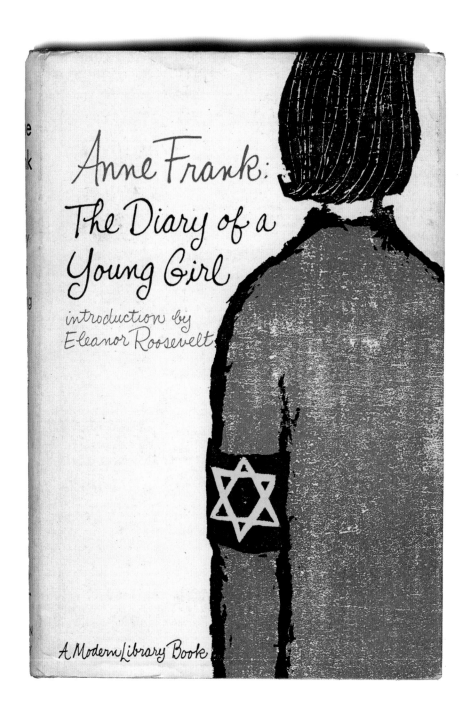

ABOVE: *A Modern Library edition from 1952, with an introduction by Eleanor Roosevelt.*

OPPOSITE: *A page from Anne Frank's diary, dated October 10, 1942: 'This is a photograph of me as I wish I looked all the time. Then I might still have a chance of getting to Hollywood.'*

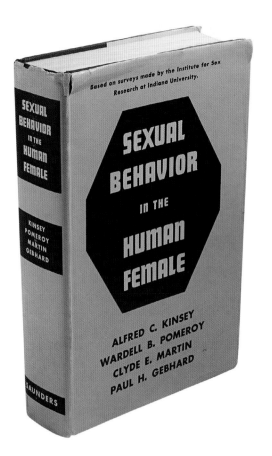

ABOVE: First editions of both books, and a photo from 1953, showing Kinsey surrounded by staff of Indiana University's Institute of Sex Research. The publication of the Kinsey reports represented the largest and most detailed set of data on human sexual behaviour collected to that point.

Kinsey Reports

(1948 and 1953)

An Indiana zoology professor spent years asking strangers about their sex habits and published two empirical reports detailing what they said. The books brought the issue out of the closet and challenged several conventional notions of male and female sexuality, thereby contributing to America's sexual revolution.

While teaching a course on marriage at Indiana University, Alfred Charles Kinsey (1894–1956) began to collect information about individuals' sexual histories. Starting in 1941, he received research grants from philanthropic institutions that were connected to the Rockefeller family, which had a longstanding interest in sexual social problems. The funding enabled the Kinsey Institute for Research in Sex, Gender and Reproduction, Inc. to compile a comprehensive report that was published by a commercial publisher in 1948 as *Sexual Behavior in the Human Male*.

The 800-page tome comprised text, charts and graphs documenting the results of 12,000 clinical interviews with a range of males of various ages, occupations and social backgrounds who were surveyed by a team of researchers about their sexual behaviour and preferences.

A reviewer for the *New York Times* squeamishly noted that the book was as difficult to read as it was to complete: 'Difficult, because of the magnitude of the subject; difficult, because it deals with man's basic drive to reproduce, a drive as strong as that for survival; difficult, because of our prejudices, taboos and preconceptions, preconceptions colored by personal experience, which gives the individual the microscopic rather than the total concept.'

The book provided a surprising antiseptic, statistical profile of the sexual mores of modern American males in the postwar era, noting when most had their first sexual experience, how often they masturbated, and what were their patterns of premarital, marital and extramarital intercourse, as well as the extent of their homosexual experiences. One comment about homosexuality was particularly controversial at the time: 'Males do not represent two discrete populations; heterosexual and homosexual,' he wrote. 'The world is not to be divided into sheep and goats, and not all things are black nor all things white … The sooner we learn this concerning human sexual behavior, the sooner we shall reach a sound understanding of the realities of sex.' However, the public airing of the findings received a mixed reaction, with some psychiatrists complaining that the project was not sufficiently grounded in Freudian theory, and methodologists critiquing the surveys' sampling techniques, while moralists huffed and puffed over the 'shocking' results. 'We are the recorders and reporters of facts,' Kinsey replied, 'not the judges of the behaviors we describe.'

Following on from the substantial commercial success of its first volume, Kinsey published *Sexual Behavior of the Human Female* (1953), which immediately prompted a firestorm of controversy on several fronts. Appearing in the McCarthy era, it triggered a wave of anti-communist hysteria and congressional hearings, as well as objections by religious organisations, which contested the report's empirical findings. Based on its interviews of more than 6,000 females, the team found women to be more sexually active than previously assumed, with 26 per cent of the women found to have had extramarital sex by their forties, and a higher percentage than men were reported to have had a homosexual experience.

Together, the books sold more than 750,000 copies, making the series one of the most widely read report-type publications in history at that time.

Many social studies credited Kinsey with helping to launch the sexual revolution of the 1960s and contributing to such developments as the appearance of *Playboy* magazine in 1953 and the first oral contraceptive for women – the Pill – in 1960.

1984
George Orwell
(1949)

The definitive political novel of our time was written in the immediate aftermath of World War II, when a veteran English essayist, journalist, critic and novelist imagined the future of life in a totalitarian society in which 'Big Brother is Watching You', lies are decreed as truth, and individuals are micromanaged and crushed by the state.

Eric Arthur Blair (1903–50) adopted the pen name of George Orwell to satisfy publishers for marketing reasons. But he was an independent thinker who had crammed enormous experience and struggle into his forty-seven years. A former imperial policeman in Burma, and an anarchist who had fought against Franco's fascists in the Spanish Civil War and survived terrible hardship and personal loss in World War II, he was desperate when he went to a primitive house on a remote island in the Inner Hebrides to write his next novel.

Although his recently published 'animal fable' – a political-allegorical novella entitled *Animal Farm* (1945) – was receiving a warm reception, the combination of tuberculosis, lack of money, family obligations and worry weighed on his mind. His ordeal was a race against time. Despite his rapidly declining health and anguish, Orwell pounded out his vision on a battered typewriter, determined to save the world from its fate.

The new novel began: 'It was a bright cold day in April, and the clocks were striking thirteen.' In its opening scene, he wrote: 'On each landing, the poster with the enormous face gazed from the wall. It was one of those pictures which are so contrived that the eyes follow you about when you move. BIG BROTHER IS WATCHING YOU, the caption beneath it ran.'

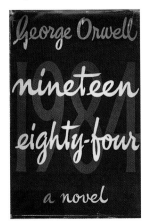

The main characters, Winston Smith and Julia, struggle to maintain their humanity in an insane world. The conflict is between ideology and emotion. The language is gritty and factual. Orwell was frantically racing to get it all down as soon as he could.

One of the best assessments of Orwell's achievement was written by the literary critic Irving Howe as follows: 'Nightmare the book may be, and no doubt it is grounded, as are all books, in the psychological troubles of the author. But it is also grounded in his psychological health, otherwise it could not penetrate so deeply the social reality of our time. The private nightmare, if it is there, is profoundly related to, and helps us understand, public events.'

Historians argue over how the publisher selected the title. Orwell's working title was *The Last Man in Europe*. Was it a homage to his idol, Jack London, whose novel *The Iron Heel*, had been set in 1984? Or was it a reversal of the numbers of the year – 48 – when the book was completed?

When *1984* was published in June 1949, it was quickly hailed as a masterpiece, but its completion proved fatal to the author. He died alone in a hospital on January 21, 1950. His chilling dystopian vision has been translated into more than sixty-five languages and made into numerous screen and stage versions. In 2017 it once again became the Amazon top best-seller, after social media commentators connected the phrase 'alternative facts' (used by Counsellor to President Donald Trump, Kellyanne Conway) with the language of *1984*.

Such terms as 'doublethink', 'the thought police', 'Room 101' and 'newspeak' are now part of everyone's political vocabulary, along with the term 'Orwellian', signifying something repressive or totalitarian.

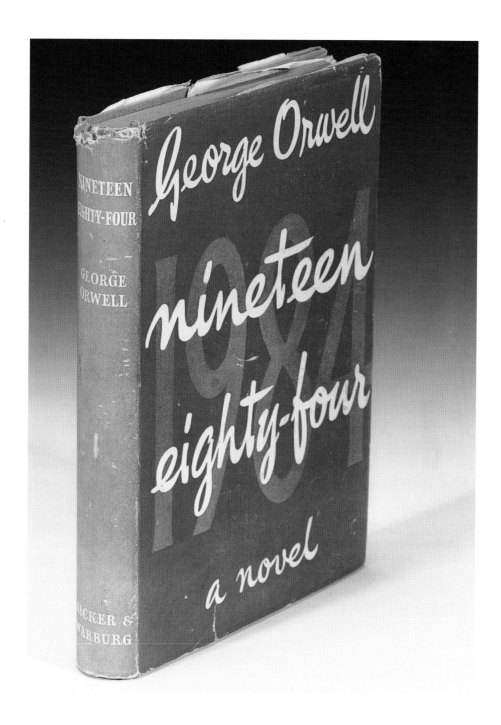

ABOVE AND OPPOSITE: The first edition, published in June 1949 by Secker & Warburg, was printed with red and green dust jackets.

ABOVE: *Simone de Beauvoir in Café de Flore, Paris, where she would spend up to six hours a day writing.*

OPPOSITE: *The title page of the first edition. The opening line of part two – 'One is not born, but rather becomes, a woman' – is regarded as a cornerstone of modern, radical feminist thought.*

The Second Sex
Simone de Beauvoir

(1949)

After World War II, one of France's rising public intellectuals extended the growing call for liberation to women. She documented their oppression throughout history in rich detail, some of which was drawn from her own life experience. Her book of feminist philosophy paved the way for a movement that used it as a lodestar in feminism's second wave.

Simone de Beauvoir (1908–86) grew up in the 1920s wanting to escape from the shackles of her stultifying, genteel French Catholic roots. While studying philosophy at the Sorbonne in Paris, she became romantically involved with Jean-Paul Sartre (1905–80), a young scholar, writer and activist who was completing his training in philosophy at the École Normale Supérieure. Their radical relationship began as they crammed together for the immensely competitive *agrégation* examination, which resulted in him scoring first and her ranking second.

In 1946 she embarked on an autobiographical essay, but the project snowballed to become a deep and intense excavation into women's treatment throughout history. Published first in Sartre's journal *Les Temps modernes*, and then as a two-volume book, *Le Deuxième Sexe* (*The Second Sex*) in 1949, it helped to establish her as one of France's leading radical voices.

After asking the question 'What is a woman?' she proceeded to answer: 'Man is defined as a human being and a woman as a female – whenever she behaves as a human being she is said to imitate the male … Thus humanity is male and man defines woman not herself but as relative to him … Society, being codified by man, decrees that woman is inferior; she can do away with this inferiority only by destroying the male's superiority.'

Her impassioned thesis contained observations about the biology of female insects, fish and other animals, including humans, describing how females of every species were dominated and subordinated by the males. She examined and rejected the views of women expounded by Sigmund Freud and Alfred Adler, saying that their treatment of eroticism was flawed.

Based on her own research, she traced the evolution of women's condition from ancient Greece and Rome, through early Christianity, Renaissance Italy and Spain, and nineteenth-century France, and found always that women were oppressed, degraded and devalued. Her historical study included women's participation in labour unions, their role in birth control and suffrage movements, and treatment in scientific fields, where she concluded that the examples of such stars as Marie Curie 'brilliantly demonstrate that it is not women's inferiority that has determined their historical insignificance: it is their historical insignificance that has doomed them to inferiority.'

De Beauvoir's study delved into socialisation, sexuality, marriage, motherhood, prostitution and other intimate subjects.

Writing that marriage 'almost always destroys woman', she quoted Sophia Tolstoy as confiding, 'you are stuck there forever and there you must sit.'

In her conclusion, she envisioned a future in which women would be treated as equals in every respect and take control of their own lives.

The Second Sex was translated into nineteen languages and enjoyed renewed popularity with the rise of the women's movement in the 1960s that was rekindled by the appearance of Betty Friedan's *The Feminine Mystique* and other works that De Beauvoir's book had helped inspire.

SIMONE DE BEAUVOIR

LE
DEUXIÈME SEXE

I

LES FAITS ET LES MYTHES

nrf

GALLIMARD
5, rue Sébastien-Bottin, Paris VIIe

A Book of Mediterranean Food
Elizabeth David

(1950)

The book that brought hope to the taste buds of Britain. When Elizabeth David returned from northern Africa to England after World War II, food rationing was still in force. Appalled at the state of British cuisine, she first wrote about Mediterranean meals to cheer herself up.

British cooking before World War II wasn't all bad, but it took being a student at the Sorbonne in Paris for Elizabeth David (1913–92) to awaken her love of good food. She studied there in the early 1930s and lodged with a French family for whom mealtimes were occasions to savour. Back in Britain, she taught herself to cook. The first cookbook she owned, a present from her mother, was *The Gentle Art of Cooking* by the eccentric Hilda Leyel, an expert in the use of herbs for both culinary and medicinal purposes.

In 1939, David and a friend were sailing around the Mediterranean when war broke out. They were arrested in Italy on suspicion of spying, and with difficulty they found their way out through Yugoslavia and Greece to Egypt, where she found work with Britain's Ministry of Information. Despite the privations of war, she discovered delicious local food everywhere she went.

Her shock on returning to England in 1946 was enormous. The German fleet had deliberately targeted ships bringing food to Britain, and rationing of almost all foodstuffs had been gradually introduced from January 1940. It was still in place. Among the horrors she found were dehydrated vegetables and eggs, soup flavoured only with pepper and flour, and meals she described as being 'produced with a kind of bleak triumph which amounted almost to a hatred of humanity and humanity's needs.'

David began to write reflective magazine articles about the Mediterranean cooking that she had enjoyed throughout the war. Collected together, they were published in 1950 as her first book, prosaically titled *A Book of Mediterranean Food*. As the title subtly

declared, it was not merely a cookbook. It was a book about food and her devotion to fresh ingredients and seasonal flavours. She wrote with a passion bordering on poetry about the aspects of Mediterranean landscape and life from which such colourful food came. When it came to recipes, she assumed an ability to cook on the part of her readers. David wrote not in the formal instructional style developed by Mrs. Beeton but with an enthusiastic conversational voice, taking knowledge of cooking times and quantities for granted.

Its publication was well received, lightening the gloom of British food lovers and delighting them with dishes of which they had never heard – gazpacho, paella, bouillabaisse, kokoretsi. As chef and author Jane Grigson noted later, 'Basil was no more than the name of bachelor uncles, "courgette" was printed in italics as an alien word, and few of us knew how to eat spaghetti…' Before David encouraged its culinary use, olive oil was most commonly supplied in Britain by pharmacies in small bottles, for cleaning one's ears.

Mediterranean Food was inspirational reading but, with the availability of ingredients still limited, not always very practical. Rationing ended at last in 1954, and in 1955, Penguin Books brought out a paperback edition. While some ingredients were still scarce, it was now at least possible to try Mediterranean cooking for yourself. The book's popularity spread rapidly, and Elizabeth David can take credit for introducing not only good food but good food writing. Cookery authors from Julia Childs to Diana Henry acknowledge their debt to her authorial voice. None have surpassed it.

ABOVE AND OPPOSITE: The first edition included dust jacket and interior illustrations by artist John Minton. Elizabeth David's approach to cooking was seen as a breath of fresh air after the austerity of World War II. Foods that are now taken for granted – garlic, olive oil, Parmesan cheese – were either unheard of or generally viewed with suspicion before A Book of Mediterranean Food.

ALDOUS HUXLEY

The Doors of Perception

The Doors of Perception
Aldous Huxley
(1954)

The Doors of Perception, which described a single hallucinogenic experience, went on to influence the rising drug culture of the 1950s and '60s. Huxley's measured report of his first mescaline trip is lucid, detailed, and philosophical about the drug's good and bad effects.

Aldous Huxley (1894–1963) settled in California in 1937 when he was already the successful author of the dystopian novel *Brave New World*. Even before he left his native England, he had shown an interest in the effects of mind-altering drugs, and in spirituality. In *Brave New World* the state keeps the people docile with a constant supply of a fictional drug called soma. The protagonist of his 1936 war novel *Eyeless in Gaza* turns to Eastern philosophy to ease his disillusionment with the world. Huxley, himself disillusioned by the path that he saw society following in the twentieth century, had turned to meditation at this time.

In 1952, Huxley's attention was caught by the research of an English psychiatrist, Humphry Osmond. Osmond was experimenting with mescaline (the hallucinogenic component of the peyote cactus) as a treatment for schizophrenic patients at his Saskatchewan mental hospital. The two men corresponded, and Huxley volunteered to take mescaline experimentally in the presence of Osmond, in the hope of removing conscious barriers to his spiritual enlightenment.

Huxley may have had another motive for experimenting with hallucinogens. Following a childhood illness, his eyesight was so bad that he was at times almost completely blind. Was he hoping to receive a different kind of vision?

The experiment took place on May 3, 1953, in Huxley's West Hollywood home. *The Doors of Perception* is the record of that day. The title is taken from William Blake's 1793 book *The Marriage of Heaven and Hell*: 'If the doors of perception were cleansed every thing would appear to man as it is, Infinite.'

Huxley had a very visual response to the drug. A vase of flowers, for example, became 'a miracle of naked existence', while a book of famous paintings opened his eyes to abstract colour and pattern, even in figurative works. Towards the end of his trip, the garden chairs took on an intense reality that threatened, he felt, to drive him mad.

He concluded that although heightened perception should be possible without mescaline, nevertheless, it helps, and certainly works better than tobacco and alcohol. Mescaline, he wrote, did not make men violent – quite the opposite: they were brought to inaction because the experience was so vivid and gripping. He conceded that some users might have bad trips, and felt that at around eight hours its effects lasted inconveniently long. But on balance it offered a change in perception that was worth having.

Huxley, who had been critical of such drugs in *Brave New World*, was converted. He took mescaline several times a year for the rest of his life, and he took LSD for the first time a year after the publication of *The Doors of Perception*. Furthermore, he is said to have introduced Timothy Leary and Allen Ginsberg to the idea of experimenting with psychedelic drugs – indeed, he and Humphry Osmond invented the word 'psychedelic'. Without such experimentation we might have missed out on the Beat poets, the Beatles' *Sgt. Pepper*, the Doors (named after the book), Woodstock and all the cultural legacies of the 1960s that are still felt today.

Lolita
Vladimir Nabokov
(1955)

Lolita is a sexually explicit and controversial tale of tragedy, lust and love. Nabokov's divisive subject and treatment tread a difficult line between pornography and literary merit.

Lolita was first published in 1955 by the Paris-based Olympia Press, which specialised in risqué and erotic fiction, after many more reputable American houses turned it down for fear of being prosecuted for obscenity. It attracted little attention until Graham Greene became an early champion of its literary quality. Vladimir Nabokov (1899–1977) succeeds in getting us to empathise with his narrator, Humbert, while still condemning his deeds. In so doing, he has written not a salacious tale but a powerful and tragic love story. It is Nabokov's exquisite prose that raises *Lolita* above mere erotica, encouraging us to look more fully into the mind of its dubious narrator.

Lolita is the story of the thirty-seven-year-old Humbert's infatuation with an underage girl, Dolores Haze (Lolita), who ages from twelve to seventeen in the course of the book. Humbert tells the story in retrospect from a prison cell. He is a sexual criminal writing down his crimes, and we have to take his version of events with a grain of salt. We only have his unreliable perspective on what has happened, never Lolita's, and must trust Nabokov and ourselves to make judgments about both characters' actions and motives. Just as Humbert uses smooth words and playful games to seduce the child Lolita, Nabokov uses verbal jokes and literary puzzles to lead his readers to the underlying truths of his novel. *Lolita* is full of puns and references to other works, as if Nabokov is playing with us.

It's not all about sex. Nabokov was a harsh critic of Freudian psychology, which was on the

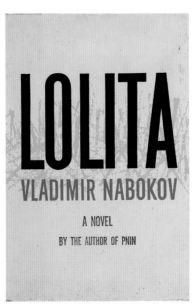

ascendency in the 1950s. He invents a fictitious psychiatrist to write a foreword for the book, extolling its psychiatric insights, but he uses many of his characters to mock the inability of psychological analysis to describe complex problems, such as the sexuality of the book's characters.

Much of the novel deals with a culture clash between European and American thinking. Humbert is a European, often at odds with the America through which he travels, and with Quilty, his American rival for Lolita's affections. Nabokov was himself a Russian who fled through Europe before settling on America's east coast, and *Lolita* is a detailed picture of his adopted nation in the 1950s.

The risk that the novel takes in getting us to empathise with Humbert is that we get too close to him to see him for the sexual predator he is. But in the end it is not Humbert who takes Lolita's virginity, or makes her pregnant, or tries to use her in a pornographic movie, or with whom she settles down. Those roles are left to other characters, and all that remains for Humbert is a warped, lost love.

Once Graham Greene brought the novel to the literary world's attention, it attracted as much scandalised damnation as critical praise. England and France both banned it for a couple of years, but not (despite those fears of prosecution) the United States, where it was finally published in 1958. The novel was hailed a classic and the word 'Lolita' entered the English language as a term for a sexually precocious young girl.

ABOVE: *The first edition was published in two volumes by Olympia Press in Paris, after being rejected by Viking; Simon & Schuster; New Directions; Farrar, Straus; and Doubleday.*

OPPOSITE: *The first American edition was published by Putnam in 1958 and sold 100,000 copies in its first three weeks.*

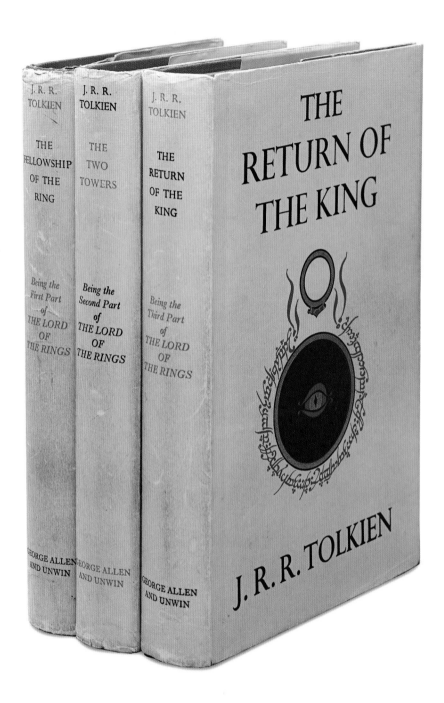

ABOVE AND OPPOSITE: The title page of The Fellowship of the Ring *(opposite) and all three volumes (above), published between July 1954 and October 1955 by George Allen & Unwin. In an interview from 1966, Tolkien brushed aside the idea of filming his trilogy: 'You can't cramp narrative into dramatic form. It would be easier to film* The Odyssey. *Much less happens in it. Only a few storms.'*

The Lord of the Rings
J.R.R. Tolkien
(1954–55)

An Oxford philologist who had survived one of the bloodiest battles in history spent twelve years penning an epic high-fantasy trilogy about brutal warring armies in a mythical medieval land known as Middle-earth. His iconic creation went on to become one of the best-selling novels of all time and the model for a huge genre of world-building fantasy books, movies and games.

Born in South Africa, J.R.R. Tolkien (1892–1973) grew up in England and taught philology at Oxford University, writing fantasy fiction in his spare time. Based on the success of his early fantasy novel *The Hobbit* (1937), his publisher asked him to write a sequel, in which he would explore other reaches of the fictional world he had been building through a process he called 'mythopoeia' (meaning the creation of myths).

Tolkien's extraordinary erudition and fertile imagination led him to draw from a huge treasury of Norse and Germanic mythology, Celtic lore, fairy tales and other ancient myths taken from several cultures. He studied *Beowulf* and other medieval texts and used his knowledge of the Welsh language to create his own names and word patterns. As a veteran of the Somme and other battles in the Great War, he also carried memories of the ravages and devastation of combat, and expressions of his deep Catholic worldview.

Tolkien's labours on *The Lord of the Rings* stretched on for more than a decade. His contractual arrangement with the publisher George Allen & Unwin provided no advance or royalties unless and until the book broke even, at which time he would begin to receive a high share of the profits. The publisher initially thought his 'work of genius' wouldn't make any money.

The novel's title refers to the story's chief antagonist, the Dark Lord Sauron, who had created the One Ring to rule over the other Rings of Power in his merciless campaign to conquer and rule all of Middle-earth. The story includes a huge cast of strange characters who are caught up in the epic struggle between good and evil: 'The world is indeed full of peril, and in it there are many dark places; but still there is much that is fair, and though in all lands love is now mingled with grief, it grows perhaps the greater.'

The Lord of the Rings was finally published in three volumes from July 1954 to October 1955. The trio included *The Fellowship of the Ring, The Two Towers* and *The Return of the King.*

Although the initial reviews were mixed, the *Sunday Telegraph* called it 'among the greatest works of imaginative fiction in the twentieth century', and W.H. Auden marvelled at Tolkien's 'masterpiece',

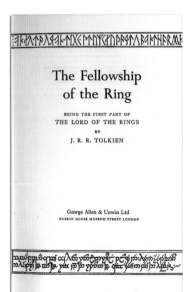

comparing it favourably to John Milton's *Paradise Lost.*

Over time, its popularity has increased, stimulated by movie adaptations, making it one of the best-selling novels of all time, with more than 150 million copies sold. It has been translated into at least thirty-eight languages. The original manuscripts, totalling 9,250 pages, are housed at Marquette University in Milwaukee.

In addition to its own success, *The Lord of the Rings* has given rise to a thriving gaming industry built on Tolkien-like world-building themes.

On the Road
Jack Kerouac
(1957)

The defining novel of the Beat Generation. Kerouac's almost-autobiographical voyage of discovery tells of the bonds and limits of friendship, of broken dreams and plans gone awry in postwar America.

After the turmoil of World War II, America settled down to a period of much-needed stability, reaping the benefits of victory and wartime industrial development in a booming peacetime economy. The focus was on steady jobs, prosperity and wholesome family units.

There was inevitable reaction to this conventional vision of white middle-class America. Authors such as Allen Ginsberg, William S. Burroughs and Neal Cassady sought greater meaning to life than mere material success. These voices of the Beat Generation felt that the bland conformity of postwar consumerism stultified the mind until it was beaten: Beat.

For Jack Kerouac (1922–69), another of the circle of Beat authors, being beaten down meant more – it reduced you to your core, an almost blissful state from which the only way was up. The Beat movement was not just the eternal rebellion of one generation against the previous one; it was a spiritual journey. In the 1940s Kerouac embarked on a series of road trips with Cassady, looking for another America and for a more spirited way of living. As he wrote to a student in 1961: 'It was really a story about two Catholic buddies roaming the country in search of God. And we found him.'

In 1950, Kerouac received a long, disjointed letter from Cassady that inspired him to develop what he called 'spontaneous prose'. Although he had already been trying to turn their trips into a novel, he now started again, telling his story in the literary equivalent of an improvised jazz solo, a stream of consciousness uninterrupted by paragraph breaks or new sheets of paper. He typed the first draft continuously on a scroll made by taping individual pages together to a length of 120 feet.

On the Road was finally published in 1957 after many revisions, including the fictionalisation of names and the removal of some sexually explicit episodes. Kerouac became Sal Paradise, Allen Ginsberg appeared as Carlo Marx, William S. Burroughs as Bull Lee, and Neal Cassady as Dean Moriarty.

In the book, Sal looks up to Dean, a wild, free spirit. Crisscrossing America in four trips, they meet a string of characters who prompt questions about class, race, conformity and change. But each journey, fuelled by alcohol, drugs and sex, is a little less carefree than the last. Dean, exciting as he is to be with, is not a reliable friend. When they part at the end, it is with little regret, and a sense that perhaps we all need to grow up, eventually.

Kerouac's new form of prose, the literary equivalent of an Impressionist painting, divided critics. Some hailed it as visionary, while others condemned it as a self-indulgent road to nowhere, a novel in which nothing really happened.

On the Road is groundbreaking in its style, the finest book of the Beat Generation, which laid the groundwork for the radical movements of the 1960s. It inspired Bob Dylan, Jim Morrison, Tom Waits, Hunter S. Thompson and many more, as well as films like *Easy Rider* and *Thelma and Louise*. Today, in a professionalised, over-regulated, overprotective world in which once again conformity and prosperity are the conventional goals, we can still be inspired by *On the Road*.

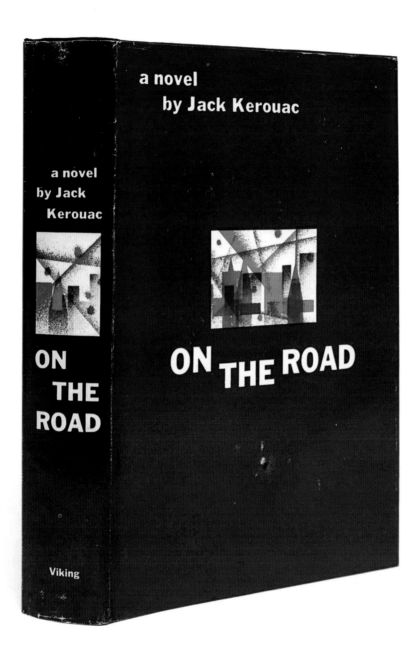

ABOVE: Theodor Giesel (Dr. Seuss), with an early edition of The Cat in
the Hat *– 'It is the book I'm proudest of because it had something to do
with the death of the Dick and Jane primers.' It was published under the
newly formed Beginner's Books imprint of Random House, which aimed
to provide books for children between the ages of three and nine.*

The Cat in the Hat
Dr. Seuss

(1957)

The book that broke the mould in young children's literature. Setting out to write an alternative to 'pallid primers with abnormally courteous, unnaturally clean boys and girls', Dr. Seuss gave us a world of fun seen through children's eyes.

Dr. Seuss (1904–91) was born Theodor Seuss Giesel, an American son of German immigrant stock. He adopted the title Dr. to please his parents, who had wanted him to study medicine, but his early career was as an illustrator of books, advertisements, and wartime propaganda. His first children's book, *And to Think That I Saw It on Mulberry Street,* was rejected by twenty publishers before getting into print in 1937.

Mulberry Street's title and text contain the trademark rhythm and rhyme that would reach their zenith in *The Cat in the Hat.* The rhythm is anapaestic tetrameter – four units of two unstressed syllables and one stressed one – much used by epic poets such as Byron and Browning to convey a dramatic, galloping mood. Its breathless pace also lends itself well to comedy.

Seuss wrote *The Cat in the Hat* in response to 1950s criticisms of the inadequate reading primers available to children at the time. The Dick and Jane series had been in use since the 1930s, and their simplistic, moralistic stories were neither remotely entertaining for children nor effective in teaching them to read. Seuss would later declare that *The Cat in the Hat* 'is the book I'm proudest of because it had something to do with the death of the Dick and Jane primers.'

Publisher William Spaulding gave Seuss a list of 348 words suitable for six- to seven-year-olds from which he should choose 225 with which to write a better primer. Frustrated by these limited options, Seuss decided that he would write a story about the first two words on

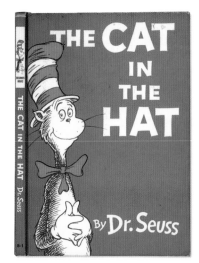

the list that rhymed. They were, of course, 'cat' and 'hat'. In the end he used 236 different words in the book.

The result was the irresistible tale of an anarchic cat in a red-and-white-striped top hat that arrives to brighten the lives of two children stuck at home on a rainy day. He brings giggle-inducing chaos and disorder to their afternoon; he juggles domestic items, including a rake and goldfish, and introduces Thing One and Thing Two, the children's reckless alter egos, who fly kites in the corridors. But when the children's laughter turns to anxiety about the mess they've made and the imminent return of their mother, he restores order and leaves.

The book has been analysed in absurd depth over the years. The disapproving goldfish, for example, has been seen as the joyless, puritanical streak in American culture, and the red-hatted cat and his red-romper-suited Things are the invasive anarchy of red communism in the McCarthyist United States of the 1950s. Today, we might see the cat as a nonconformist punk, twenty years ahead of his time.

Dr. Seuss certainly approved of him – his face is not unlike Seuss's, and the sorrowful expression he wears when he has to tidy up seems to express Seuss's own regret. The book has endured, and its simple rhythms and rhymes have proved effective in encouraging children to read for themselves. Above all, it is a testament to Seuss's ability to see the world through children's eyes, to understand more than Dick and Jane ever could what children find funny.

Things Fall Apart
Chinua Achebe
(1958)

As his country stood on the brink of gaining its independence from Great Britain, a Nigerian writer penned a masterpiece that would become a landmark in world literature – the first great African novel, told from an African's perspective, yet presented in the language of the colonial oppressor, about a former society undergoing radical cultural change.

Chinua Achebe (1930–2013) was an orphan who was raised by his grandfather in a part of Nigeria known as Igboland, which British colonists had occupied about forty-five years before he was born. He grew up exposed to two worlds – white Christian colonial culture and the traditional Igbo culture that had survived imperial British rule. While studying English literature at University College, Ibadan, Achebe was required to read works that dealt with African themes – Rudyard Kipling, Joseph Conrad and Joyce Cary – and came away appalled by the way they depicted his people. 'It began to dawn on me,' he later wrote, 'that although fiction was undoubtedly fictitious it could also be true or false, not with the truth or falsehood of a news item but as to its disinterestedness, its intention, its integrity.'

Thus, he embarked on an effort to write a novel about his homeland that would tell the truth from the perspective of the Africans who had been colonised. He crafted his work in a way that would help to reclaim his country's precolonial identity by setting his story in the days before his parents' birth, when Igboland was becoming colonised – when traditional village life was 'falling apart'.

The timing of his book coincided with Nigeria's official decolonisation from British rule, when, after centuries of being targeted by the slave trade and various forms of British control and influence, that part of West Africa was about to become an independent nation.

Without a single native language in which to tell his story, Achebe explained that he chose to write his

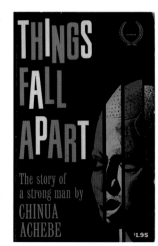

novel in English as a way of striking back at the culture that had forced that language 'down our throats'.

The book's first line transported its readers back to an earlier period of major change in which its characters would find themselves. 'Okonkwo was well known throughout the nine villages and even beyond', he wrote.

The narrator described Okonkwo's life in the village of Umuofia as it was being colonised by Christian missionaries. Rather than conforming to the stereotype of Africans that had been presented in previous novels written by whites, Achebe's protagonist was portrayed as a character with positive qualities – a hardworking man of honour who exhibited strength and pride.

Instead of presenting Western culture as enlightened and worldly, he depicted it as 'arrogant and ethnocentric', showing how the colonizers destroyed one local institution after another in order to extinguish the native culture.

Achebe's novel became widely embraced as the first major novel written by an African. Translated into fifty languages, it has sold more than ten million copies and been recognised as one of the most noteworthy books of twentieth-century literature. Its appearance blazed a trail for other African writers. Chimamanda Ngozi Adichie has credited his influence on her novels: 'Reading him emboldened me, gave me permission to write about the things I knew well.'

Achebe published several more books, and in 1990 he moved to the United States, where he taught at Bard College in Annandale-on-Hudson, New York, until his death in 2013.

ABOVE AND OPPOSITE: *The first UK edition (above) was published by Heinemann in 1958. A subtitle – 'The Story of a Strong Man' – was added to the first American edition of the novel (opposite), which was published the following year.*

To Kill a Mockingbird
Harper Lee

(1960)

The amazing success of her mesmerising first novel, about race and justice in a small Alabama town in the 1930s, propelled an unknown author to international fame and helped to inspire the civil rights movement and public defenders.

Harper Lee (1926–2016) grew up in tiny Monroeville, Alabama, close to her childhood friend, Truman Persons, aka Truman Capote (1924–84), and they both aspired to become full-time writers. When Capote travelled to Kansas to conduct the research for the article and book that would become *In Cold Blood*, the first 'non-fiction novel', she went along for support and as cover to muddle his image as a flaming gay eccentric. He already was an established author and a master of self-promotion.

In Cold Blood (1966) enjoyed remarkable success and brought him increased celebrity. Yet Lee's even greater success – a Pulitzer Prize and more copies sold – made him envious and deepened her tendency to both shun publicity and lack the will to publish more fiction. 'I was his oldest friend,' she later confided in a letter to a friend, 'and I did something Truman could not forgive: I wrote a novel that sold. He nursed his envy for more than twenty years.'

Lee had laboured for years on her first novel, living off the charity of friends and shovelling revisions to her editor at J.B. Lippincott, and the book's prospects to become a best-seller didn't seem very good. But *To Kill a Mockingbird* became a huge favourite with readers, required reading in schools and was later made into a blockbuster movie starring Gregory Peck.

Basing her book on characters and events in her old hometown, Lee told a story in the voice of a precocious six-year-old girl, Jean

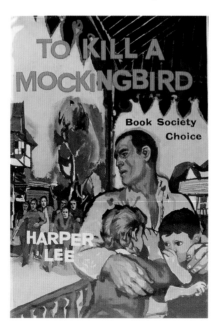

Louise Finch (Scout), who lives with her brother, Jem, and her widowed father, Atticus Finch, who is a lawyer in the small town. The story takes place from 1933 to 1935 and probes disturbing issues of race and justice in the Deep South, revolving around a case of alleged interracial rape that Atticus is called upon to defend.

Appearing at the dawn of the modern civil rights era in America, just as a rising generation of young people were starting to come of age, Lee's timing and treatment of a vexing and important social issue could not have been better. Its core theme of innocence resonated with readers and viewers. Many youths were inspired to enter the legal profession to be like Atticus Finch, or to become a writer like Harper Lee. The book has gone on to sell more than thirty million copies, and the motion picture remains a classic. It has also been one of the most controversial, due to its treatment of race and rape and its use of profanity, in the tradition of *Huckleberry Finn*.

In 2015, as Lee neared the end of her life, she published a second novel, *Go Set a Watchman*, which shocked readers by turning the iconic character of Atticus Finch, the great paragon of liberal values, into a bigot. In fact, it was her first novel, which had gone unpublished before *To Kill a Mockingbird*. The work, which some consider to be a first draft of *Mockingbird*, received mixed reviews.

Silent Spring
Rachel Carson

(1962)

A determined marine biologist and nature writer's shocking account of how pesticides were poisoning the environment elicited vicious personal attacks from the chemical industry. But her solid reporting and courageous example inspired a new environmental protection movement and led to sweeping reforms.

Rachel Carson (1907–64) was an unlikely American hero. An unmarried woman of modest means, who worked in a series of research positions and as editor for the US Fish and Wildlife Service, Carson achieved some success as a freelance writer, which enabled her to become a full-time author.

Over the years, she had become concerned about the rampant and largely unregulated use of synthetic chemical pesticides that had developed as an adjunct and after-use to wartime chemical production in World War I, World War II, the Korean conflict and the arms race. The use of toxic substances to eradicate pests was spearheaded by the US Department of Agriculture, which employed aerial spraying of pesticides over public and private land. In the course of her fish and wildlife studies, Carson became particularly concerned about the effects of a specific chemical insecticide, dichlorodiphenyltrichloroethane (DDT), a colourless, tasteless and almost odourless organochlorine that was being widely used to kill mosquitoes.

In January 1958, Carson read a letter to the editor that her friend Olga Owens Huckins had written to a Boston newspaper, decrying the death of birds, bees, grasshoppers and other creatures in her local nature sanctuary, which she continued to blame on recent spraying. Carson began researching the subject in earnest, gathering extensive evidence from scientists and government officials, some of which led her to medical sources that showed the effects of cancer-causing chemicals. Meanwhile, she became ill and underwent a mastectomy and other cancer treatments, yet she continued

to work on a book about the poisoning of the natural environment.

First serialised in *The New Yorker* magazine on June 16, 1962, and published in book format soon after by Houghton Mifflin, *Silent Spring* was embraced by scientists and conservationists. But the powerful chemical lobby mounted a brutal attack, which accused her of being a shoddy scientist. Former US Secretary of Agriculture Ezra Taft Benson said that because she was unmarried, despite being physically attractive, she was 'probably a communist'.

Although she was suffering from cancer, she appeared before a Senate subcommittee to testify about the need for laws to regulate harmful chemicals, prompting Senator Ernest Gruening of Alaska to comment: 'Every once in a while in the history of mankind, a book has appeared which has substantially altered the course of history.' Carson warned the human race: 'Our heedless and destructive acts enter into the vast cycles of the earth and in time return to bring hazard to ourselves.'

Silent Spring went on to sell more than two million copies, becoming recognised as one of the most consequential science books of all time and Carson was hailed as the most influential environmental writer since Henry David Thoreau. Her book spawned a revolution, but it did not end controversy: industrial forces have continued to denigrate her work and the ideas she championed, claiming that alarms about the effects of chemicals in air, water, soil and living organisms are overblown, and calling for cutbacks in environmental laws and regulations.

Carson died in 1964; she was fifty-seven.

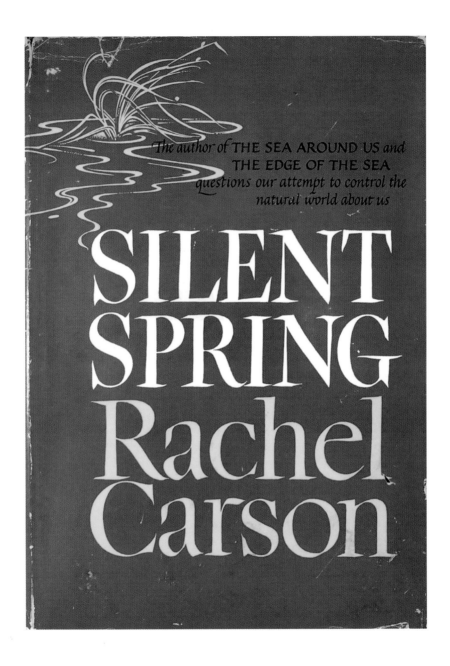

ABOVE: *The first edition of* Silent Spring. *The title was inspired by a John Keats poem, 'La Belle Dame sans Merci', with its suggestion of a barren future.*

OPPOSITE: *Rachel Carson with a copy of* Silent Spring. *Naturalist Sir David Attenborough rated* Silent Spring *as the most important scientific book after* On the Origin of Species *by Charles Darwin.*

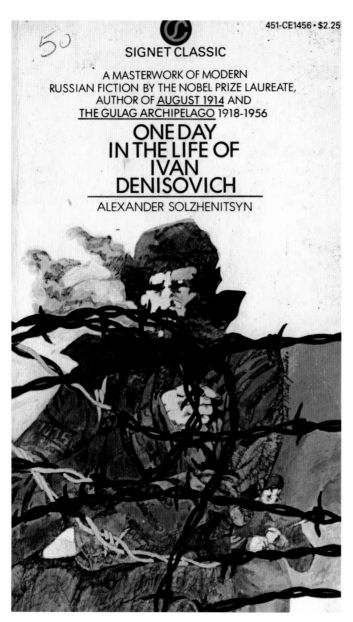

ABOVE: The US (left) and UK (top right) editions, both published in 1963. Solzhenitsyn as a prisoner in the Ekibastuz labour camp (right) that inspired One Day in the Life of Ivan Denisovich. *The impact of his novel was underlined by writer Vitaly Korotich: 'The Soviet Union was destroyed by information – and this wave started from Solzhenitsyn's* One Day.' *Solzhenitsyn was expelled from the Soviet Writers' Union in 1969 and awarded the Nobel Prize for Literature the following year.*

One Day in the Life of Ivan Denisovich
Alexsander Solzhenitsyn

(1962)

A Nobel Prize–winning indictment of the totalitarian state. Solzhenitsyn's description of Soviet life in a forced labour camp stemmed from personal experience. More than most, this book changed the world about which it was written.

Alexsander Solzhenitsyn (1918–2008) was a serving officer in the Soviet army during World War II. He was arrested in 1945 and sentenced to eight years in the gulags – secret labour camps. His crime had been writing private letters to a friend that were critical of Stalin's conduct of the war against Germany. He was charged under Section Fifty-Eight of the Soviet penal code, by which almost any action could be classified as a crime against the state. After his release from prison he was sent into external exile in Kazakhstan, but following Stalin's death and Khrushchev's policy of de-Stalinisation of the USSR, he was allowed back to Moscow in 1956, where he began to write *One Day in the Life of Ivan Denisovich.*

The day in question is just one of the 3,653 that Ivan Denisovich will serve as part of his ten-year sentence in a labour camp, his crime under Section Fifty-Eight being that he allowed himself to be taken prisoner by the German army. The novella describes Ivan Denisovich's waking hours in twenty-four parts, alternating between episodes in his day and more philosophical consideration of the brutality of the Soviet criminal system.

The camp's regime is harsh, cruel, and physically and mentally punishing. Although there is cooperation and even kindness among the fellow prisoners in Ivan Denisovich's work team, the 104th, nevertheless, the guiding principle is survival of the fittest. Ivan Denisovich gets by through hard work and small rewards for helping other prisoners. He must conceal a bonus ration of bread by sewing it into his mattress, and his kindest act of the day is to give a whole biscuit to a fellow convict.

The book is a measured, understated description of the struggle to retain human dignity in the face of perpetual and unjust punishment. Cruelty is routine; privacy and individuality is denied to the two dozen men of the 104th, most of them convicted under the catch-all Section Fifty-Eight.

Solzhenitsyn can surely not have imagined that it would ever be published in his totalitarian home country. And yet in 1962 he submitted it to Moscow's leading literary journal, *Novy Mir* (*New World*). More surprising still, its editor recognised its merit and asked the Communist Party for permission to publish. It is said that Khrushchev himself gave the go-ahead, seeing an opportunity to discredit Stalin's legacy. The impact of *One Day in the Life* was immediate and cathartic. It was the first-ever public acknowledgement of the existence of the gulags, of which Soviet citizens dared not speak and of which the wider world knew nothing.

Solzhenitsyn's novel became a sensation, but when Khrushchev fell from power in 1964, his Stalinist enemies came out of the woodwork and began to dismantle his reforms. Attempts were made to discredit Solzhenitsyn, and even to poison him, and his subsequent novels were published only in the West. In 1970 he was awarded the Nobel Prize for Literature, and the citation specifically mentioned *One Day in the Life.*

In 1974, Solzhenitsyn was arrested and deported to West Germany. He settled eventually in the United States, returning to Russia only after the dissolution of the USSR – a political collapse set in motion, via Gorbachev's perestroika, by the revelations of *One Day in the Life of Ivan Denisovich.*

The Feminine Mystique
Betty Friedan
(1963)

The Feminine Mystique is a foundation stone in the second wave of feminism. At the time of its publication, the backlash alone was enough to show that Betty Friedan had hit her mark.

The first wave of feminism, the suffragette era, fought for the rights of women to own property and vote. The third, beginning in the 1990s, deconstructed feminism, recognising its successes and failures to date. It focuses on diversity and individuality among women concerning sexuality, race, religion and culture. The crucial second wave, addressing women's rights at home, in the workplace and over their bodies, began in 1963 with the publication of Betty Friedan's book *The Feminine Mystique*.

Betty Friedan (1921–2006) walked away from a PhD and a promising career in journalism to raise a family – she was fired when she became pregnant with her second child. But by the 1950s she was beginning to feel stirrings of dissatisfaction with her domesticated life. When she surveyed her fellow female alumni at a college reunion, she found the same vague unhappiness among women who, according to society at large, had lives of perfect domestic bliss.

The results of that survey formed the basis of *The Feminine Mystique*. The 'mystique', she argued, had been created by media and advertisers, who portrayed women as unemployed, undereducated wives, mothers and sex bombs. Women were being defined by their biology alone, while men had their pick of roles in society.

Women were encouraged by advertising images to see their housekeeping role as a job, for which manufacturers and advertisers offered the tools. The impression was given in magazine articles that overeducated women would be too unfeminine to be attractive to men. Instead, they were given an ideal of attraction: the slim, dumb blonde – which, incidentally, doubly discriminated against black women.

As a consequence, women got married sooner, and had more children, for fear of being left on the shelf. Yet they were not happy in their role. In *The Feminine Mystique*, Friedan urged women to find happiness and fulfilment beyond the home in the larger community. In particular, she argued for their increased involvement in politics. 'We can no longer ignore that voice within women that says: "I want something more than my husband and my children and my home."'

The book had an immediate impact. Within a year the United States introduced equal pay legislation, and in the first twelve months of publication *The Feminine Mystique* sold more than a million copies. A backlash followed. It introduced many white middle-class women to feminism, but prompted complaints that Friedan had neglected other sectors of society. Women who were happy in their domestic roles complained that they were being unfairly painted as being dissatisfied with their lot. Men attacked her theories as pseudoscience and her writing as too strident.

In the decade that followed, Betty Friedan was directly involved in the founding of the National Organization for Women, the National Association for the Repeal of Abortion Laws and the National Women's Political Caucus – three organisations that still work for women today.

THE
FEMININE
MYSTIQUE

BETTY FRIEDAN

"I found *The Feminine Mystique* absorbingly interesting, pertinent, relevant to my own problems and those of every woman I know, and far and away more real, truer and more moving than Simone de Beauvoir's *The Second Sex*. Betty Friedan has both grasp and passion—and has put her finger on the inner wound we all carry around. But to name the suffering is relatively easy. What Mrs. Friedan has done is to show both cause and cure. The book should be read by every anxious woman in the country, and all of us are troubled about ourselves and where we belong. She has done a great service in underlining the fact that *before* we are women, we are human beings."
—*Virgilia Peterson*

ABOVE AND OPPOSITE: The first edition (above) and a June 1963 advertisement (opposite) from the New York Times, *promoting the seventh printing: 'Mrs. Friedan swings a cool and sharp-edged axe at the dolls' houses that all too many of her countrywomen have been conned into occupying almost a century after Ibsen's Nora slammed the door on hers.'*

LEFT: *The interior and red vinyl cover of an original 1964 edition. The embossed red star, a common symbol of Communism, is said to represent the five fingers of the worker's hand or the five social groups (workers, youth, peasants, military and academics).*

OPPOSITE: *Later editions include the now-iconic portrait of Mao.*

Quotations from Chairman Mao Tse-tung

(1964)

At its height, *Quotations from Chairman Mao Tse-tung* was the most widely printed book in the world. Mao's 'Little Red Book' became almost accidentally a sacred text as the cult of his personality gripped the Chinese nation. It fell from favour after Mao's death but remains highly quotable in both the East and West.

Quotations from Chairman Mao began life, like so many books, as a newspaper column, a motivational 'thought for the day' in the *People's Liberation Army Daily* in the early 1960s. Two hundred 'thoughts' were compiled in a small book for those attending a conference in the first days of 1964. After a series of revisions and expansions, the final version contained 427 quotations from Mao Tse-tung (1893–1976), chairman of the Communist Party of China (CPC) and the country's guiding revolutionary light since 1949, when he proclaimed the People's Republic.

Topics ranged from the Communist Party ('We must have faith in the masses and we must have faith in the Party') to 'education' ('Our attitude towards ourselves should be "to be insatiable in learning" and towards others "to be tireless in teaching"'), via 'arduous struggle', 'self-criticism' and twenty-nine other headings. The book was originally intended to bolster the resolve of the People's Liberation Army (PLA), on whom Mao had relied heavily to suppress dissent during his disastrous Great Leap Forward drive towards industrialisation in the 1950s.

In 1965, anticipating the launch of the Cultural Revolution the following year, Mao began to distribute the book to all non-military Chinese too. It was a fantastically ambitious programme; the population at the time was in the region of 740 million. The Chinese print industry was stretched to the limit and faced frequent shortages of paper and ink. It became known in the West as the 'Little Red Book' because the most

common edition, designed to fit into a soldier's pocket, was small with a red vinyl cover.

As the book spread in availability, it became at first popular, then advisable, then compulsory to know its contents well. Quotations were painted onto banners, walls and cliffs, and cited at every opportunity in casual conversation and official documents. The book became an icon, held aloft by chanting guards or clutched in propaganda posters by Chinese children. It is impossible to get an accurate figure of the numbers printed, but estimates range from two to six billion, far more than the population of China alone, in nearly forty languages.

The book's power as the sole source of political truth in the country is impossible to overstate. In the radical 1960s, it was also taken up by alternative cultures in the West. But following Mao's death in 1976, the practice of quoting from it began to fall into disuse.

Mao's achievements in modernising his country cannot be ignored, and it is no small irony that quotations from his Little Red Book have been used by the capitalist West in manuals for business success. Although China's politics have softened over the decades, there are still many Maoists within the CPC. A new expanded edition of *Quotations of Chairman Mao Tse-tung* was published in 2014 on the fiftieth anniversary of its launch. Some commentators believe it was something of a weather balloon to test the conditions for a return to a stricter regime. But perhaps, with China's economy booming, Mao's work is done.

One Hundred Years of Solitude
Gabriel García Márquez
(1967)

A masterpiece of magic realism, Márquez's history of a fictional South American town has a universal message about progress and decay. In Márquez's imagination, time can be both fast and slow, linear and cyclical. Memory is as burdensome as forgetfulness, but those who do not learn from their mistakes are doomed to repeat them.

The 1960s saw the entry of Latin American literature onto the world stage. It was characterised by the use of magic realism, the creation of naturalistic worlds in which fantastic, magical events were possible. This literary form perfectly captured the condition of South America at the time, caught between the invasion of modern industrialisation and potent native traditions in which myth was an alternative reality.

One Hundred Years of Solitude tells the story of a small Colombian town, Macondo, and seven generations of the Buendia family, who founded it. The qualities of strength and wisdom that established Macondo are diluted in each successive generation, until neither its descendants nor the town are recognisable. Time comes full circle as the latter disappears and the former revert to an animal state.

In *One Hundred Years of Solitude* Gabriel García Márquez (1927–2014) uses magic realism, which he described as 'outsize reality', to toy with our perceptions. He writes convincing descriptions of poverty, for example, but within that squalid world, can a child really be born with a pig's tail? Did a priest really levitate? He toys with time, too. Children grow up quickly, but for adults time stands painfully still, and plagues of insomnia or rainfall may last many years.

Márquez further challenges our grip on reality by using only a handful of first names for the Buendias, which recur in each generation. This confuses our sense of time passing, and reinforces two central themes of the novel. First, the mere passage of time does not necessarily imply progress, when even the names remain the same, and second, by passing on only their own names, the isolated Buendias are shown to be always inward looking, never engaging with the wider community or the outside world. The words 'solitude' or 'solitary' occur on almost every page of the novel.

Macondo descends into dictatorship. While *One Hundred Years of Solitude* is rooted in South America, the moral and physical collapse of Macondo mirrors the decline of other civilisations, notably ancient Greece, and serves as a warning to us all. Modernity without ethics is not progress.

The name Macondo has entered the language of many Latin American countries as a byword for a place where extraordinary news events happen, or for one's own slightly quirky hometown. Chilean refugees in Vienna, Austria, fleeing the dictator Pinochet in the 1970s, named their refugee settlement Macondo. Their descendants, and refugees from other regimes, live there still.

At its publication in 1967, it was immediately applauded as the greatest novel in the Spanish language since *Don Quixote*. The first English translation was published in 1970, and since then it has topped lists of world literature and received many awards, the highest being the 1982 Nobel Prize for Literature. Its influence has been widespread. V.S. Naipaul, Toni Morrison and Salman Rushdie, for example, all owe Márquez a debt for outsizing their reality, and ours.

RIGHT: The first edition (top left), published in 1967 by Editorial Sudamericana, Buenos Aires; the first English-language edition (top right), published in 1970 by Harper & Row, New York; and a 1975 photo of Márquez (bottom) with another South American edition of One Hundred Years *on his head.*

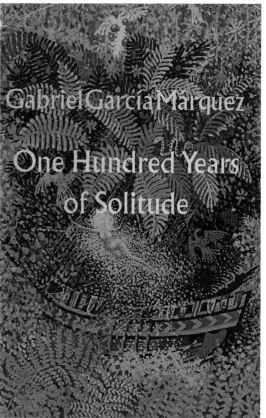

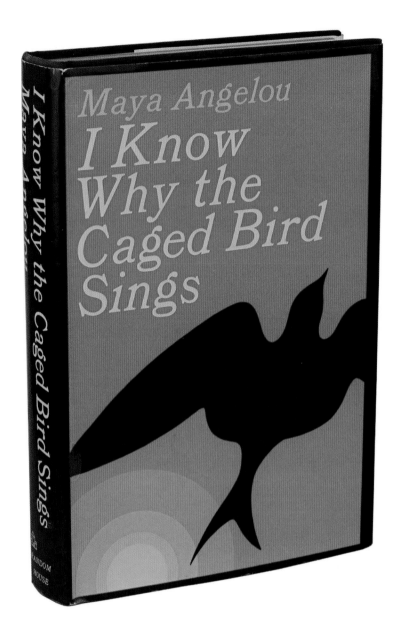

ABOVE AND OPPOSITE: *The original Random House hardback edition (above)
and the Bantam Press paperback (opposite), subtitled 'The Moving and
Beautiful Autobiography of a Talented Black Woman'.*

196_____100 Books that Changed the World

I Know Why the Caged Bird Sings
Maya Angelou

(1969)

Rejection and determination, prejudice and triumph. The first of seven volumes of Angelou's autobiography takes her from infancy to young motherhood. Its frank retelling of incidents of racism and abuse have made it an essential element of many reading lists but have also seen it banned from others.

In the 1960s Maya Angelou (1928–2014) was a successful poet and playwright and an active campaigner for civil rights for African-Americans. She had worked with both Malcolm X and Martin Luther King Jr., only to see both of them assassinated – Malcolm in 1965 and MLK on April 4, 1968, her fortieth birthday. Both deaths threw her into depression, and it was in an attempt to lift her out of it that her friend James Baldwin suggested she write a literary autobiography – one approached with the sensibilities of a novelist rather than simply a chronological narration of history.

I Know Why the Caged Bird Sings was the result. It took its title from a verse by the poet Paul Laurence Dunbar, and was written with a poet's feel for the power of words. Indeed, one of the book's themes is the redemptive power of poetry and drama in the young Maya's life. She discovers Shakespeare while growing up in a segregated Southern town; and after being struck dumb by guilt at having lied in court, she regains her voice by reading literature out loud.

Instead of ordering the key events by time, Angelou uses episodes at a point in the book where they will have the greatest impact. So an incident of racial abuse experienced by the ten-year-old Maya occurs earlier in the book than her traumatic sexual abuse and rape by her mother's boyfriend when she was eight. In this way, Angelou regains control over events, which at the time she was helpless to prevent, by making them serve her purpose now. The narrative thrust of the book is the determination with

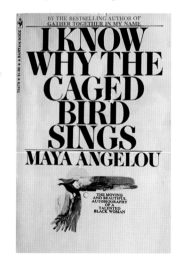

which Maya does take control of her life. It is in one sense a series of lessons in how to resist oppression, both as a woman and as an African-American. It is therefore a triumphant book. Speaking of her mother, she says, 'She comprehended the perversity of life, that in the struggle lies the joy.'

Maya becomes San Francisco's first African-American tram ticket collector by persistent badgering of a racist employment clerk; and *Caged Bird* ends with the birth of her only son, the result of her decision to try sex with a teenage classmate. Although neither particularly pleasurable nor exciting, it is a positive choice, unlike the earlier rape. Maya overcomes her experiences of both sexual and racial abuse by sheer strength of character. As she writes: 'You may encounter many defeats, but you must not be defeated.'

The book was an immediate best-seller, at a time when women's liberation and black equality were high on the radical agenda. Its success validated the experiences of women and blacks, who had hitherto been marginalised. Angelou's graphic descriptions of sex, sexuality and racism have led to the book being banned from some libraries and schools. But those descriptions are the same reasons why it is often included in syllabuses, either in its own right or as a companion piece to other books dealing with similar issues. *I Know Why the Caged Bird Sings* speaks of the shameful African-American experience of the 1930s and 1940s and is therefore relevant reading for people of all colours.

Ways of Seeing
John Berger
(1972)

Ways of Seeing is a pivotal work of art criticism and feminism. Berger made a connection between the context in which we view art and the way in which it is made, and changed the way we look at paintings, especially those depicting women.

Artist, art teacher, art critic, novelist, playwright, essayist, poet – John Berger (1926–2017) was a man of many parts, most of which were on show to good effect in 1972. In January that year he presented a BBC television series in the UK, *Ways of Seeing*, and in December he received the second of two major prizes for his experimental novel *G.* In between he found time to write seven essays containing the ideas expressed in the television programmes, which were then published as a book of the same name.

Berger's sociopolitical way of looking at art transformed our way of seeing. His *Ways of Seeing* chimed with the radical, left-wing thinking of the late 1960s and early 1970s. He was himself a committed Marxist: an early collection of his essays was titled *Permanent Red*, and the cover of his 1972 novel *G.* was plain red with white lettering. He donated half of the Booker Prize money he won for *G.* to the British Black Panther movement.

Ways of Seeing is a series of philosophical discussions about how we view fine art. The 'seeing' that Berger refers to is both the way in which the artist approaches his subject and the way the viewer considers the work of art thus produced. It is a relatively short book, which draws on several existing theories as well as his own, presenting them in a simplified, readable way. It is still an essential read for students of both art and social or political studies.

Berger argues that an artist's perception is based on the beliefs and values of his time. So, for example, medieval artists painted hell as a place in flames because that was what people thought it was. Other scenes are also painted in particular ways depending on the cultural values of the age. Still-life compositions become not merely objects but lavish displays of luxury, wealth and ownership.

Portraits, which, after all, were often painted to please the patriarchs who commissioned them, are also intended to convey ownership – of title, of place in society, of family. Figures in allegorical, biblical paintings do so with apparent piety, but do so nevertheless. Berger takes time to consider the nude in painting, particularly the female nude. He notes the semantic difference between the words 'naked' and 'nude' – the one meaning merely not wearing any clothes, the other being seen to be naked; the one the state of simply being without costume, the other of becoming one's costume.

Most classical painters depict idealised forms of nude women, which often looked not at other figures in the composition but out of the painting at the viewer – in the first instance the man who commissioned the painting, the owner. Berger suggests that women have learned to look at themselves as the paintings' owners did, from a man's point of view, rather than a woman's. He states: 'Men look at women. Women watch themselves being looked at. This determines not only most relations between men and women but also the relation of women to themselves.'

Modern advertising, he concludes, works in the same way, imposing a male ideal on images of women and objects, which is concerned with ownership, not reality. If beauty is in the eye of the beholder, John Berger encourages us to look beyond the oil paint to understand the context of that beauty for the artist, the patron and the modern viewer.

RIGHT: Ways of Seeing, *based on John Berger's BBC television series of the same name, argued that when we see paintings, photographs and graphic art, we are not just looking, we are reading the language of images.*

WAYS OF SEEING

Based on the BBC television series with

JOHN BERGER

Seeing comes before words. The child looks and recognizes before it can speak.

But there is also another sense in which seeing comes before words. It is seeing which establishes our place in the surrounding world; we explain that world with words, but words can never undo the fact that we are surrounded by it. The relation between what we see and what we know is never settled.

The Surrealist painter Magritte commented on this always-present gap between words and seeing in a painting called The Key of Dreams.

The way we see things is affected by what we

ABOVE: The subtitle of the original hardback edition, published by Morrow in 1974, was 'An Inquiry into Values'. The 1976 Corgi paperback, shown here, replaced the subtitle with a more direct claim.

Zen and the Art of Motorcycle Maintenance
Robert M. Pirsig
(1974)

Popular psychology for the post-hippie age. Pirsig's semi-autobiographical, era-defining novel weighs up different approaches to enlightenment from the back of a Honda Superhawk motorcycle, during a road trip from Minnesota to the West Coast. It was the right book, in the right place, at the right time.

Seventeen years after Jack Kerouac's *On the Road*, Robert Pirsig's *Zen and the Art of Motorcycle Maintenance* found another author on another road trip, looking for answers in a very different America. The 1960s – the laid-back, drug-fuelled destination of Kerouac's generation – had ended violently at the 1969 Altamont Speedway Free Festival and in the social unrest of civil rights movements.

In a more serious world, the sudden need for the flower children of the 1960s to adapt to the 1970s left many at a philosophical loss. Hippies opposed the industrialisation and militarism of the 1970s, which carried on without them. Musically adrift between flower power and punk, awash with second-wave heavy rock, bubblegum pop and soulless disco, their philosophy of 'living in the moment' no longer seemed adequate.

It was this sense of spiritual inadequacy that Robert Pirsig (1928–2017) explored in *Motorcycle Maintenance*. The book fictionalises a seventeen-day journey made in 1968 by Pirsig and his son Christopher in the company of another couple, the Sutherlands. The Sutherlands took a romantic approach to life and to motorcycle maintenance. They lived for the moment, accepting what life threw at them; if their bike broke down they would simply call a mechanic. Pirsig, on the other hand, perpetually tinkered with his bike to ensure that it ran smoothly and did not break down in the first place.

The book contrasts the irrational style of the Sutherlands, who seek a passive, transcendent enlightenment, with Pirsig's approach – as a philosophy lecturer he sought to understand the workings of the mind in the same way that he understood motorcycle maintenance. Pirsig tried to reconcile these two schools of thought – the 1960s and the 1970s, the passive and the active, the instinctive and the learned – in a situation that he likened to the American Civil War: 'Two worlds growingly alienated and hateful towards each other, with everyone wondering if it will always be this way, a house divided against itself.' He was attempting to do no less than unite Eastern and Western philosophies. 'It's so big,' he acknowledged. 'That's why I seem to wander sometimes.'

The split in thought was mirrored in Pirsig himself. Diagnosed years earlier with schizophrenia, he had undergone several bouts of electroconvulsive therapy that had affected his memory, cutting him off from his earlier self. Pirsig describes this therapy in the book, and his journey is also an attempt to reunify his two halves – personified in *Zen and the Art of Motorcycle Maintenance* by the novel's nameless narrator and a ghost called Phaedrus.

The book alternates between philosophical meditations and a more straightforward travelogue of the party's experiences of America on the road. It was, Pirsig claimed, rejected by 121 different publishers before finding one who recommended it to his board with these words: 'This book is brilliant beyond belief, it is probably a work of genius, and will, I'll wager, attain classic stature.' It sold a million copies in its first year. Since cultural shifts between decades and the resulting spiritual dislocation happen on a fairly regular basis (about every ten years), Robert Pirsig's *Zen and the Art of Motorcycle Maintenance* seems certain to run and run with very little tinkering.

A Brief History of Time
Stephen Hawking
(1988)

A Brief History of Time offered big science without the equations. Subtitled 'From the Big Bang to Black Holes', Hawking's attempt to explain the universe and everything in it to nonscientists has been hugely successful, selling around twenty million copies to date. It's a colossal achievement for a man whose own time has not, mercifully, been as brief as expected.

Stephen Hawking (born 1942) was diagnosed at the age of twenty-one with motor neuron disease. It slowly paralyses the body, and Hawking was expected to live for only another two years. Now well into his seventies, Hawking continues to write, deliver public lectures and make regular guest appearances on popular TV series such as *The Big Bang Theory*, *Star Trek: The Next Generation*, and *Futurama*. His electronically generated 'voice' is instantly recognisable, controlled by a muscle in his cheek.

A Brief History of Time was his first book. In it Hawking sets himself the ambitious task of explaining cosmology to ordinary readers: how the universe began, how it works, and how it may end. First he takes a historical look at how our perceptions of the universe have changed over the few millennia that we have been part of it. The history of space is the history of the time that has elapsed since the Big Bang, and Hawking deals with the nature of three kinds of time in an expanding universe – four if you count imaginary time. Later editions of the book even discuss the possibility of time travel.

Not content with leading us through the infinitely large, Hawking also tackles the smallest particles in space, the many colours and flavours of quarks and anti-quarks that are the building blocks of matter. And finally, concerning the two scientific theories that apply to the cosmos – quantum mechanics and general relativity – he considers the possibility of one big theory that might unify them both and explain everything.

'What did God do,' he asks, 'before He created the universe?' St. Augustine was asked this and replied that there was no 'before', since God invented time only as a property of the universe. It's a little too evasive for Hawking. As if all the science were not enough, he asks the big philosophical questions, too, although he comes out unapologetically as an atheist. Scientists, he writes, are too busy explaining it all to ask 'Why?' and philosophers are too wrapped up in the whys and wherefores to keep up with the science. So in a sense Hawking is also looking for a unifying theory for philosophy and science.

Hawking's publisher rejected the first draft that he submitted. It was a much more technical work, and as the publisher pointed out, every equation that he included (and there were many) would halve Hawking's readership. Nobody wants to read mathematics. In the published version, helpful diagrams abound, and Hawking removed all but one equation, Einstein's famous $E=mc^2$.

In 2005 he worked with popular science author Leonard Mlodinow on *A Briefer History of Time*, a shortened version of the original. The full-length 1988 book remained on the best-seller lists for five years after its publication. Stephen Hawking, recognised since the 1970s as a brilliant scientist, was now applauded as a great ambassador for science. He introduced millions of nonscientists to the biggest science of all, and to some philosophy, too.

RIGHT: The first edition of A Brief History of Time, *which remained on the London* Sunday Times *best-seller list for five years. Hawking's succinct, entertaining and lucid text introduced readers to wormholes, spiral galaxies and superstring theory.*

A BRIEF HISTORY OF TIME

FROM THE BIG BANG TO BLACK HOLES

STEPHEN W. HAWKING

INTRODUCTION BY CARL SAGAN

The Satanic Verses
Salman Rushdie

(1988)

The most controversial novel of modern times. Its admirable qualities as a work of magic realism are still overshadowed by its perceived offences against Islam and the resulting threats, injuries and deaths. Its author still has a price on his head.

Salman Rushdie (born 1947) had his first success with his second novel, *Midnight's Children*, which won both the Booker Prize and the James Tait Black Memorial Prize in 1981. The publication of his fourth, *The Satanic Verses*, was eagerly anticipated.

When it appeared in the UK in February 1988, it was a monumental work – 550 pages of extraordinary magic realism. The story follows two Indian actors who survive a plane crash and are changed into an angel and a demon. Rushdie uses their different experiences of arrival in England to explore themes of immigration, racism and Indian identity.

They and several other characters undergo transformation or reincarnation, either genuinely or in the minds of others, and the author implies that illusion, delusion and dreams are as important to the human experience as reality is. Doubt about what is real makes us ask questions, and so we grow. Lack of doubt, or an excess of unquestioning faith, leads to ignorance and a corruption of personal beliefs. This is at the heart of Rushdie's magic realism.

Throughout *The Satanic Verses* there is a second storyline about a religion called Submission, of which both actors are followers. Parallel narratives follow the founding of Submission and the modern-day crises of faith of the actors in secular England. Submission is a thinly veiled disguise for Islam, a word that translates as 'submission' in English. The book's title and a passage within it refer to a disputed episode in the life of Muhammad (or, in the novel, Mahound). The prophet is supposed to have been fooled by the devil into including verses into the Quran that advocated worshipping three goddesses. Muhammad later realised his mistake and removed the verses. Islam worships only one god, and strict Muslims believe that the verses in question must be the work of unbelievers. For them, Rushdie's use of the title suggested that the Quran was a devilish book.

Other elements of the book were also open to interpretation as blasphemy, and some were quick to cry heresy. India banned Rushdie's novel in October 1988, and the first organised book-burning took place in Bolton, Lancashire, in December. In February 1989, after a large demonstration against Rushdie in Islamabad, Pakistan, Iran's spiritual leader Ayatollah Khomeini issued a fatwa – a call for Muslims everywhere to kill the author and anyone knowingly associated with the book's publication.

While a verbal battle raged between authors and religious leaders of all beliefs about the rights and limits to free speech, very real violence was conducted in the name of the fatwa. Bookshops were bombed; publishers were threatened and attacked. In 1991, Hitoshi Igarashi, the translator of the Japanese edition, was stabbed to death. Rushdie himself went into hiding, guarded twenty-four hours a day by Britain's security forces.

Although there have been several attempts to diffuse the situation, the fatwa remains in place because only the person who declared it can rescind it – and Khomeini died in June 1989. A bounty of $2.8 million is still on offer, and almost any news item about Salman Rushdie is greeted with renewed calls for his death. Sales of *The Satanic Verses*, which had been relatively slow by the end of 1988, soared after the declaration of the fatwa, and the book is now Viking Penguin's all-time best-seller.

LEFT: *When published in 1988,* The Satanic Verses *met with favourable reviews, was shortlisted for the Booker Prize and won the Whitbread Award. In 1989, at the height of* The Satanic Verses *controversy, or Rushdie Affair, a fatwa was issued by the Ayatollah Khomeini of Iran ordering Muslims to kill Rushdie.*

Maus
Art Spiegelman
(1991)

Using interviews with his father as a starting point, Spiegelman found a new way to write about the Holocaust, and with it the graphic novel came of age. This genre-defying book is now a modern masterpiece.

The term 'graphic novel' was coined in 1964, but cartoons and comic strips have been compiled into book form since the early nineteenth century. In the twentieth century, superhero stories and fantasy tales took the genre in new directions, thanks to the likes of Stan Lee, and from the 1970s Raymond Briggs drew more philosophical novels about the humdrum lives of his characters.

Maus, however, took the graphic novel to a new level. It has been subjected to serious academic debate about its form, its content, and its style. It captures real, horrific events in history by focusing largely on the painful memories of one man, portraying difficult intimacy and wholesale inhumanity with equal power. Its overriding theme is guilt.

Maus describes one Jewish Pole's experience of the Nazi Holocaust. It is a true story. The man, who survived Auschwitz, is Art Spiegelman's father, Vladek, and his memories are framed by modern scenes in which Spiegelman (born 1948) interviews his father in order to capture his wartime memories for inclusion in *Maus*. These interview scenes are further framed by a meta-narrative in which Spiegelman wrestles with how to use the material that he has gathered in the interviews.

Spiegelman explores guilt in several ways. There is the obvious but unfelt guilt of the Nazis who ran the concentration camps. Art's relationship with his father is not an easy one, and Art feels guilty for not being a better son. He also feels guilt at not being able to do his father's story justice. Vladek too bears some guilt, for having burned the invaluable wartime diaries of Art's

mother after she committed suicide in 1968 – something Art also feels responsible for.

Art and Vladek both experience survivor guilt – Vladek because so many of his fellow Jews died, and Art because his older brother was killed in the war, before Art was born. Art suffers further guilt about having had such an easy life compared to his parents and about how he should feel about the Holocaust, which happened before he was even alive.

Spiegelman presents the Jews in *Maus* as mice ('maus' is the German for 'mouse') and the Germans as cats – a reference to the Nazis' intention to eradicate the Jews like vermin. The different species are a powerful metaphor for separations of class and race in Nazi Germany. Racism is perpetuated in one modern scene: Vladek, the victim of Nazi racism, is furious because Art picks up a black hitchhiker one day.

Spiegelman originally published *Maus* in magazine instalments between 1980 and 1991. In book form it first appeared in two parts, in 1987 and 1991. It has the literary depth of a classic novel, and the graphic skills of a master draughtsman, and there was much confusion about how to classify the book and where to shelve it in bookstores. It was art, biography, autobiography, history, memoir and comic book. The book industry only adopted the category 'graphic novel' in 2001, and when Spiegelman won a Pulitzer Prize for *Maus* in 1991, they avoided classification by giving it a 'special award'. This special book, which has now been translated into more than thirty languages, continues to move and provoke.

ABOVE AND OPPOSITE: Maus, *which was published in two volumes, in 1987 and 1991, went on to become the first graphic novel to win a Pulitzer Prize.*

"A terrific read and a stunning first novel" *Wendy Cooling*

Harry Potter and the Philosopher's Stone
J.K. Rowling
(1997)

The book that got children reading again. Author Joanne Rowling changed her name to J.K. because her publishers thought that boys preferred male authors. To date, some 400 million boys, girls and grown-up men and women have bought copies of the book and its six sequels.

Can there be anyone who hasn't either read the book or seen the movie? The ubiquitous success of *Harry Potter and the Philosopher's Stone* has launched a global industry of films, books and merchandise worth an estimated $15 billion, and earned its author J.K. Rowling (born 1965) a personal fortune of around $1 billion. Renamed *Harry Potter and the Sorcerer's Stone* for publication in the US, it stayed at number one in the *New York Times* fiction list for nearly a year in 1998. Its run only ended when the newspaper split the list into adult and children's fiction, at the request of adult fiction publishers who wanted their books to have a chance of being number one.

Harry Potter is an orphaned boy who discovers that he was born a wizard when he is admitted to Hogwarts School of Witchcraft and Wizardry at the age of eleven. *Harry Potter and the Philosopher's Stone* follows the exciting events of his first year at the school. In particular, he must thwart the evil Lord Voldemort, who murdered his parents and wants to steal the magical Philosopher's Stone, the source of eternal life and unlimited wealth.

On the surface, the book is a fast-paced thriller about the prevention of a crime. Its phenomenal success is in the richness of its underlying themes, all of universal concern to young people, and quite a few older ones too. The importance of friends and family pervades all seven books and is introduced from the very start with the contrast between Harry's unpleasant foster parents and his mother, who saved his life by giving hers out of love. Many of his teachers at Hogwarts are important father figures. The circle of close friends that he makes at the school, notably Hermione and Ron, give him strength and support in all his adventures.

Harry enjoys success and popularity at school, as any child wants to, but is always modest about his achievements. He obeys the school's strict but sensible rules, unless there is a strong and selfless reason for breaking them. Humility and submission to authority are generally good things, but one should always do one's best and think for oneself about the right course of action. Power in the forms of spells and potions is useful when exercised selflessly, but in the service of greed at the hands of Voldemort, it is dangerous.

The novel does have a dark strand, and it is death. Rowling's characters spend much time debating it philosophically. It is part of the cycle of life. As Harry's headmaster Professor Dumbledore says near the end of book, 'Death is but the next great adventure.' Harry's mother's love prevents his death, and the desire to defeat death is what drives Voldemort, whose very name means 'flight from [or of] death', but his attempts to achieve immortality without love are at great personal cost.

Harry Potter and the Philosopher's Stone prompted protests from religious conservatives around the world who feared that it promoted black magic. But it displays very clearly the sense that children possess good and bad qualities. The battle between good and evil, between Harry Potter and Voldemort, is sharply drawn. *Harry Potter and the Philosopher's Stone* is, behind all its sorcery, an old-fashioned and highly moral tale.

LEFT: *The first edition, which was published by Bloomsbury in 1997, had a print run of only 500 copies. Life sales of the book are now estimated to be around 107 million.*

Capital in the Twenty-First Century
Thomas Piketty

(2013)

Thomas Piketty's *Capital* has drawn comparisons with Karl Marx's book of the same name, offering a radical approach to wealth inequality. Its success can be measured by the number of books that have already been written about it, and the furious reaction of the libertarian right to Piketty's economic bombshell.

Thomas Piketty (born 1971) is a French economist. His publications include *Long Live the American Left!*, *Towards a Tax Revolution*, and *High Income in Twentieth-Century France: Inequality and Redistribution*, all issued only in France. The English translation of his 2013 work *Le Capital* gave him a global audience for his theories in 2014, prompting much-needed debate about the very definitions of wealth and income, and the permanence or otherwise of economic inequality. *Capital in the Twenty-First Century* topped US non-fiction lists and became the best-selling book of all time for its publisher, the Harvard University Press.

Piketty's central argument is that when the rate of return on capital exceeds economic growth, inherited wealth will inevitably grow faster than wealth earned through labour. An ever-widening gap of financial inequality will be the result, as demonstrated by Western capitalist economies, where wealth is increasingly concentrated in a small elite.

It is the evidence of history that gives *Capital* much of its persuasive power. Like other theorists, Piketty presents useful data, but he does not rely merely on mathematical modelling. To support his ideas, he takes a long view, reviewing more than two centuries of economic activity, over which the tendency has been for greater and greater inequality. A brief blip in the mid-twentieth century interrupted this trend, caused by wars, economic depression and recession, which drained much of the elite's wealth. A more powerful labour force and the higher taxes required to run a welfare state also contributed, but from the late 1970s onwards, the trend has been restored.

Piketty concludes that strong economic growth promotes a fairer distribution of wealth in the population and reduces society's focus on wealth. Slow growth, on the other hand, impoverishes the population and concentrates the wealth in the elite, creating social and economic division. The power is all in the hands of capitalists who have no incentive to change the system, and it will require the intervention of governments to redress the balance. He calls for a worldwide tax, not just on income but on wealth itself.

Piketty's position is clearly and forcefully argued, and has triggered both admiration and fury. His opponents have challenged not his argument but his basic premises, his notions of wealth, income and capital. They point to people like Bill Gates and Mark Zuckerberg, whose wealth is undeniably earned and not inherited, and they question whether history is evidence of the future.

Comparisons have been drawn between Piketty's ideas and those of the author of another book of the same title. In *Das Kapital*, Karl Marx also challenged inherited wealth, but he was more concerned with the means of production than distribution. He was interested in social relationships between labourer and employer, between serf and lord; Piketty does not discuss divisions of class, only divisions of income and wealth.

Capital in the Twenty-First Century has shaken up the world of economic theory. In its wake the battle lines have been redrawn. On the one hand, libertarians who think inequality is the normal outcome of capitalism, acceptable as long as the rich are getting richer and the poor are not getting poorer; on the other, egalitarians who believe that capitalism is inherently unfair, and equality does matter.

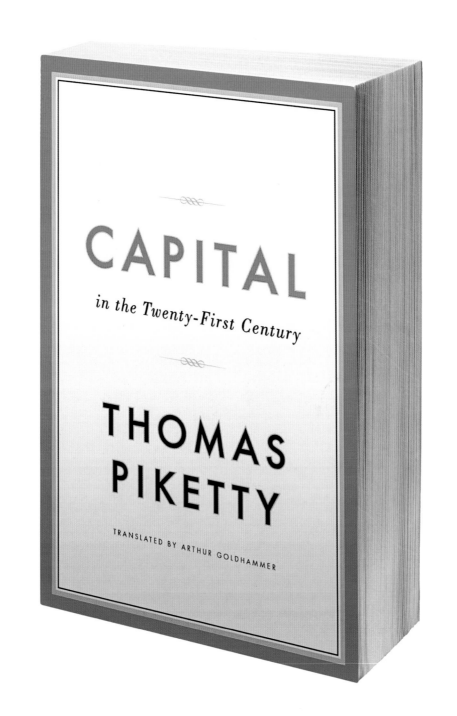

CAPITAL

in the Twenty-First Century

THOMAS
PIKETTY

TRANSLATED BY ARTHUR GOLDHAMMER

ABOVE: The American edition of Capital *reached the top of the New York Times hardback non-fiction best-sellers list and became Harvard University Press's biggest-selling book.*

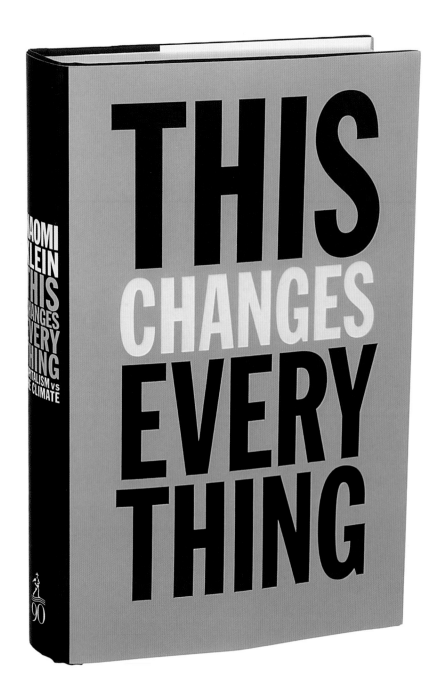

ABOVE: This Changes Everything *was described by the* New York Times *as 'the most momentous and contentious environmental book since* Silent Spring.*'*

212_____100 Books that Changed the World

This Changes Everything: Capitalism vs. the Climate
Naomi Klein

(2014)

In a world whose economic model is infinite consumption of finite resources, Klein claims that profit has taken precedence over survival. *This Changes Everything* is an urgent rallying call for collective action on the environment, and a recalibration of our aspirations.

Canadian author Naomi Klein (born 1970) has a reputation for taking on the big boys. She made her name with *No Logo* (1999), a scathing attack on corporate globalisation. In *The Shock Doctrine* (2007) she criticised the tendency for neoliberals to exploit national and global crises by introducing controversial policies when populations are too distressed or distracted to oppose them. *This Changes Everything* is the third book in this unofficial trilogy of left-of-centre polemics.

Klein once again has in her sights the global damage done by a rampant and increasingly unregulated capitalist market. But this time her concern is not social but environmental. As the body of scientific evidence for global warming becomes incontrovertible, corporations cannot be relied on to take responsible actions for the preservation of the planet. Their own survival depends on unrestrained consumerism, on shareholders who demand constant growth, and on continued exploitation of the limited natural resources on which their products depend.

Governments cede power to corporations because the measures of success in most Western economies require the perpetuation of the status quo. Damaging monopolies and cynical trade agreements are the result. As Klein writes: 'Our economic system and our planetary system are now at war. Dealing with the climate crisis will require a completely different economic system.'

We all have our part to play. As consumers we must learn to consume less and not define ourselves simply by the quantity and newness of our possessions. Our governments must invest in environmentally friendly systems, from bicycle networks to renewable energy. And our corporations must redefine success to include ecological and social aims and not unsustainable, eternal growth. Since we cannot rely on government and big business to take a lead, we must. Klein makes a compelling, passionate case for ordinary people to act for the planet and not for themselves, to make shared sacrifices for the sake of the future.

This Changes Everything – the most optimistic of Klein's anti-globalisation trilogy – was published a week before the 2014 UN Climate Summit, which was convened in New York. Some of the collective action for which the book calls began during the summit. In New York and around the world, more than half a million people took part in the People's Climate March.

One of the consequences of the summit was a UN conference on climate change in Paris the following year, at which the Paris Agreement was declared. Signatory countries agreed to take measures to tackle global warming. Although there were no specific targets for each country and no means of enforcing any commitment made by any of them, it was at least an encouraging start by governments.

But unfettered capitalism will not give up without a fight. In June 2017, President Donald Trump withdrew the United States from the Paris Agreement. Dismay was felt not only in Europe but in many US states, some of which formed the United States Climate Alliance to continue to pursue the agreement's aims. Klein's next book, *No Is Not Enough: Resisting Trump's Shock Politics and Winning the World We Need*, was published the same month.

Acknowledgements

The publisher wishes to thank the following for kindly supplying the images that appear in this book:

Alamy: 129, 131, 142 top, 148, 199, 203, 206, 207. Anne Frank Zentrum: 162. Astor-Honor Inc: 182. Bantam Press: 197. Beginner's Books/Random House: 181. Biblioteca Nazionale Marciana: 21. Bob Schutz/AP: 186. Bridgeman Images: 28. British Library: 41, 46, 103. Corgi: 200. C.W. Barton/ Heinemann: 183. Dutton Books: 14, 29. Editorial Sudamericana: 195 top left. Estate Brassaï-RMN: 168. Getty Images: 9, 23, 31, 76, 180, 204, 208. George Allen & Unwin Ltd: 176, 177. Harper & Row: 195 top right. Harvard University Press: 211. Heinemann: 185. Hodder & Stoughton: 40. Houghton Mifflin Co/ Lois and Louis Darling/Samuel H. Bryant: 187. Isabel Steva i Hernández/Colita: 195 bottom. John Minton/John Lehmann Limited: 171. John Woodcock/Chatto & Windus: 172. Library of Congress: 10, 43, 107. Metropolitan Museum of Art: 45. Modern Library: 163. National Palace Museum: 27. Orange County Regional History Center: 178. Penguin Books: 13, 153, 188 top right. Perkins School for the Blind: 94. Peter Pauper Press: 223. Pierpont Morgan Library: 92. Putnam: 174. Random House: 196. Royal Society: 216. Shirley Smith/J.B. Lippincott Company: 184. Signet: 188 left. Simon & Schuster: 213. Sotheby's: 39, 69, 147, 156, 166, 167, 175, 192. Sulaymaniyah Museum: 16. University of Birmingham: 38. Viking Press: 179. W.A. Dwiggins/Random House: 136. Wallaby Books: 160. Warnock Library: 53 bottom. W.B. Saunders: 164 top. Wellcome Library: 34, 64 bottom, 114, 117, 118, 119. W.W. Norton & Company: 191. Yinqueshan Han Tombs Bamboo Slips Museum: 25.

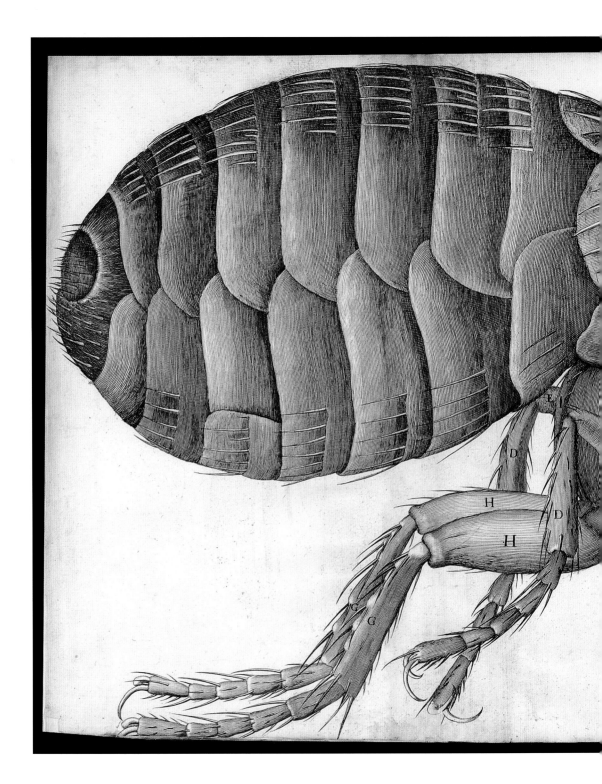

Schem XXXIV

Index

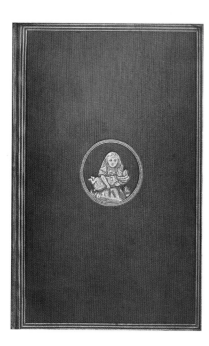

ABOVE: *The first edition of Lewis Carroll's* Alice's Adventures in Wonderland, *published in 1865 (see page 124).*

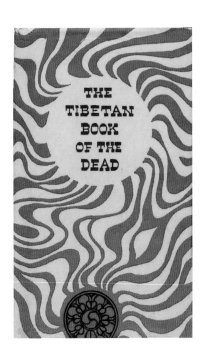

ABOVE: A Peter Pauper Press hardback edition of The Tibetan Book of the Dead *from 1972 (see page 150).*